Copyright © 2022 by P.J. Hanley

This book is protected under the copyright laws of the United States of America. This book may not be copied or reprinted for commercial gain or profit. The use of short quotations or occasional page copying for personal, or group study is permitted.

Lowercase is used in the name "satan" out of disrespect.

Unless otherwise noted, all Scripture quotations are from the New American Standard Bible. Copyright©1960, 1962, 1963, 1968, 1971, 1972, 1973, 1975, 1977 by the Lockman Foundation (Emphasis Mine).

Scripture quotations marked NIV are from the Holy Bible, New International Version. Copyright©1973, 1978, 1984, International Bible Society (Emphasis Mine).

New Testament Scriptures that appear with block capitals are quotes from the Old Testament.

Cover design by Rachel Chahanovich

Layout by Jenny Hanley

The Prophets of Israel

The prophets were just ordinary people like you and me. They were not angels or entities sent directly from heaven. Neither were they chosen because they had great charisma. They had dedicated their lives to the Lord. They were the ones who were willing to be radical during a time of idolatry and wickedness. Putting everything aside to pursue the Lord, they went against the grain of the surrounding lifestyle. They walked with God and talked with Him. Like David, they had come into a place of knowing the heart of Yahweh. They were intimate with Him in such a way that they were moved by what moved Him. The things that burdened His heart were impressed on their own, just as close friends can feel each other's burdens. The messages the prophets spoke were not just words they heard from God. They were not just messages, but an impregnation of the very heart of God into their lives. Through these men and women (2 Kings 22: 14-20) the Lord spoke to His people, expressing the depths of His feelings for them. This is why the prophets themselves were so passionate with the messages they presented. Not only did they verbalize the heart and emotions of the Lord, they also experienced them. They were not primarily concerned about foretelling the future, but rather turning the hearts of the people back to God - to show them how far they had strayed from Him and yet how much He still cherished them.

The above painting of Elijah being taken to heaven, is included in our introduction since he was perhaps the father of the Prophets, even though Samuel was the first to have a school or company of prophets. Elisha who was the protégé of Elijah, was also mighty in the Lord and in godly character. And there were many others throughout the early history of Israel. Yet, except for a verse here or there and a record of their activities, they have no writings or books of the Bible. David wrote several prophetic Psalms that are part of Scripture, and Moses wrote some also, including the five books of Torah and its many prophetic passages. Yet as the time came for the judgment of Israel and its Diaspora, God raised up a host of prophets to proclaim the burden of the Lord and write it down for a witness to future generations. Central to that message was the revelation and message of the Messiah and His unveiling to the world. Upon this foundation the true church of Christ is built[1] and through these God breathed words the State of Israel will be brought to His side. May the Lord bless you with wisdom and understanding as you study the Prophets of Israel!

---

[1] Eph 2:20

Pre-Exilic Prophets

Authors: The prophetic books were written or dictated by the prophets themselves. Most of their writings are records of the words they spoke to the Lord's people, but some of them also include historical accounts.

Time: The prophets Jonah, Amos, Hosea, and Obadiah were contemporaries living during the eighth century BC. Their ministry was to the Northern Kingdom of Israel just before it was taken captive by the Assyrians in 722 BC. Joel's ministry began earlier in the ninth century and was to the Kingdom of Judah.

Samuel - Abraham de Bruyn, mentioned on object, print maker (1540–1587)

David 1000BC	Elijah	Elisha		606BC-586BC	536BC – 432BC
		852			
United Kingdom	Divided Kingdom			Exile	Return

	PROPHETS BEFORE THE EXILE		EXILE PROPHETS	PROPHETS AFTER THE EXILE
	To Israel:	To Judah:	To Jews in Babylon:	To the Remnant after returning:
	Amos (760)	Joel (835)	Daniel (605)	
	Hosea (755)	Isaiah (740)	Ezekiel (592)	Haggai (520)
		Micah (735)		Zechariah (520)
	To Nineveh:	Zephaniah (630)		Malachi (432)
		Jeremiah (627)		
	Jonah (760)	Habakkuk (607)		
	Nahum (660)	Lamentations (586)		
	To Edom:			
	Obadiah (840)			

Joel
(Yahweh is God)

Theme: The Day of the Lord at the end of the age!

Read Chapters 1-3

Traditionally, Joel is said to have been written in 835 BC, the year that Joash was placed on the throne after his grandmother Athaliah was killed. The mention of Judah's enemies as Philistines, Phoenicians, Egyptians, and Edomites, rather than Assyrians and Babylonians, confirms this. Joel was a prophet to Judah and thus was primarily concerned with the leadership of Judah. His book is often understood to be a description of an intense locust plague that occurred during his life. It is supposed that Joel then used the devastation of his day to point to the Day of the Lord, and that the great locust plague was a foreshadowing of what was to come. It undoubtedly speaks of the destruction from Babylon in the immediate future, yet it switches to, and majors in, the judgment of God at the end of the age, repeatedly referred to as the Day of the Lord. The words of Joel have parallels to the book of Revelation which is also about the Day of the Lord. Consider the description of the locusts in Revelation Chapter 9.

What are these locusts that come against Israel in the Day of The Lord? From the description in Joel and Revelation 9, they are definitely not literal locusts. They sound like horses and chariots, have teeth like lions, march in line, rush on houses, and climb in windows. They are released by the armies coming against Jerusalem at the end of the age. Therefore, they are likely modern, computer driven, weapons, such as helicopters, or more likely drones. They burn everything and leave blackness behind them, and they usher in the cosmic signs which appear at the end of the Tribulation – the Sun turns to darkness and the Moon to blood. The technology already exists (and continues to be tested) to release "swarms" of tiny drones from aircraft to accomplish missions. Not only do they look like locusts they are called LOCUST (Low-Cost UAV Swarming Technology).

Joel	Revelation 9
Please note: Zion is Jerusalem (leadership of Judah - tribe representative of all Israel)	
1:6 - A nation has invaded MY land (note the MY Land focus and compare to the 3:2 judgment on the nations for dividing up MY LAND - Teeth of Lions	9:8 - teeth like Lions 9:13-16 - armies being released
1:15 - the Day of The Lord is near	The context of the whole book of Revelation - Rev 1:10 9:7
2:4 - their appearance is like the appearance of horses	- the appearance of the locusts was like horses prepared for battle
2:2, 2:10-11, 2:30-31 - darkness on the land - cosmic signs	9:2 - the sun and the air were darkened by the smoke of the pit
The call to repentance - chap 1 & 2 and the promise of restoration 2:18-32	
Though this could also refer to the immediate destruction coming from the North, it undoubtedly refers to the end of the age. In fact, it may exclusively refer to it. Note: the context in 3:1, the last days - division of the land, nations coming against Jerusalem, the cosmic signs, never again (2:19), outpouring of the Spirit.	The chapter is all about the armies coming against Israel in the Day of The Lord, and the destruction they bring, and then God destroys them.
The armies of Locusts are not the army of the Lord, as those who espouse Replacement Theology often say. Yes, they are the army of the Lord, in the sense that God is sending them to carry out His judgment, but they are not His people.	

Compare Joel 2:30-32 with Acts 2:17-21

This prophecy of the Spirit being poured out on both Jew and Gentile, began then and will be completed on the Day of The Lord, when the full number of the Gentiles is brought into the Bride of Messiah (Rom 11:25).

Joel 2:31 says that the cosmic signs (Sun to Black, Moon to Blood), will happen before the Day of the Lord. They happen at the end of the Tribulation period (Mt 24:29), which is the Day of the Lord, and before the Millennium, which is also the Day of The Lord.

The Remnant of Israel is delivered in Joel 2:32.

Chapter 3:1-3
After God has brought back Israel and restored the fortunes of Judah and Jerusalem, then (at that time) He will gather all the nations to the Valley of Jehoshaphat (Jerusalem) and enter into judgment with them for the way they have treated Israel and divided up His Land. This scenario takes place at the end of the age, after He has restored Israel and Jerusalem, which is our day. Nothing like this happened after the exile from Babylon.

Valley of Jehoshaphat (YAHWEH judges)
Many believe this valley is the Kidron in Jerusalem. All the nations will be gathered against it. Jerusalem is the focal point of the battle, but it is too small to be a gathering place for the armies of the nations. The staging area, or camp, will be the Valley of Megiddo in the center of the country.

"And they gathered them together to the place which in Hebrew is called HarMagedon." Rev 16:16

This is the mountain of Megiddo - *(Armageddon)*.

Chapter 3:13

- Winepress of God's wrath - see Rev 19:15-19 - see also Ezekiel 38 & 39
- God finally avenges all the violence done to the Jewish people throughout history (3:21).
- Restoration of Zion - the nation of Israel reigns – Millennium
- House of The Lord (Temple) restored - water flows out of it (3:18) - see also Ezekiel 4

Notes

Obadiah

Obadiah is the shortest book in the Hebrew Scriptures. It seems to have been written in the 9th Century B.C. The message is one of coming destruction for Edom. Edom (the descendants of Esau) was very vicious in her hatred of the descendants of her brother Jacob. They persecuted Israel every chance they got and gloated when Israel suffered. In verses 11-13 they are pictured as gloating over the destruction of Jerusalem, which was at the time, at least three centuries in the future. Edom was famous for their cities in the mountains cut out of the rocks. The city of Petra is a perfect example. Many believe that the remnant of Israel will flee there during the Tribulation. Notice the reference to the house of Jacob possessing their possessions (verse 17). Some believe that the judgment on Edom was not complete and that there are at least two more stages. The people of Edom moved westward during the Babylonian exile of Judah and settled in what became known as Idumea. After the revolt of Bar Kokhba in 135 AD, when Hadrian renamed the land of Israel after one of the Jew's arch enemies the Philistines (Palestine), Idumea disappeared. It is likely that many of the so-called Palestinians are in fact Edomites, which makes the End-Time portion of the prophecy very interesting.

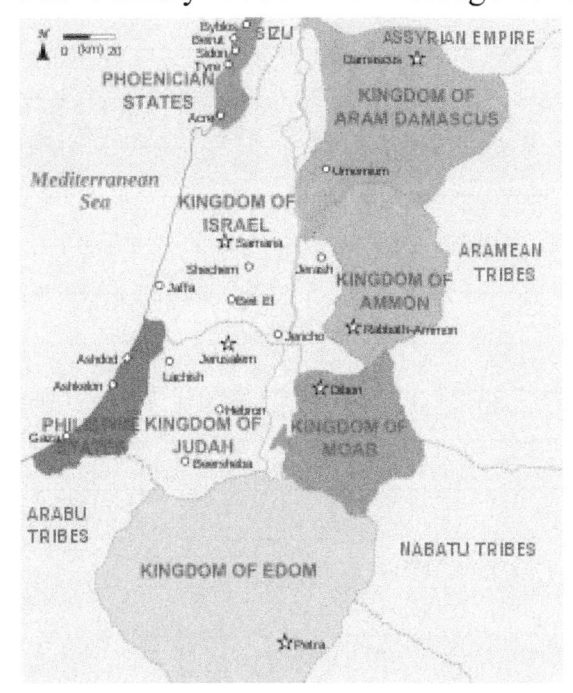

In verses 15-21 there is a description of the Day of The Lord.

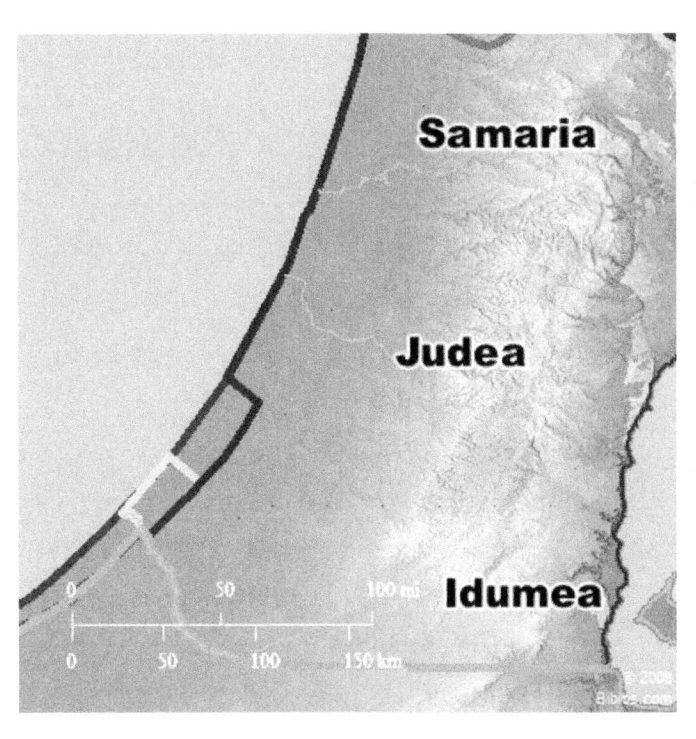

Also, an interesting reference in verse 20 to Sephardic Jews. *"The exiles of Jerusalem who are in Sepharad" (Spain – Spanish Jews)*. Many Sephardic Jews live in the Negev today!

Notes

Hosea

"Then the Lord said to me, 'Go again, love a woman who is loved by her husband, yet an adulteress, even as the Lord loves the sons of Israel, though they turn to their gods and love raisin cakes" (Hosea 3:1).

The book begins with a painful glimpse into the heart of God through the personal story of Hosea. Hosea, who probably lived in the Northern Kingdom, was a prophet who had been told by the Lord to marry a prostitute. This can be difficult to understand. Why would the Lord issue such an order? Yet it is clear that the Lord wanted Hosea to enter into and experience, the pain of rejection that was in His heart, and as a result, to deliver the message of coming judgment to the people. Indeed, all who would address God's people, especially with judgment, must be able to not only bring a message, but deliver the very burden of the Lord's heart. Thus, all the prophets to some extent endured suffering and rejection to be the Lord's messengers. Indeed, one could say, that it is impossible to be a genuine prophet or messenger of the Lord, unless one has not only come to know the message, but also the heart of God for His beloved.

Chapters 1-2

Hosea is told to marry Gomer because Israel is unfaithful. God wants the prophet to be a message for Israel. He wants him to experience the same thing He is experiencing with Israel's unfaithfulness. He is not just the messenger; his life is the message.

His wife Gomer gave birth to three children and each of them received prophetic names.

Verse 4

A son named Jezreel is born. The message is punishment on the house of Jehu and the end of the kingdom of Israel. Yet, there seems to be a hint that Jezreel will be a place of great victory in the future restoration (verse 11).

The Jezreel valley is the fertile valley east of Mount Carmel. It was the place where Israel fought many battles, and the place where Jehu slew the kings of Israel and Judah, and Ahab's entire house. It is also referred to as the plain of Megiddo. It will be the place where the armies of the earth will gather for the last great war known as Armageddon.

Verse 6: A daughter is born. Prophetic name -"Lo-ruhamah" - "I will not have compassion"

Verse 9: A son is born named: "Lo-ammi" - "not my people"

No sooner does God speak of "not my people" and "no compassion," than He begins to speak of restoration. In verse10, He talks about the remnant at the end of the age and the uniting of both kingdoms, which, of course, has happened in our day.
Peter quotes these verses when he speaks of the restoration in Christ (1 Pet 2:10)

Chapter 2:1-13
God will punish Israel for her spiritual adultery. Though He loved them and blessed them, they gave credit to the Baal and worshipped him.

Verses 14-23
God promises to restore Israel. Note the reference to the Valley of Achor, which was the valley near Jericho, where Achan sinned and brought trouble on Israel. Achor means "trouble." It's the valley of trouble. Of course, it is also in the wilderness, and it is likely the way the remnant returns with Messiah after the Tribulation period. The reference to God taking her into the desert, and speaking kindly with her, refers to their scattering throughout the nations and His bringing them back. The valley of trouble becomes a door of hope. Israel will be restored to the Lord and call Him her husband. It is the Millennium Reign, as is clear from verses 19 and 20.

The rest of the chapter is all about blessing after the Lord restores her to the land and to her God. The reference to Jezreel in verse 22, has the connotation of sowing and harvest. Jezreel is the fertile pain and the breadbasket of Israel.

Chapter 3
Hosea is told to buy back Gomer who has gone again on one of her adulterous missions, becoming involved with another man. Then Hosea tells her that she will be with him for many days without any harlotries or any relationship with him. Then comes the message for Israel.

"For the sons of Israel will remain for many days without king or prince, without sacrifice or sacred pillar and without ephod or household idols. Afterward the sons of Israel will return and seek the LORD their God and David their king; and they will come trembling to the LORD and to His goodness in the last days." Hos 3:4-5 NAS

The sons of Israel will be for many days (a long time) without King or Prince (without a kingdom), without sacrifice or sacred pillar (no priests or temple worship), and without idols. This is the exile of Israel throughout the nations which we call the Diaspora. Israel has been this way from 70AD until today. But then comes the promise that they will return and seek the Lord, and David their king, and will come trembling to the Lord and His goodness in the last days. This is precisely where we are at today. Israel has come back to her land and is in the process of turning back to the Lord. As a result, the Temple will be rebuilt, and the priesthood restored. Then they will come to the Messiah, Yeshua (Jesus) and the kingdom of David will reign on the earth.

Chapters 4-5

God details the sin of the people in idolatry. Both the princes and the priests are implicated in it. They have polluted the land with their violence and bloodshed. Even the land mourns. God has withdrawn from them on account of their harlotries.

"They will go with their flocks and herds to seek the LORD, but they will not find Him; He has withdrawn from them. They have dealt treacherously against the LORD, for they have borne illegitimate children." Hos 5:6-7 NASU

Some think that Gomer's last two children were not Hosea's because of the way their conception is mentioned in chapter 1. I do not think this conclusion is necessary, but it could be true. However, here we have a reference to "illegitimate children" which speaks to the fruit of Israel's harlotry.

At first Judah is left out, but in chapter 5, she is also included. Then there is the sad conclusion for Israel (Ephraim)[2] and Judah. It is a repeat of chapter 3. Please note that the famous chapter 6 is a continuation of chapter 5 since there are no chapters and verses in the original.

"For I will be like a lion to Ephraim and like a young lion to the house of Judah. I, even I, will tear to pieces and go away, I will carry away, and there will be none to deliver. I will go away and return to My place until they acknowledge their guilt and seek My face; in their affliction they will earnestly seek Me. "Come, let us return to the LORD. For He has torn us, but He will heal us; He has wounded us, but He will bandage us. He will revive us after two days; He will raise us up on the third day, that we may live before Him. So let us know, let us press on to know the LORD. His going forth is as certain as the dawn; and He will come to us like the rain, like the spring rain watering the earth." Hos 5:14-6:3 NASU

This is a beautiful, yet sad prophecy, of the destruction and scattering of Israel and her restoration at the end of the age. God says that he will tear them in pieces like a lion, and then He will go away to His place and leave them, until they acknowledge their guilt and seek His face again.

Chapter 6 - The Third Day

"Come, let us return to the LORD. For He has torn us, but He will heal us; He has wounded us, but He will bandage us. He will revive us after two days; <u>He will raise us up on the third day,</u> that we may live before Him." Hosea 6:1-2 Emphasis Mine

---

[2] Israel was also called Ephraim because its capital was in the territory of the tribe of Ephraim.

The early rabbis understood this passage to refer to the Messianic era. The Jewish people would be wounded for two days, but on the third day they would be healed. For two thousand years they would suffer, and in the third millennium the Kingdom would come. Jesus Himself seems to have verified this by the following statements:

"And He said to them, "Go and tell that fox, `Behold, I cast out demons and perform cures today and tomorrow, <u>and the third day I reach My goal</u>. Nevertheless I must journey on today and tomorrow and the next day; for it cannot be that a prophet should perish outside of Jerusalem." Luke 13:32 Emphasis Mine

Careful examination of the text tells us that Jesus did not reach His goal on the third day after this statement. He was not referring to twenty-four-hour periods at all, but rather the "Third Day" or Third Millennium - a theme well known to the Jews at that time. He said that He would perform cures and cast out demons for two millennia, and then He will reach His goal - the Kingdom of God. One would be hard pressed to interpret this passage any other way.

This prophecy concerning the "Third Day" has caused the church, particularly in the last century, to come up with many dates. It is rightly supposed that if one knows the beginning of the first day, then one can also determine when the third day comes. This is the reason why so many expected something to happen in the year 2000. However, the church has misunderstood this prophecy, because we have assumed the day to begin with Jesus. It was first thought to begin with Jesus' birth, and since 2000 years from that date passed without incident, it was then supposed that some other date, such as the beginning of His Ministry, or His death, constituted the beginning of the first day. Now that all those dates have come and gone, and the skeptics are all saying, "I told you so," there is no more discussion of the prophecy. However, the prophet's words stand, and it is up to us to understand them.

The reason the prophecy has been misunderstood is surprisingly simple. We have gotten it wrong because, as usual, we took it out of its Biblical context. Like all the prophets, Hosea is revealing God's heart over the sin of Israel and the fact that their sin would lead to terrible consequences. But as always there is the promise to restore them at the end of the age. Let's look at it again now in its context. I will begin with some verses from chapter 3 and chapter 5 that illustrate that context.

"For the sons of Israel will remain for many days without king or prince, without sacrifice or sacred pillar and without ephod or household idols. <u>Afterward</u> the sons of Israel will return and seek the LORD their God and David their king; and they will come trembling to the LORD and to His goodness in the last days....."

For I will be like a lion to Ephraim and like a young lion to the house of Judah. I, even I, will tear to pieces and go away, I will carry away, and there will be none to deliver. I will go away and return to My place until they acknowledge their guilt and seek My face; in their affliction they will earnestly seek Me..... Come, let us return to the LORD. For He has torn us, but He will heal us; He has wounded us, but He will bandage us. He will revive us after two days; He will raise us up on the third day, that we may live before Him." Hos 3:4-5, 5:14, 6:3 Emphasis Mine

God is saying that He will punish the people for their sin and idolatry. They will go a long time without king or prince or sacrifice or temple. He said that He Himself will be as a lion to them and will wound them and go away to His place. Then after a long period of time, in the last days they will turn back to Him and say, "Come let us return to the Lord. For He has torn us, but He will heal us; He has wounded us, but He will bandage us. He will revive us after two days; He will raise us up on the third day that we may live before Him." When we keep the prophecy regarding Israel in its proper context, the beginning of the first day becomes clear. God will wound the people for two days, or two millennia, and revive them on the third day, or third millennium. Therefore, since the wounding starts the first day, then the beginning of the first day starts with the wounding and scattering of Israel. Messiah doesn't enter the prophecy until the third day.

In the Bible, the number 7 represents "completeness" and the number 10 means "weighed in the balance" and either "accepted" or "rejected." Therefore, ten times seventy represents either complete acceptance or complete rejection. In 66AD, the War of the Jews began the wounding and scattering of Israel. In 70AD, Jerusalem and the Temple were destroyed, and she was scattered to the nations. Israel was rejected as a nation, but only for a season albeit a long one. She would be wounded for two millennia and healed on the third. Then she would be completely accepted again. Since we know the date the first millennium began, 66AD, then we can determine when the Third Millennium will begin.

2000 years of 360 days (Biblical years) = 720000 days
720000 days/365.25 (days in our years) = 1971 our years
*66 A.D. + 1971 = **2037***

According to this understanding, the year 2037 would be the year when the Third Millennium begins. This is also 70 years after the return of Jerusalem to the nation of Israel. Therefore, since we know that the Millennium occurs 3½ years after the beginning of the Tribulation, then we merely subtract 3½ years to find the year it begins.

Verses 4-11 & Chapter 7:1-16
This passage continues to address the sin of Israel and Judah in forsaking the Lord.

Chapter 8

Chapter 8 begins with the sounding of the Trumpet or Shophar, which in this case, is declaring that the enemy is coming to destroy them in battle. He comes like an eagle from the north. This is the Assyrian Empire coming to take them captive (8-9). Note in verse 1, how the people pride themselves in knowing God, yet they rebel against Him.

Chapter 9

The Lord continues to contemplate their wickedness and idolatry, and remembers them at their youth, when He took them out of Egypt. Yet, even then, they were idolatrous.

"I found Israel like grapes in the wilderness; I saw your forefathers as the earliest fruit on the fig tree in its first season. But they came to Baal-peor and devoted themselves to shame, and they became as detestable as that which they loved." Hos 9:10

Grapes in the wilderness are a picture of something very pleasant, since the wilderness is so barren.

Then He mentions the awful occurrence with Baal-peor, when Balaam counseled Balak to entice the Israelites to sin with fornication, and they participated in idolatry (Num 25).

Notice again in verse 3, how they will be taken captive to Assyria. The mention of Egypt is a typical Hebraism denoting return to bondage and slavery. Once again, the Diaspora is mentioned.

"My God will cast them away because they have not listened to Him; and they will be wanderers among the nations." Hos 9:17 NASU

Chapter 10

The lament over Israel's idolatry and soon destruction continues. The people will be carried into exile and their princes cut off. Even the idols that they worship will be carried off as gifts for the king of Assyria. Notice the continual reference to what happened at Gibeah.[3]

Then in verse 12, there is a call to repent and return to the Lord. Throughout all the promise of destruction, the offer of restoration through genuine repentance is always extended to them.

Chapter 11

The chapter begins with the Lord speaking of Israel as He found him in Egypt.

---

[3] The horrible affair with the concubine (Judges 19).

"When Israel was a youth I loved him, and out of Egypt I called My son. The more they called them, the more they went from them; they kept sacrificing to the Baals and burning incense to idols." Hos 11:1-2 NASU

The Father speaks as though He is lovesick. The more the prophets called Israel, the more they followed the Baals. This verse is also applied to Jesus, by Matthew, as a sort of dual fulfillment of prophecy, in that Israel was called out of Egypt and also Jesus came out of Egypt.

"Yet it is I who taught Ephraim to walk, I took them in My arms; but they did not know that I healed them. I led them with cords of a man, with bonds of love, and I became to them as one who lifts the yoke from their jaws; and I bent down and fed them." Hos 11:3-4 NASU

Notice the heart of the Father and His love for His people. It is clear that the prophet also feels this pain.

Then in verse 5 we are told clearly that they will not return to Egypt, but that Assyria will be their king because they refused to return to the Lord and have not listened to the prophets (verse 7). Then there is a lament. The Lord is grieving over what He must do and asking, "How can I give you up?" In verses 9-11, there is a promise that it will never happen again, and that God will bring them back and restore them.

Chapter 12

The Lord says that He will punish Ephraim (Israel) and Judah and all the sons of Jacob for their sins. Then He reminisces about Jacob, and how he wrestled with his brother in the womb, and with the angel in his maturity at the brook Jabbok, and how he sought the Lord and spoke with Him at Bethel. Bethel, of course, was one of Israel's high places where they are worshiping idols. Again, the call goes out to return to the Lord and seek Him, as Jacob did at Bethel. They are to return by doing righteousness and justice and seeking the Lord continually. They are to stop oppressing the poor and the widow and being greedy with false weights and balances (verses 6-8).

"I have also spoken to the prophets, and I gave numerous visions, and through the prophets I gave parables." Hos 12:10

They are reminded that the Father has spoken to them and reached out to them continually through the prophets, but they have not listened.

The Lord says that Jacob (Israel, the man) fled to Aram (Assyria) and worked for a wife there. But that God delivered Israel (the nation) from Egypt by a prophet. This time the Lord will take them to Assyria.

Chapter 13

The lament continues over Israel's sin and coming exile. The Lord speaks tenderly of how He brought them from Egypt and loved them from the beginning.

"Yet I have been the LORD your God since the land of Egypt; and you were not to know any god except Me, for there is no savior besides Me. I cared for you in the wilderness, in the land of drought. As they had their pasture, they became satisfied, and being satisfied, their heart became proud; therefore they forgot Me." Hos 13:4-6

Does that sound like the heart of someone rejected? The heart of the Father is broken over His people. Now there is the mention of the lion again. The Lord says He will become a lion to them and tear them to pieces. This is the wounding spoken of in Chapter 6.

"So I will be like a lion to them; like a leopard I will lie in wait by the wayside. I will encounter them like a bear robbed of her cubs, and I will tear open their chests; there I will also devour them like a lioness, as a wild beast would tear them. It is your destruction, O Israel, that you are against Me, against your help." Hos 13:7-9 NASU

Then the Lord asks again, "Shall I ransom them from death?" He is asking, "How can I save them? Shall I ransom them from the power of Sheol?[4] Surely death and destruction must come." But He says, "O death where are your thorns? O Sheol where is your sting?"

Here the Lord makes a momentary prophetic statement that points to when, in Christ, death and sin will be defeated, and we will dwell with Him forever. This is regular practice in biblical prophecy, where a portion of the dialogue speaks of distant future, and then returns to the immediate application; for example, the following statement is; "Compassion will be hidden from My sight." We know this to be true here because Paul quotes from verse 14 in 1 Corinthians 15:55

Chapter 13 concludes with a graphic description of the suffering coming from Assyria.

"Samaria will be held guilty, for she has rebelled against her God. They will fall by the sword, their little ones will be dashed in pieces, and their pregnant women will be ripped open." Hos 13:16

---

[4] Sheol is the underworld or Hades.

Chapter 14
There is a final call to repent and return to the Lord. They are asked to repent for looking to Assyria for help instead of the Lord, to stop worshiping the work of their own hands (idols), and to care for the orphan and the widow.

Verses 4-9 prophesy the return of Israel to the Lord and the restoration of the last days. She is again prospering on the land and knowing Yahweh alone as her God.

Notes

Amos

Amos was a shepherd who lived in Tekoa, just south of Bethlehem. He was an ordinary man living in the rural country, yet God called him to speak to the nation. His prophecies were to both Israel and Judah. In Amos, God rebukes the Israelites for rejecting Him and turning to the idols which Jeroboam constructed in Bethel and in Dan. The Lord speaks of all the things He had done trying to persuade them to turn back to Him. But they had not listened and had held onto their wickedness. In a time of prosperity, greed and dishonest gain had overtaken their hearts. They sacrificed to God and to their idols simultaneously. Through Amos, God warned that Israel would be carried into exile; that the land would be laid desolate, and the sacrifices and temple worship would be put to an end. Amos prophesied even further into the future, speaking of the dispersion of the Jews into all the nations (70 AD). Again, as is typical of the prophets, his words contain a double meaning, as he pendulums between the judgment of Israel in the seventh and eighth centuries, and the Day of the Lord at the end of the age. In the end, Amos speaks of Israel's promising future, when God will bring her back to her land, and her ruins will be rebuilt never to be torn down again.

Chapters 1-2
Amos begins with prophecy of judgment on the surrounding nations.

"The Lord roars from Zion and from Jerusalem He utters His voice…"

Here, we have what is called a Hebrew parallelism, where the same thought is repeated twice using different words. This is common throughout the Bible and is often misunderstood. Zion is another name for Jerusalem.

Amos declares judgment on the surrounding nations for their sins, and the way they have treated Israel. However, Israel will also be judged, something that the affluent at the time were unwilling to accept; but if God is going to judge the surrounding nations, why would He not judge Israel?

First it is Aram (Assyria, Syria), then Gaza (Philistines & their cities Ashdod and Ashkelon), Tyre, Edom, Amon, Moab, and finally Judah and Israel. The sins of Israel and Judah are idolatry, and oppression of the poor and needy. The prophet speaks of destruction coming on both kingdoms as a result. God reminds the people that He brought them up from Egypt and drove out the Amorite before them. Again, the point is, if I punished the Amorite how can I not punish you for your sin?

Chapter 3:1-8

Continuing the theme, God reminds them that they are chosen from all the families of the earth, and therefore, or on account of that choice, He will punish them for their sins.
Then there are questions which all have an obvious answer.

- Do two men walk together unless they have made an appointment (or in agreement)? Answer, NO!
- Does a lion roar in the forest when he has no prey? Answer, NO!
- When a trumpet sounds as an alarm in the city, do not the people tremble? Answer, YES!

It's the same as saying, "Where there is smoke there is a fire."

God is the one roaring from Jerusalem, and there is a reason why He is roaring. Amos is saying to the people, "Why won't you listen?" And since the roaring of the Lord is so obvious, "Who can but prophesy?" The prophet is compelled to speak.

Verses 9-10

Here he addresses the Philistines and the Egyptians in a sort of sarcastic way. "Just take a look, come and see for yourselves what is going on in Samaria." As if to say to the Israelites that even the godless can see what's going on.

Verses 11-15

A nation, an enemy will come and snatch them away (Assyria) and there will be very little left ("like a shepherd pulling a piece of finger from the lion's mouth)".

The pagan altars at Bethel will be destroyed as well as the summer and winter houses inlaid with ivory, which speaks of their opulence and indifference.

The horns of the altar refer to horns at each of the four ends of the altar, which signify strength and power, and thus are going to be cut off. The Israelites had made Bethel (house of God),[5] into a High Place, where they worshiped idols. This was done by the wicked king Jeroboam (the first Jeroboam). It was venerated as an important High Place and apparently the king had a residence there.

Chapter 4:1-3

Calling them "Cows of Bashan," was like saying "You fat cats." Bashan was the fertile land of Northern Israel, near Syria, which is today the Golan Heights. All they wanted to do was eat and drink, but the enemy will come with meat hooks and take them away. In other words, they will be taken away to slaughter like cows, by the enemy from the north (note the reference to Mt. Hermon in verse 3).

---

[5] Bethel had been viewed as holy since Jacob had his vision there, and later the Tabernacle of Moses was there.

Verses 4-5
Is sort of like saying, "So carry on then with all your idolatry, since that's what you love to do."

Verse 6-13
God outlines all the things He has done to get them to turn back to Him, but they have not. So, He is going to drive them away, "Prepare to meet your God."

Chapter 5:1-17
God continues explaining what He is going to do and why He is going to do it. It is because of their idolatry on the High Places, and their oppression of the poor and the needy, and not caring for them.

There are continual references to the House of Joseph. The capital of the northern kingdom was called Samaria, and it was in Ephraim. Thus the northern kingdom known as Israel was also called Ephraim. Also, the House or Tent of Joseph was another way of referring to Israel since Ephraim was Joseph's son. Bethel and Gilgal were also in Ephraim.

Verses 18-20
Now there is a shift to the Day of the Lord. Of course, they all were aware of the promise to David and the future time when God would establish His kingdom over all the nations. This time, which we call the Millennial Reign, was something they were looking forward to; however, the prophet tells them that it is also a time of judgment on those who do evil, and that includes them. We know this time to be the Tribulation at the end of the age, but the prophet identifies it as the Day of The Lord. So, in this passage, we see a clear reference to both the Tribulation and the Millennium being the Day of The Lord.

Verses 20-27
God says He hates their festivals and offerings and worship. Israel continued to worship God and hold to Torah, even though they sacrificed to their idols as well. God says He hates the sacrifices because while they offer them, they walk in unrighteousness.

"But let justice roll down like waters and righteousness like an ever-flowing stream." Amos 5:24

Another parallelism. Note all the parallelisms in the chapter. This is very typical in the prophets.

Verses 25-26
These verses tell us that even during the wilderness journey, Israel was still carrying and hiding household idols. See Acts 7:42-43

Verse 27
They will be taken captive by Assyria

Chapter 6
"Woe to those who are at ease in Zion and to those who feel secure in the mountain of Samaria, the distinguished men of the foremost of nations, to whom the house of Israel comes." Hosea 6:1 NASU

In this case the parallelism is framed to include both the leaders of Judah (Zion) and Israel (Samaria). The leaders of both kingdoms live at ease and in luxury. Because they are God's people and are living in prosperity and security for the moment, they have become proud and arrogant, thinking they are invincible. They live their lives of pleasure and opulence and have no regard for the poor and needy. Again, there is the promise to send a nation against them and afflict them from the northernmost part (Hamath) to the southernmost part (Arabah).

Chapter 7:1-9
God shows Amos three visions. In the first, a locust swarm comes to devour everything, and in the second, fire comes to consume everything. On both occasions Amos cries out in intercession and God relents. Finally, He sees the Lord on a vertical (straight) wall with a plumbline. The point seems to be that God has punished them many times and relented, but since they have not turned back to Him, destruction is now coming.

"Behold I am about to put a plumb line in the midst of My people Israel. I will spare them no longer. The high places of Isaac will be desolated and the sanctuaries of Israel laid waste. Then I will rise up against the house of Jeroboam with the sword." Amos 7:8-9 NASU

I believe the plumb line speaks of God's righteousness and justice making things right! Again, there is the promise to bring the sword against Israel (this time referred to as the "House of Jeroboam") and destroy its High Places.

Verses 10-17
Amos is confronted by Amaziah, the priest of Bethel, and told to stop prophesying. He is told by the king to go back to Judah; in other words, "go home." Amos does not receive the rebuke. Instead, he informs them that he is not a "professional" prophet but is only

there because the Lord told him to go and prophesy. Then he goes on to repeat the word and this time he includes Jeroboam's family directly in Israel's destruction.

Chapter 8:1-3
God showed Amos a basket of summer fruit and then asks him what it was. The message here is that summer fruit is good, but it does not last long. It will quickly rot and spoil and be useless. Then He says:

"The end has come for My people Israel. I will spare them no longer." Amos 8:2 NASU

The songs of the palaces - all the rejoicing and reveling will turn to wailing like the summer fruit!

Verses 4-8
God again addresses the hypocrisy and callousness of the people. They are pictured as unable to wait for the feast days to be over so they can get back to their business of making money dishonestly.

"When will the new moon be over, so that we may sell grain, and the Sabbath, that we may open the wheat market, to make the bushel smaller and the shekel bigger, and to cheat with dishonest scales, so as to buy the helpless for money, and the needy for a pair of sandals, and that we may sell the refuse of the wheat?" Amos 8:5-6 NASU

Verses 9-14
Though the prophet continues to prophesy about the destruction coming from the north, he also jumps to the Day of The Lord, which he has already mentioned.

"It will come about in that day," declares the Lord GOD, that I will make the sun go down at noon and make the earth dark in broad daylight. Amos 8:9 NASU

The Day of the Lord is also characterized by mourning and weeping and a thirst for God and His word.

Chapter 9:1-8
The Lord smites the capitals (pillars) so that the house falls on top of them. This is a shaking from the Lord, which likely refers to the coming catastrophic earthquake,[6] that shook the region, causing the destruction of the temple and altar at Bethel. It also, of course, refers to the coming shaking throughout the nations, and the shaking of the Day of the Lord.

Though most of the discussion has been concerning the northern kingdom, Judah is also included. At this point, it would seem that there is no difference as they are both identified by the term "House of Jacob."

---

[6] Zech 14:5, Amos 1:1, 3:14-15, 6:11, 8:8, 9:1

Notice the totality and inescapability of the punishment. God says that wherever they are it will find them.

Verses 8-15
Just as the Lord emphasized the totality of the punishment, He now promises to restore Israel and Judah in the last days. Here the sons of Jacob are identified together with Jerusalem and the city of David, which God promises to restore fully.

Verse 9
"For behold, I am commanding, and I will shake the house of Israel among all nations as grain is shaken in a sieve, but not a kernel will fall to the ground. All the sinners of My people will die by the sword, those who say, 'The calamity will not overtake or confront us.'"

Israel will be scattered among the nations and shaken like a sieve, but a remnant will survive and not be lost.

Verse 11
"'In that day I will raise up the fallen booth of David, and wall up its breaches; I will also raise up its ruins and rebuild it as in the days of old; that they may possess the remnant of Edom and all the nations who are called by My name,' declares the LORD who does this."

There is much talk today about the "Restoration of the Tabernacle of David" as having to do with twenty-four-hour praise and worship. These verses in Amos 9 are often used to teach this. This is Replacement Theology which views the church as "Spiritual Israel" and "Zion."

Though the increase of worship and praise is a wonderful thing, it is not the restoration of the Tabernacle of David. The Tabernacle of David is the house and city of David. It is Jerusalem. This manner of speaking regarding the House of Joseph, the House of Israel, and the House of Jeroboam occurs throughout the book. Thus, the Tabernacle of David is the place where David resided - the capital of his kingdom. This is clearly illustrated by the mention of rebuilding its ruins, which obviously a tent could not have. The remnant of Edom is the remnant of Israel, rescued by the Messiah at the end of the Tribulation (the Day of the Lord), that is pictured as coming from Edom (Bozrah, Is 63:1).

Verse 13-15

"'Behold, days are coming,' declares the LORD, 'When the plowman will overtake the reaper and the treader of grapes him who sows seed; when the mountains will drip sweet wine and all the hills will be dissolved. Also I will restore the captivity of My people Israel, and they will rebuild the ruined cities and live in them; they will also plant vineyards and drink their wine, and make gardens and eat their fruit. I will also plant them on their land, and they will not again be rooted out from their land which I have given them,' says the LORD your God."

The plowman overtaking the reaper portrays the suddenness with which the harvest will come. In other words, there will be no more delay! Again, notice the rebuilding of the ruined cities which follows the rebuilding of Jerusalem. There will be much destruction during the Day of The Lord. Israel, rejoice in the Lord!

Notes

Jonah

The story of Jonah and the "whale" (really a big fish) is a Sunday school favorite. Jonah was a prophet in the Northern Kingdom. In an unusual assignment, the Lord told Jonah to go out of Israel to Nineveh and prophesy against it. Nineveh was the capital of the ruthless Assyrian Empire. It was the center of the world at the time and encompassed the many pagan practices and rituals of the nations. The wickedness of the city had reached such a point that it had to end. But instead of wiping the city out, God decided to give the people there a chance to turn from their ways. Thus He commissioned Jonah, but he went in the opposite direction.

It must have taken an enormous amount of trust in God to march over to the capital of the largest empire in the world and tell the people that they were going to be destroyed. But that was not what bothered Jonah. He was not afraid to do it. He had another reason for running away. Jonah knew the Lord, and he knew the heart behind God's message. He knew that if God wanted to wipe out Nineveh, He could surely do that. The only reason God would send him with such a message, would be to show mercy on the people of Nineveh, and give them a chance to repent of their sin. Jonah did not like this idea. After all, the Assyrians had been Israel's greatest enemy at the time, constantly harassing them and causing great affliction to the people. Jonah did not want them to receive the mercy of God. He did not want God to show love to Israel's enemies. This was why he tried to run away. But the Lord pursued Jonah until he had to surrender. The fact that Jonah was swallowed by a fish and called out to God from there is attested to by Jesus Himself.[7]

It was a very reluctant Jonah that traveled to Nineveh to warn the people of the judgment about to fall on them. However, unlike the Israelites who had become so stubborn in their ways, the people of Nineveh repented immediately, which angered Jonah. However, the story ends with the illustration given him by God, regarding his love and compassion for Jew and Gentile.

"Then the LORD said, 'You had compassion on the plant for which you did not work and which you did not cause to grow, which came up overnight and perished overnight. Should I not have compassion on Nineveh, the great city in which there are more than 120,000 persons who do not know the difference between their right and left hand, as well as many animals?'" Jonah 4:10-11

---

[7] Mt 12:39-41

It appears Jonah trusted God, since he told the men on the ship to throw him overboard, and he did not seem afraid. He knew the maker of heaven and earth was behind it all. Therefore, it is curious why he ran, especially in the other direction. Perhaps he thought he could waste time or that God would change His mind or choose someone else.

Notes

Nahum

The book of Nahum denounces Nineveh and predicts its destruction in three short chapters. Only a few decades before Nahum, the mighty empire of Assyria had overrun the northern tribes of Israel and had taken them into captivity. Judah was not captured but was under the oppression of Assyrian imperialism. They were the world power of the time.

More recently, Assyria had just conquered the great Egyptian city of No-Amon (Thebes). Who could revolt against such a great power? Yet, Nahum prophesied its destruction. The absurdity of Nahum's message left him in a place of ridicule, which was not uncommon for God's prophets. However, it was a clear and hopeful message for Judah for at least a little while. This enemy will never bother them again (1:15).

The Ninevites had forgotten the mercy God had shown them through Jonah. Forgetting how they had been saved from the brink of destruction, they returned to their wickedness, and now the time for God's wrath had come.

Shamas Gate Nineveh Ruins, Iraq

Assyria was a particularly cruel empire. They terrorized people with torture and exceptional brutality. That is why Nineveh is referred to as "the bloody city." Since they had no mercy on the people they conquered, God will have no mercy on them – they were to be completely destroyed and obliterated.

"But with an overflowing flood He will make a complete end of its site, and will pursue His enemies into darkness." 1:8

Just as Nahum had spoken, the capital of this world empire was destroyed by the Babylonians in 612 BC.

In the midst of his short word regarding the coming destruction of the wicked Assyrian Empire, and it's capital Nineveh, Nahum also speaks of the wrath of God which will be poured out on the entire world at the end of the age (Ch 1:1-6). This is surely a reference to the Day of The Lord.

Notes

Micah

Micah was a prophet in Judah during the reigns of Jotham, Ahaz and Hezekiah (last third of the 8th century BC - 735BC). He was a contemporary of Isaiah in Judah and Hosea in Israel.

Chapter 1

As in all the prophets, we see the judgment that was about to come on the Northern kingdom, and Judah, as well as Assyria and Babylon jumbled up together with the Day of the Lord at the end of the age. Chapter 1 starts with God coming out of His place to make the earth tremble. Then the rest of the chapter talks about Israel's "incurable wound" and the invasion and exile soon to come under Tiglath-pileser and Sennacherib. Note it will reach as far as "the gate of Judah" which is Jerusalem. Sennacherib devastated many cities of Judah and laid siege to Jerusalem in 701BC.[8] This was the time when Hezekiah's Tunnel was built as the siege was anticipated. Also notice the prophetic play on words with the names of the various cities of Judah, i.e., Bethleaphrah (house of dust) roll yourself in the dust.

Sennacherib (as crown prince) on a relief from the Khorsabad, now in the Louvre.

Chapter 2

The prophet chastises Israel for her sin. It's the same message delivered by the other prophets. They scheme evil on their beds. They oppress the poor and the widows (verse 2 & 9). The prophets speak a warning, but no one listens (verse 6). The Lord is planning calamity. They will be taken captive and their fields given to "apostates" (backsliders or perverse ones - obviously their enemies).

Verses 12 & 13 are indeed curious. They seem to be talking about the remnant that will be gathered together by the Lord and led by the Messiah, the "breaker." However, it's also possible that this verse is talking about them being led as sheep into exile by the false prophet of verse 11, who is their king.

Chapter 3

A word is spoken to the leaders of Israel. They are scolded as those who hate good and love evil and who "eat the flesh of my people." The Lord holds the leaders accountable for the wickedness and injustice they are perpetrating.

Then the false prophets are confronted (verse 5-7). They lead the people astray with false words saying "peace." They say everything will be alright and calamity won't come! He says that darkness will come on the false prophets, and they will see nothing.

---

[8] 2 Kings 18 & 19, 2 Chron 32

In verse 8 Micah says that he is filled with the word of the Lord and with justice and courage to proclaim to "Jacob his rebellious act."

Then he speaks a word to Judah and to its leaders, priests, and prophets who "build Zion with bloodshed and Jerusalem (Zion) with injustice." They say, "Don't worry, calamity won't come on us, the Lord is in our midst." Then he gives an astonishing prophesy:

"Therefore, on account of you, Zion will be plowed as a field, Jerusalem will become a heap of ruins. The mountain of the Temple will become high places of a forest."

In Micah 3:11-12, the prophet Micah said that Jerusalem would be destroyed and that "Zion" - a central part of Jerusalem - would be "plowed like a field." Micah's prophecy is believed to have been delivered in about 730BC (about 2700 years ago). Since that time, Jerusalem was destroyed in 586BC by the Babylonians and by the Romans in 70AD. The Romans destroyed it again in 135AD to crush a Jewish rebellion for independence. According to a text in the Gemara (a collection of ancient Jewish writings), the Romans ran a plow over Zion on the 9th day of the Jewish month of Ab. It also states that Turnus Rufus, a Roman officer, plowed the area of the Temple. This prophecy was fulfilled in literal detail. Incidentally, there was a Roman coin minted during that era that shows an image of a man using a plow. The coin was intended to commemorate the founding of the pagan Roman city called Aelia Capitolina, on the site of Jerusalem. The Romans minted coins showing the plowing motif as a symbol of the establishment of the new Roman city.

Hadrian minted this bronze coin to commemorate the refounding of Jerusalem as a Roman colony named Colonia Aelia Capitolina. Symbolizing the beginning of a new Jerusalem, Hadrian is shown plowing the land with a bull and a cow.

The Jews fast (go without food) on the 9th day of the Jewish month of Ab (sometimes spelled Av) in remembrance of five historic events that are recorded as occurring on that date. One of those events is the plowing of all or part of Jerusalem by the Romans.

Chapter 4
Chapter 4 is almost identical to Isaiah chapter 2. Since they were both contemporaries it is possible, of course that they conferred. They were obviously hearing the same thing. The picture changes drastically from the end of chapter 3, where Zion is being destroyed and the Temple Mount is becoming a forest, to its being raised above the hills and all the nations streaming to it. This is a picture of the restoration of Zion and the Millennial reign. Jerusalem will be restored, and the Temple will be restored (mountain of the House) and all the nations will go up to Jerusalem to learn Torah. The remnant of Israel will be brought

back, the outcasts and lame will be made a strong nation, and the Lord will reign over them in Jerusalem forever.

Then there is the "birth pains" which begin the Day of The Lord. The statement "for now" (verse 10) speaks of Micah's present day, declaration that Judah and Jerusalem will be taken into exile to Babylon; yet in the same verse is the promise of God's future redemption and restoration. Verse 11 to chapter 5:1, are about the battle at the end of the age – the Armageddon Campaign. All the nations will come against Jerusalem and God through Israel will pulverize them.

Chapter 5
In the middle of verse 1 there is a switch from the Campaign of Armageddon to the rejection of Jesus. Remember, all these events are far in the future for the prophet.

In this chapter we see the Remnant Bride as in Revelation chapter 12.

"Writhe and labor to give birth, daughter of Zion, like a woman in childbirth, for now you will go out of the city, dwell in the field, and go to Babylon. There you will be rescued; there the LORD will redeem you from the hand of your enemies. And now many nations have been assembled against you who say, 'Let her be polluted, and let our eyes gloat over Zion.' But they do not know the thoughts of the LORD, and they do not understand His purpose; for He has gathered them like sheaves to the threshing floor. Arise and thresh, daughter of Zion, for your horn I will make iron and your hoofs I will make bronze, that you may pulverize many peoples, that you may devote to the LORD their unjust gain and their wealth to the Lord of all the earth. Now muster yourselves in troops, daughter of troops; they have laid siege against us; with a rod they will smite the judge of Israel on the cheek. But as for you, Bethlehem Ephrathah, too little to be among the clans of Judah, from you One will go forth for me to be ruler in Israel. His goings forth are from long ago, from the days of eternity. <u>*Therefore, He will give them up until the time when she who is in labor has borne a child. Then the remainder of His brethren will return to the sons of Israel.*</u> *And He will arise and shepherd His flock in the strength of the LORD, in the majesty of the name of the LORD His God. And they will remain, because at that time He will be great to the ends of the earth." Mic 4:10-5:4 Emphasis Mine*

Jesus leaves the Temple (Mt 23) – gives them up! Movie, Jesus of Nazareth"

This passage is clearly talking about the end of the age (Micah 4:1), the battle of Armageddon (4:13-5:1), and the time of Jacob's distress (4:10). Then there is a digression (which is typical of the Hebrew prophets) to the rejection of the Messiah and the statement that "he will give them up until the time when she who is in labor has borne a child." Just

36

as in Isaiah 66, this passage has also been interpreted to be referring to Mary, the mother of Jesus, giving birth to Messiah. But this simply does not fit for several reasons:

➤ The Messiah is being spoken of as the one who is being rejected by Israel in 5:1, born in Bethlehem, going forth to be ruler in Israel in 5:2, and the one who does the giving up (of Israel) in 5:3. Therefore, since He is the one who gives her up "until the time when she who is in labor gives birth," how can He be the one born?

➤ It says that He (the Messiah) gives them up "until she who is in labor has borne a child." The word "until" means that after the child is born, He will no longer give them up, but will instead begin to shepherd His flock and usher in His Millennial reign (5:4). If Jesus is the One spoken of as being the child that is born, then why did He not establish His rule and why did He give them up at that time?

➤ In verse 4 we are told that, after the time that the child is born, Israel lives securely and enters into a time of great peace and prosperity. If Mary was the one spoken of in the prophecy and Jesus the child born, then where did the peace go and why were the Jews scattered to all the nations?

I believe that the prophecy is telling us the following:

➤ Messiah gave up the nation of Israel after His rejection. This is consistent with the rest of Scripture (Mt 23:36-39, Mt 21:43, Rom 11:25). He did not reject Israel forever, but He allowed the prophesied judgment to come on them, and He turned His focus on the Gentiles. Jerusalem and sadly the Jewish people were trodden underfoot by the Gentiles.

Revelation 12

➤ The "time when she who is in labor" refers to the Day of Jacob's Distress. This is the context of the passage (4:10). The child born to Israel at this time is the Bride of Christ, made up of Jew and Gentile.

➤ "Then the remainder of His brethren will return to the sons of Israel" (5:3). This is a reference to the remnant being brought back by Jesus from the ends of the earth to join their brothers in Israel. Thus, He will arise and shepherd His flock (5:4).

➤ The one born of Israel at this time cannot be the remnant that is sealed (Rev 7:3-8), because it is said that He gives up the sons of Israel until after this one is born. This giving up is not complete rejection. Neither does it imply that God is not working on behalf of Israel. That is obviously not the case. He continues to watch over Israel, however He is not fellowshipping with them as a nation, until that time when the veil is removed and there is healing in their relationship. It is interesting to note the key role the rapture of the Bride plays in the repentance of Israel, and the removing of the hardness that is still over their hearts.

Verse 6-15 speak of the ascendancy of Jacob and how the nations will be subdued, and God will cut away idolatry from them completely.

Chapter 6
This chapter returns to the present situation and calls on the nation to repent. They are asked to remember how God brought them up from Egypt and how He dealt with them over the sin of Balak, and Balaam son of Beor, when they committed idolatry and fornication with idols.

Verses 6-16 are a call to true repentance and a promise that God will bring a curse on those who pervert justice in the land. Then there is the much beloved and quoted passage indicating what God really wants from them.

"He has told you, O man, what is good; and what does the LORD require of you but to do justice, to love kindness, and to walk humbly with your God?" Micah 6:8 NASU

Chapter 7
Verse 1-6 are again describing the evil of the land, "both hands do it well." It is a situation where all are untrustworthy and looking out only for themselves. Verse 6 was quoted by Jesus and used to describe the persecution that would come on account of Him. "A man's enemies would be the members of his own household."

Verses 7-20 return to the theme of Israel's restoration at the end of the age. The prophet speaks in the first person, but he seems to be speaking for the nation. The Lord will punish Israel but bring them out to the light (verse 7-8). Then their enemies who scoffed at them will be put to shame. Israel will be built up and the nations will come to her (verse 11-12). In verse 13 there is a reference to the destruction of the Day of The Lord. Then there is the call for the Lord to shepherd His people as in the days of old. The Lord will display miracles and wonders (verse 15), and the nations will be ashamed and come trembling to the Lord and will be afraid before Him. The Lord has restored the remnant of His people (verse 18). "He delights in unchanging love." He will again have compassion on them and tread their enemies underfoot. He will cast their sins into the depths of the sea. The time has come. God is fulfilling this word!!!! Amen!!!!

Notes

Zephaniah

Zephaniah was a prophet during the time of Josiah king of Judah (640-609 BC). This would make him a contemporary of Jeremiah. His short, but significant book, seems to record the words that he spoke in the early years of the king's reign, before Josiah carried out his purging of idolatry from the land.

The major theme of the book is the Day of the Lord.

The Day of the Lord is Coming
Though the theme of the Day of the Lord concerns the judgment which God was about to bring upon the land of Israel at that time, it always seems to jump to the end of the age and the final judgment upon the nations for their treatment of the Jews. This pattern is typical throughout the prophetic writings, and we must be careful to see it. The prophets were shown the future not only of Israel, but of the whole world. And sometimes there were long gaps of time between these "coming" events that was not clear to them. Those of us who have the benefit of hindsight, can see which of these events have happened in history and which ones are still future.

Chapter 1: 1-6
The chapter begins with God's promise to bring judgment on all the inhabitants of the earth. He will stretch out His hand against Judah and Jerusalem and all the "remnant of Baal" as He calls them. They worship all the host of heaven from their rooftops and swear to Yahweh but by the name of Milcom or Molech, the god of the Ammonites. Also, those who have turned back from following Him or who have not sought Him or inquired of Him.

Verses 7-14
The Day of the Lord is near for Judah and Jerusalem. He will punish the idolaters and those who act wickedly towards the Lord with violence and deceit. He will punish the kings and princes who clothe themselves in foreign or strange apparel – i.e., the customs of the pagans. The Lord will search Jerusalem with lamps, and He will expose all wickedness that is done in the darkness. Nothing will escape or be covered up. The Lord will punish all the men who are settled in complacency and say that He will not do good or evil. In other words, they are saying that the Lord is ok with the way things are.

Verses 14-18

Though these verses refer to the immediate judgment about to come from the Babylonians, they also seem to jump to the Day of the Lord at the end of the age, when all the nations who come against Israel will be judged.

"Neither their silver nor their gold will be able to deliver them on the day of the LORD'S wrath; and all the earth will be devoured in the fire of His jealousy, for He will make a complete end, indeed a terrifying one, of all the inhabitants of the earth." Zeph 1:18

Also, these verses are almost identical with Isaiah 2:12-22, which is clearly referring to the Tribulation period also known as the Day of the Lord.

Chapter 2:1-3

The call goes out to Israel, the "nation without shame," to humble themselves and seek righteousness. Though the wrath is coming, perhaps if they humble themselves the Lord might hide them during it.

Ashdod today

Verses 4-7 – Judgment on the Philistines

The Philistines of the seacoast are warned that they will not escape. They will be driven out of their cities and there will be none left. This all took place under the Babylonians in 604BC.[9] The Lord executed His judgment against them for all their evil deeds. Their territory in Canaan was never conquered by Israel and they oppressed the people of God throughout their existence. But now they will be no more, and the remnant of Israel will inherit their territory. Though Gaza today is inhabited by what are likely Arab tribes and the remnant of Edom, they are still at war with Israel. Yet these Scriptures are clear! Just as Ashdod and Ashkelon are Israeli cities today, Gaza will also be possessed by the Jewish remnant.

Verses 8-10 - Judgment of Moab and Ammon

Moab and Ammon, the descendants of Lot, were always enemies of Israel. The Lord gave them many chances to repent but they continued in their idolatry and hatred. They are said to taunt the people of God, reviling them and their territory. It is likely that they thought they would escape the destruction of the Babylonians. But the Lord says that because of their pride and their arrogance toward Israel, they would be destroyed and be like Sodom and Gomorrah. Thus they disappeared of the pages of history and their land was occupied

---

[9] See Jeremiah 47, Pg. 93

by Arab tribes.[10] It is likely that the territory of Moab and Ammon, which is the Hashemite kingdom of Jordan today, contains a remnant of the original people mixed together with Arab's and Syrians. Nevertheless, their territory will be occupied by Israel soon.

Verse 11 states that God will judge the gods of Ammon and Moab, but then the verse seems to reach forward to the end of the age when God will starve the gods of all the nations and the coastlands will bow down to Him.

Verses 12-15 – Judgment upon Ethiopia and Assyria

The Ethiopians will be slain by the sword we are told. They are not slated for destruction or exile as the others, and thus the nation continues to this day. Assyria on the other hand was to be annihilated without trace remaining. This was a just punishment for what they had done to the northern kingdom.

Chapter 3:1-7 -The Rebellious City

Jerusalem is described as the rebellious, tyrannical city, who refuses the Lord's correction. Her princes are like roaring lions who devour the people. Her prophets are reckless and treacherous. Her priests have profaned the sanctuary and done violence to the Law. The Lord is righteous within her bringing His justice to light every morning, but the unjust within her know no shame. Therefore, the Lord will bring His judgment upon her.

In verse 8, while declaring the injustice and recklessness of Judah which is refusing to listen to Him, the Lord speaks of the distant future when He will gather all the nations against Jerusalem and enter into judgment with them.

"Therefore wait for Me "declares the LORD, "For the day when I rise up as a witness. Indeed, My decision is to gather nations, to assemble kingdoms, to pour out on them My indignation, all My burning anger; for all the earth will be devoured by the fire of My zeal." Zeph 3:8

Verses 9-20 – Restoration at the End of the Age

Though the Lord plans to bring Judgment upon Judah and Jerusalem, His focus changes to the end of the age when He will bring them back to the land. He will purge them of their haughty godless ones, and He will bring back a humble remnant to Himself. A remnant that will do no wrong. A humble and lowly people that take refuge in the Lord and do no wrong and tell no lies and neither will a deceitful tongue be in their mouths. They will feed and lie down with no one to make them afraid. They Lord will have taken away His judgments against them and cleared away their enemies and they will fear disaster no more. Then comes this wonderful passage about the Lord rejoicing over them with shouts of joy, which is often used by the church to speak of itself with no mention of Israel. However, these passionate words must not be lifted from their context. The Lord will gather back the remnant of Israel from all the nations and establish them in Zion and rejoice over them

---
[10] See Jeremiah 48 & 49, Pg. 94

with singing. For He is a victorious warrior who saves. He will deal at that time with all their oppressors after he has purged the nation of her haughty ones. He will gather the lame and the outcast, and we are the generation that has seen this throughout the 20th Century. But the Lord has not yet finished His work. He is about to bring them back to Himself and remove all their shame.

"At that time I will bring you in, even at the time when I gather you together; indeed, I will give you renown and praise among all the peoples of the earth, when I restore your fortunes before your eyes," says the LORD." Zeph 3:20

Notes

Habakkuk
"In wrath remember mercy."

Habakkuk prophesied during the time just before the exile. The people of Judah had come to such a wicked state that the judgment of God was inevitable, and the prophet knew it. In fact, God had revealed to Him the details of His plan to allow the Babylonians to conquer Judah and take the people into exile. But, despite this knowledge, Habakkuk appears to have had some mixed feelings over this imminent judgment.

Chapter 1 – The Chaldeans are Coming

The book begins with what is called the oracle or burden which the prophet saw. Verses 1-4 seem to be highlighting the rebellion and wickedness of Judah. How long must he have to look on this violence and injustice? The law is ignored, and justice perverted. Then comes the answer – the Babylonians are coming to bring judgment.

The answer to Habakkuk's prayer is revealed.

"Look among the nations! Observe! Be astonished! Wonder! Because I am doing something in your days— You would not believe if you were told. For behold, I am raising up the Chaldeans, that fierce and impetuous people who march throughout the earth to seize dwelling places which are not theirs." Hab 1:5-6

This is the burden that he is carrying. God is sending the Chaldeans to judge Judah. Then the passage goes to describe the warfare of the Babylonians and how they seize property that is not theirs and operate on their own authority. They mock rulers and laugh at every fortress. They lay siege and capture every city. Their horses run like leopards and they swoop down like the eagle. A great and mighty army is coming that will sweep through like the wind and pass on. But they will be held guilty, those whose god is their own strength.

Then the prophet seems to question why God is allowing this. He acknowledges that the Lord has appointed them to judge Israel but finds it hard to understand why they are not judged as well since they are worse.

"Your eyes are too pure to approve evil, and You can not look on wickedness with favor. Why do You look with favor on those who deal treacherously? Why are You silent when the wicked swallow up those more righteous than they?" Hab 1:13

It's the age-old question and one that we hear a lot today. Why do the wicked seem to prosper? Or why does God allow evil? Habakkuk asks the Lord why He allows men to be like fish in the sea with no ruler over them. The Chaldeans, he says, bring them up with a hook and drag them away with a net. Then they feast and worship their net and offer incense to it. In other words, they give glory to themselves and their own power and skill. Then the prophet asks will they be allowed to continue this practice and slay nations without sparing?

Chapter 2 – The Wicked will be Judged

Habakkuk says he will stand guard on the rampart and keep watch to see what the Lord will say to him and how he may reply when he is reproved. From this we see that the prophet knows he deserves a rebuke and yet his struggle is genuine. Then he tells us that the answer comes from heaven.

"Then the LORD answered me and said, "Record the vision and inscribe it on tablets, that the one who reads it may run. For the vision is yet for the appointed time; it hastens toward the goal and it will not fail. Though it tarries, wait for it; for it will certainly come, it will not delay." Hab 2:2-3

This admonition seems to be saying that what matters is the vision and goal of God – His plan and purpose which He intends to accomplish. There is an appointed time for the judgment of Judah and for the Chaldeans. We must be patient when that judgment tarries and not assume it's not coming. All the proud and arrogant will die but the righteous man will live by his faith.

This portion of verse 4 that says, "the righteous man will live by his faith," is quoted by Paul in Romans 1:17 to underscore that the righteous are always justified based on faith and never by works under both the Old and New Covenants.

The rest of the chapter lays out the case that the wicked will not escape. Whatever a man sows he will also reap. The Chaldeans may be prospering now, and may seem to be getting away with evil, but the time of their judgment will come. They will not escape. They have looted many nations but those who remain will loot them. As they have measured out it will be measured back to them. The righteous must be patient, God's judgment on evildoers may tarry but it will surely come. The plan and purpose of God will be completed. The vision is certain, but we must wait for it and trust the Lord who is working His plan. Then comes the reminder of God's promise and the kingdom of Messiah.

"For the earth will be filled with the knowledge of the glory of the LORD, as the waters cover the sea." Hab 2:14

The Lord also addresses idolatry saying there is no profit in idols. The one who fashions it trusts in his own handiwork. It may look good, but it is speechless and though he overlay it with gold there is still no breath in it. Woe to those who worship idols. However, the prophet is reminded that God is in His holy temple and all the earth should be silent before him.

Chapter 3 – In Wrath Remember Mercy

This chapter seems to be a psalm and prayer of Habakkuk the prophet. "Shigionoth" seems to be a wild passionate song. The prophet is rejoicing over the majesty and splendor of the almighty who judges the earth in righteousness. The prayer is that, in the coming wrath to be poured out on Judah, the Lord would remember mercy.

"LORD, I have heard the report about You and I fear. O LORD, revive Your work in the midst of the years, in the midst of the years make it known; in wrath remember mercy." Hab 3:2

The Lord comes from Teman and Paran (the East). His splendor covers the heavens, and the earth is full of His praise. This beautiful psalm goes on to sing of God's majesty and power in judgment. In verse 12 it seems to reach to the judgment of the end of the age.

"In indignation You marched through the earth; in anger You trampled the nations." Hab 3;12

As the Psalm ends the tone seems to change to acceptance of God's judgment that must come on Judah. The prophet says that even though he is trembling about what is to come he must wait quietly for the day of distress.

"I heard and my inward parts trembled, at the sound my lips quivered. decay enters my bones and in my place I tremble. Because I must wait quietly for the day of distress, for the people to arise who will invade us." Hab 3:16

Then comes the declaration of faith and trust in the Lord.

"Though the fig tree should not blossom and there be no fruit on the vines, though the yield of the olive should fail and the fields produce no food, though the flock should be cut off from the fold and there be no cattle in the stalls, yet I will exult in the LORD, I will rejoice in the God of my salvation." Hab 3:17-18

Regardless of what destruction may come and how hard things may get, the prophet is trusting and depending on the Lord who is His deliverer. He will trust in Him and be secure no matter what comes. The Lord is his strength. The Lord is his refuge. He will make him an overcomer and give him hinds'[11] feet so that he can walk on high places and climb the craggy rocks. Those of us who are living at the end of the age and facing persecution and judgment in our nations, can take great courage from these words. The Lord is our refuge and help. He is our deliverer. As His wrath is being kindled for the final judgment, how blessed are those who take refuge in Him![12]

---

[11] A female deer
[12] Psalm 2:12

Notes

Isaiah

Author: This book was written by the prophet Isaiah and is a compilation of his prophecies as well as miniature historical accounts. Isaiah's wife was called a prophetess. They lived in Jerusalem with at least two sons. It is apparent from his writing that Isaiah was well educated and was of noble birth.

Time: Isaiah's ministry began in 740BC near the end of Uzziah's reign and spanned sixty years, through the reigns of Jotham, Ahaz, and Hezekiah. This would make Isaiah a contemporary with Hosea and Micah.

Isaiah is probably the most prominent prophet in the Bible because his written work is the longest and the most often quoted. The many prophecies in the book of Isaiah have the appearance of being sporadic and even repetitive at times, but it must be remembered that this is a collection of his many prophecies spoken throughout the sixty years of his ministry. Isaiah's prophecies have a broad perspective, encompassing events of the near as well as the distant future. Like the other prophets, Isaiah addressed the wickedness of his people and their imminent exile from the land. But the insight of Isaiah into future events is intensified by his many references and descriptions of the birth of the Messiah and the Day of the Lord. Just as prominent as the punishment of Judah, is its deliverance and establishment through its Savior. Although Isaiah's primary subject is the plight of his people the Jews (which is foremost on God's heart), many of his prophecies also concern the neighbors of Israel and Judah, and the fate God has for them. The judgment of these, and all the nations, is based upon how they treat God's people, and what they will do to the Jews in the future. Thus, the theme of the Day of the Lord at the end of the age runs throughout the book.

Chapter 1

Isaiah begins with the sick condition of Judah and Jerusalem and speaks of the coming overthrow and exile (verses 7-9), and the surviving remnant (verses 9,26,27). He laments their condition and compares it to leprosy (verses 5,6,18), which when it runs its course, becomes "white as snow." They are reprimanded for injustice, idolatry, and not caring for the orphan and widow. God says He hates their festivals and prayers because their hands are filled with blood. He appeals to them to repent and return and seek justice and righteousness. Their leprosy can be healed if they will seek the Lord and listen to Him (18). As always there is the promise of testing, sifting, refining, and restoration at the end. As with all the prophets, the coming judgment and restoration is a foreshadowing of the Day of the Lord and the restoration at the end of the age!

Chapter 2
Verses 1-4 are the same as Micah 4 and make it clear that at the end of the age, the Mountain of the House of the Lord (the Temple Mount in Jerusalem) will be the center of the earth, and all the nations will flock to it to learn the Law of the Lord and walk in his ways. Please note, that it is the mountain of the House of the Lord that will be exalted, meaning that the Temple will be rebuilt and rededicated by the Messiah. The people not only say, "Let us go up to the mountain of the Lord" but also, "to the house (Temple) of the God of Jacob."

Verses 5-9 are a call to repentance and a lament over Israel's current condition.

Then the rest of the chapter introduces the theme of the Day of the Lord at the end of the age. All the events of the sixth seal of Revelation 6 take place (Rev 6:12-17).

Chapter 3
This chapter is about God's judgment which is coming on the nation. God is going to remove "supply" and "support." The lack of competent leadership is the result of their sin. Their pride and wealth will be removed, and they will be taken captive and put to the sword. The city will be destroyed ("deserted she will sit on the ground").

Chapter 4
Verse 1 is a continuation of chapter 3, showing how the women will be begging to have their reproach removed. This is a contrast to their pride in the previous verses.

Verses 2-6 are a glorious prophecy of the restoration of the remnant at the end of the age and the Day of The Lord (in this case the glorious Millennial rule). The "Branch" is likely a reference to the Messiah. Notice in verse 4, how the Lord will have cleansed Jerusalem by the spirit of judgment and burning (the Day of The Lord - Tribulation part).

Chapter 5
Verses 1-8 are the parable of the vineyard which is the house of Israel. The Lord wanted fruit but found nothing but bloodshed, therefore, He will lay it waste. Jesus tells this parable again to the religious leaders of His day, whose generation was about to see a repeat of destruction on the city and the exile of the people throughout the nations (Mt 21).

Verses 13-30 are about the exile and destruction coming upon them from Babylon.

Chapter 6
Isaiah has a vision of the Lord in the Temple with the Seraphim above Him. Upon seeing the glory of the Lord, he becomes aware that

he is unclean - he feels ruined. Whenever the glory appears, we are captivated with our own need for Him. Isaiah realizes that his lips are unclean and that he is living among a people of unclean lips. The angel touches his lips, and he is cleansed from his iniquity (lawlessness). The lips reveal what is in the heart and when the lips are cleansed so also is the heart. Notice that God cleanses his lips before He sends him with the message. Isaiah volunteers to go. Then he is told that the people will not listen to the message although he is to speak it anyway (9 & 10). He then asks, "How long Lord?" He is told until the land is destroyed, and the people exiled (verses 11-12). However, verse 13 is the promise of a remnant - "the holy seed is its stump" (The Messiah is the Branch that comes from this stump).

Chapter 7 & 8

Ahaz king of Judah was a wicked king, and in his days, God sent the king of Aram (Syria) and Pekah son of Remaliah, king of Israel (Northern Kingdom), against Judah and Jerusalem to conquer it.[13] Even though they afflicted great casualties, Isaiah told Ahaz king of Judah not to fear for the Lord will not allow their plan to succeed. He will not allow His promise to David to be annulled for they intended to put "Tabeel" on the throne. Isaiah told him that within sixty-five years Ephraim (Israel - Northern Kingdom) would no longer be a nation.

Then the Lord (through Isaiah) told Ahaz to ask for a sign, presumably to confirm these prophesied events. Ahaz gave a sickening answer, saying "I will not test the Lord." This is the same man who forsook the Lord and offered his son in the fire to idols, and is now looking to the king of Assyria for help, that is acting so self-righteous. He really didn't believe the Lord would help him. Then the prophet said, "The Lord Himself will give you a sign."

"Behold, a virgin will be with child and bear a son, and she will call His name Immanuel. He will eat curds and honey at the time He knows enough to refuse evil and choose good. For before the boy will know enough to refuse evil and choose good, the land whose two kings you dread will be forsaken." Isa 7:14-16 NASU

This prophecy, like all the Messianic and Day of The Lord prophecies, has a dual meaning. It is a message for the present and the distant future. The present message is undoubtedly given in Chapter 8:3-4. The wife of Isaiah, the prophetess, conceived and bore a son who was called "Mahershalalhashbaz" and before he was able to know right from wrong, the land of both kings (Ephraim, with its capital of Samaria, and Aram/Syria, with its capital of Damascus) would be forsaken and taken over by the king of Assyria. Chapter 7:17-25 and 8:5-8, talk about the king of Assyria destroying both lands (Ephraim and Aram) and even coming up to Jerusalem and laying siege, which happened in the days of Ahaz' son, Hezekiah. The name of the child, "Immanuel", is not understood to be literal but symbolic; it means "the Lord is with us" and it is here with reference to the Lord being with Judah.

---

[13] 2 Kings 16, 2 Chron 28

The people of Israel (northern kingdom - Ephraim) are said to have rejected the "gentle flowing waters of Shiloah" (the waters of the Gihon spring in Jerusalem where Solomon was anointed) and have looked to the "River" (Euphrates in Aram/Syria and Assyria). Therefore, God will bring on them the waters of the Euphrates (the armies of the king of Assyria) which will even flow up to the neck (Jerusalem).

The second and future meaning is of the Messiah, Jesus, who is born of a virgin and is the promised son of David.[14] The prophecy, and its fulfillment, was to proclaim that God is with Judah, not because of Ahaz, but because of His promise to David. In the Messiah the meaning of the name "Immanuel" is even more clear; God is with them and among them. The prophecy is affirmed very emphatically in Chapter 8:9-10. In other words, nothing shall prevent its fulfillment. The passage goes on to talk about the Messiah as does the rest of Isaiah.

Verses 11-13
Don't listen to all this conspiracy talk or be afraid of these kings. The Lord is the one you should be afraid of.

Verses 14-15
He (the Lord, but in this case the Messiah) will become a sanctuary (Temple). It is clear Peter had this in mind when he wrote his epistle.[15] To both houses of Israel, the Messiah will be a stone of stumbling and a rock of offense.[16]

The fortified city of Samaria was destroyed.

Verses 16-22 - Isaiah says that the testimony and the revelation he has received, which was written on scrolls, was to be sealed, and kept among his disciples. God is hiding Himself from those who are not seeking Him. As for Isaiah, he will wait for the Lord who is hiding His face from Jacob. This passage is also Messianic (referring to Messiah) as the author of Hebrews points out.[17] Instead of seeking the Lord they are seeking after the idols of Assyria and the occult. Thus their destruction is imminent, because they do not seek the Lord or listen to the testimony of the prophet; they have "no dawn."

Chapter 9 - Verses 1-7
Now the prophet jumps to the distant future and the ministry of Messiah, Jesus. The land of Zebulun and Naphtali are the areas around the Galilee where Jesus ministered (Mt 4:14-16). This passage is very famous among Messianic passages. The Messiah's kingdom is

---
[14] Mt 1:23
[15] 1 Pet 2:5-8
[16] Is 28:16
[17] Heb 2:13

coming, and its increase will be without end. Notice, how Jesus is to reign on the throne of David his father. It is a literal kingdom. Also, notice how Jesus' first coming and second coming are intertwined. His ministry around the Galilee (first), and then His kingdom reign (second). Verses 4 and 5 are a reference to the Day of The Lord and the Armageddon campaign. The Lord will break the rod of the oppressor as on the day of Midian. Remember, that when Gideon fought this battle, the Midianites were confused and turned on each other. This will also happen again at the end of the age when the armies of the nations come against Jerusalem.

Verses 8-21 are about the northern kingdom of Israel and how they just say, "We'll put it all back together better than it was (10)." Because they do not seek the Lord, He will bring the very armies that they look to for help against them and they will be destroyed.

Chapter 10
Verses 1-4 chastise the people again for injustice and greed against the poor, the orphan, and the widow. They are asked, "What will you do in the day of punishment?"

Verses 5-19
The Lord says that although Assyria is like a rod in His hand that He uses to chastise His people, He will turn around and destroy her because of her pride and arrogance against Him. In other words, "Your turn is coming."

Verses 20-34
The Lord promises that the remnant of Israel will return (to the land) and be saved. We know it is speaking of the end of the age because it says, they will "never again rely on the one who struck them" but will rely on the Lord. This one is antichrist whom they will look to in our day, just as they looked to Assyria back then. The Lord says in a little while His anger will be spent against them, and He will turn on their enemies. Today the Lord is no longer angry with Israel, and those who attack them or cheat them now, will incur His wrath very swiftly.

Verses 28-32 show the progression of how the king of Assyria came up to Jerusalem to shake his fist at the mountain of the Lord.

Please note: Passages that refer to the end of the age are usually identified by the fact that they have not yet happened in full! Also, as I've said earlier in this book, it is very common for prophecies to jump from the prophet's present day to the distant future and back again.

Chapter 11
The passage continues about the end of the age and the ministry of Messiah. The "shoot from the stem of Jesse" and the "branch from his roots," are a reference to Jesus who is from the remnant and offspring of David, and of Jesse his father. Notice how the Holy Spirit rests on Jesus in a 7-fold measure (complete) and how He ministers to the poor and

afflicted, as opposed to what the current leaders are doing. Also notice, the first and second parts of His coming. In His second coming, He will strike the earth with the rod of His mouth[18] and usher in the kingdom reign, or Millennial reign (6-16). His resting place (Jerusalem) will be glorious!!

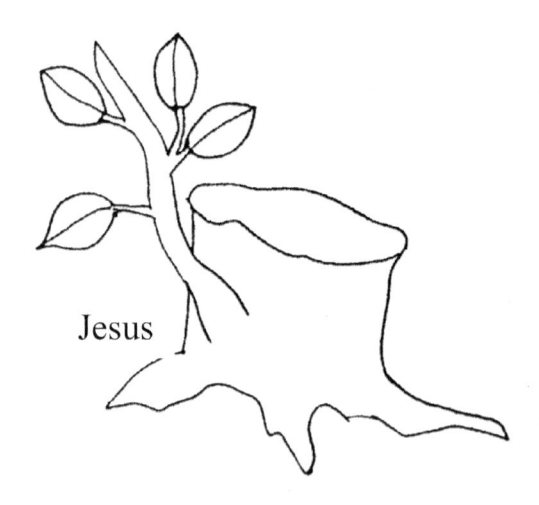

Verses 11-16 have begun to be fulfilled in our day. Notice, "He will bring them back a second time" – this is now past tense for us. The first time was after the Babylonian captivity. This time He has brought them back from all the nations. Verses 14-16 will yet be fulfilled; regardless of all the current threats the land will not be taken away from Israel again!

Chapter 12
This is a continuation! It talks of Israel rejoicing in the Lord because of what He has done for them at the end! The Lord will be in their midst, in Zion forever!

Chapter 13
In this chapter, Isaiah predicts the destruction of Babylon by the kingdom of the Medes and Persians. This is astonishing since it was not an empire in his days. The complete destruction of Babylon is predicted, however, from the context it is clear that it is not just about the conquest of Babylon by Cyrus the Great in 539BC, but also about the Day of The Lord at the end of the age (verses 6-13). Babylon represents the last great human Empire that will receive the wrath of the God. It is the head of gold in Daniel Chapter 2 that is representative of all other kingdoms.[19]

Chapter 14
Verses 1-3 are a continuation from the previous chapter. When the Lord has settled Israel again in her land and has poured out judgment on Babylon, they are to take up a taunt against the king of Babylon. The passage goes on to talk about the attitude and destruction of the king of Babylon, which although it is about the actual king of Babylon, seems also to refer to the Empire at the end of the age. Note, verses 1-3 show Israel being brought back by other nations who become their servants. Though Persia did assist in the first return, Israel continued to be servants of the resulting empires until the present day when all the nations have assisted them in their return.

Many believe that verses 12-14 are about satan, as they could not be about a human.

"How you have fallen from heaven, O star of the morning, son of the dawn! You have been cut down to the earth, you who have weakened the nations! But you said in your heart, 'I

---
[18] Rev 19:15
[19] See Rev 13, 17 & 18

will ascend to heaven; I will raise my throne above the stars of God, and I will sit on the mount of assembly in the recesses of the north."

The star of the morning is Lucifer who will fall from the heavens at the beginning of the Tribulation period. He is the one who energizes the Antichrist whose kingdom is the final manifestation of Babylon. (Rev 17-19, Dan 2:38).

Assyrian siege ramp at Lachish.

Verses 22-26 refer to the destruction of Assyria. It could be that these two empires are being lumped together because Assyria ruled over Babylon and then Babylon conquered Assyria. It could also refer to Sennacherib's (King of Assyria) defeat during the siege of Jerusalem in 701BC, when 185,000 men were slain by the angel of the Lord (2 Kings 18-19, 2 Chron 32 - "My land" and "My mountains").

Verses 29-31 warn Philistia not to be happy at Judah's demise since they will also be destroyed by the Babylonians. Verse 32 seems to be telling Philistia that the Lord has founded Zion and the afflicted of His people will seek refuge in it!

Chapters 15 & 16
The destruction of Moab is predicted in great detail. Moab was across the Jordan river from Israel and south of Ammon. Both Moab and Ammon comprise the kingdom of Jordon today. It seems that Moab is being told to send tribute to Judah (Zion) and seek help (16:1-5). However, Moab will experience devastation because of her pride. It appears that this took place under the Assyrians! In 16:5 we have this beautiful promise of the Messiah's reign from Jerusalem, the tent of David.

Chapter 17 concerns the destruction of Damascus, the capital city of Aram (Syria). Damascus was allied with Israel (Northern Kingdom) against the Assyrians, but to no avail – both were overcome by the Assyrians. Verse 4 says Jacob would be like a fat man that wasted away (verse 4).

Many feel that this prophecy (verse 1) regarding Damascus has yet a future fulfillment, since the city was not completely destroyed to become "a ruinous heap." This is remotely possible, but it is more likely that the destruction under Tiglath-Pileser III in 732BC was the fulfillment. Notice how the destruction of Ephraim (Samaria) and Damascus are together. This is the context of the chapter and Assyria only overcame them both once in history. Some argue that although Damascus was damaged and lost its seat of power (verse 3) it did not become a heap of ruins and limped on as a city.[20] Thus they conclude that the

---
[20] The ancient city of Damascus is likely not the same site as modern-day Damascus, and the original site is probably in ruins.

prophecy is not yet fulfilled. However, the same was said of Babylon (Jer 51:37) since it was not completely destroyed in battle, only abandoned, yet it is a heap of ruins today.

Chapter 18 contains prophecy concerning Ethiopia. It seems that it is referring to the invasion of the Assyrians. This also seems to have a fulfillment in the Day of The Lord.

Chapter 19
The first half (verses 1-15) was likely fulfilled by the Assyrians. The latter half is to be fulfilled in the future. God has promised that Israel will govern the nations. It appears that the ancient highway from Damascus to Egypt will be established and that Assyria (not just Syria), and Egypt, will be a blessing along with Israel. Amen!

Chapter 20
Isaiah was instructed to walk about naked and barefoot as a sign that Egypt and Cush (believed to be Ethiopia), together with Israel, would be taken captive and led away naked and barefoot by Assyria.

Chapter 21
Verses 1-10 are about Babylon. Some feel that this was fulfilled when the Babylonian Empire was taken over by the Medes and Persians. It could also be about Babylon's rebellion against Assyria which was crushed. However, as with the others, there appears to be more reserved for the Day of The Lord.

Verses 11-17 warn Edom and Arabia that they too will be overrun by the Assyrians.

Chapter 22
This word is about Judah. The valley of vision is likely Jerusalem. Isaiah is referencing the attack on Judah and Jerusalem by Sennacherib. Though he had conquered many of the cities of Judah he was unable to take Jerusalem. During the siege, Hezekiah sought the Lord and Isaiah the prophet. As a result, the Assyrians were routed by the angel of the Lord.[21]

It was at this time that Hezekiah diverted the water from the Gihon spring inside the city through a marvelous tunnel (which can be seen today) to the lower parts of the city, thus enabling them to endure the siege (verses 9-11). Also, he strengthened the walls and extended them, knocking down houses to build a new wall. Portions of this wall, which actually goes right through some houses, can still be seen in the Jewish Quarter of the Old City today. However, though God delivered the people, they did not repent as they were

---

I'm inclined to believe that this prophecy is fulfilled. We need to remember that the prophets were people devoted to God, and thus the statements are filled with passion and emotion, resulting in them sometimes being slightly exaggerated to make the people aware of the passion in the heart of God. Although much of prophecy is literally fulfilled, we need to remember that it is not exact computer speak, rather words from God's heart.

[21] You can read about it in chapters 36 and 37.

supposed to. Instead, they partied and missed the whole point of the Assyrian invasion, which brings their ultimate destruction from Babylon.

The latter part of the chapter is a prophesy against Shebna who is over the king of Judah's house. He is to be replaced by Eliakim son of Hilkiah (see 36:3). However, although Eliakim was better than Shebna, he too would eventually fall. Notice the reference to the key of the house of David. Jesus, the ultimate king of Judah, who rules in righteousness used this verse to refer to Himself (Rev 3:7).

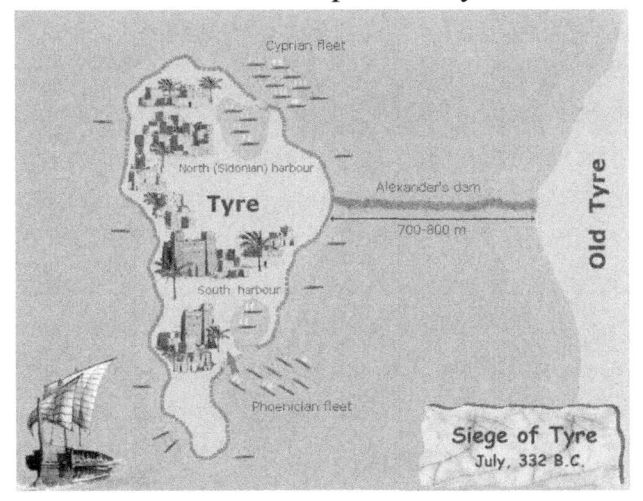

Chapter 23 is a prophecy against Tyre, a major influential port in the Mediterranean. The city had two parts, the mainland and an island off the coast. The city was surrounded by Nebuchadnezzar in 586 BC (the same time as Jerusalem was destroyed). He laid siege for 13 years and destroyed the mainland city. This is undoubtedly the reference to the 70 years it was forgotten, which was the period Babylonian rule. Nebuchadnezzar wasn't able however, to destroy the island portion and it lived on, having a resurgence under Persian rule. It was eventually destroyed by Alexander the Great in 332BC.

From Chapter 24 onwards the theme of The Day of The Lord rises to the fore. It is the destruction of all the nations that come against Jerusalem at the end of the age and then the Messianic reign begins. The imminent destruction of Israel and the nations round about spoken by the prophet, will be nothing compared to the destruction that the whole earth will feel in the Day of The Lord. This is the whole point. Make no mistake, Israel will be restored and will reign!

Chapter 24
The Day of the Lord (the Tribulation) is described. "Behold the Lord lays the earth waste, devastates it, distorts its surface and scatters its inhabitants" (vs 1). It won't matter in that day who is the priest and who is not, who is the servant and who is the master, for all will be mourning. The West and "the islands of the sea" cry out at the majesty of the Lord. And those in the East (Israel), or literally, "the region of light," are told to praise the Lord.

The destruction of the earth is very severe, and the prophet seems to suggest "it will never rise again." However, this is to emphasize the severity of the destruction. We know that the earth is not completely destroyed since it is restored by the Messiah. Notice in verse 21, how the Lord will punish satan's host in heaven and will reign in Mt. Zion (Millennium). When it says that the sun and moon will be ashamed it means that the light of Israel will shine so bright because of the presence of God.

Chapters 25, 26 & 27 sing praises in advance, if you would, for all that the Lord will do for His people in that Day. The Lord has destroyed their enemies and begun to reign. They will rejoice in the Messiah when the mourning has ended!

"And it will be said in that day, Behold, this is our God for whom we have waited that He might save us. This is the LORD for whom we have waited; let us rejoice and be glad in His salvation." For the hand of the LORD will rest on this mountain…" Isa 25:9-10 NASU

Notice the banquet in the beginning of the Millennium for all the earth. This feast was commonly anticipated by the Jews and may be the wedding feast.[22] Look how the Lord will utterly destroy His enemies (their enemies) in 26:11. Notice, how the land will be extended to the Biblical boundaries (26:15). Chapter 26:16-21 are about the Tribulation (Day of The Lord) - Jacob's distress. See how it ends with the resurrection of the righteous Jews, something the enemies said would not happen (verse. 14). Notice, the hiding (protection) of the Remnant nation in 26:20. The Lord is about to come out of His place (Messiah). This leads into Chapter 27. The Lord will punish Leviathan (the twisted serpent), the dragon that lives in the sea. This is obviously symbolic language for the pride of men, although it may also refer to Satan (Job 41). There seems to have been a creature called Leviathan, a sea monster, as well, although I think here it is symbolic. In Chapter 27:1-6 the prophet returns to the vineyard theme. This time the Lord's vineyard will bring forth fruit (verse 9).
Verses 8-11 are about the scattering and punishment.

Verse 12
The Lord promises to gather them one by one, and in verse 13 the Messiah will blow the Shophar and all the Jews remaining in the nations will be brought home.

Chapters 28-33 return to the theme of the coming judgment on Israel (Ephraim and Judah) and all the nations round about by the Assyrians. It is interspersed with restoration promises.

Chapter 28:1-4 are about the destruction of Ephraim for its corruption. The "proud crown of the drunkards of Ephraim" is Samaria at the head of the "fertile valley." The overflowing waters are armies, and the proud crown is thrown down (verse 3) - swallowed up like the first fig. The "drunkenness" is a picture of their living luxuriously and recklessly. They have no sense and are babbling like fools and babies.

---
[22] Mt 8:11

Verses 5-6

There appears to be a shift to Judah and the Lord being their crown at Jerusalem and their defense when the battle comes to the gate – likely Sennacherib's siege of Jerusalem. Could also be a reference to the remnant at the end of the age with the same meaning?

Verses 7-8

Judah also is living recklessly in wanton pleasure and drunkenness. The priest and the prophet reel from strong drink – meaning they are speaking falsehood and babbling like fools.

Verses 9-13 are often misunderstood. They have nothing to do with order. These are Hebrew monosyllables imitating the babbling of a child. This is how they view the message. With these they taunt the prophet, but the Lord will laugh back at them in the same way imitating their mocking with the unintelligible language of a conqueror.

Notice it's a play on words:

Sav Lasav, sav lasav - Order on order, order on order
Kav lakav, kav lakav – Line on line, line on line
Ze'er sham, ze'er sham – A little here, a little there

The Lord will speak to them with stammering lips and the language of foreigners. Paul uses this passage to say that the gifts of tongues are for a sign.[23] The Lord spoke rest and repose to them, but they would not listen. Since they would not listen to the Lord they will now have to listen to the tongue of a foreigner.

Verses 14-15 could be referring to Hezekiah's attempt to make a deal with Sennacherib.[24] But they are also referring to the covenant Israel makes with Antichrist hoping to escape the "overwhelming scourge" (attack of nations – 'flood' or 'floods' refers to armies). Notice how the prophecy jumps to the future in verse 16, and then to the end of the age in verse 17. This is the "Peace Treaty" Israel will sign in the days ahead, to avoid the scorn and attack of nations. But they will become the nation's trampling place (verse 18) and the Lord will cancel the covenant with Sheol (death).

Verses 16 & 17 are famous words about the Messiah "the tested stone." Those who trust in Him will not be disappointed.[25]

Verses 19-21 continue to talk about the Tribulation (Day of the Lord) when the Lord will do his extraordinary, strange work. He will rise up as at Perazim,[26] and in the valley of

---

[23] 1Cor 14:21
[24] 2Kings 18:14-16
[25] 1Pet 2:6
[26] 2Sam 5:20

Ayalon (also Gibeon) where the sun stood still, and God rained down hail on the Amorites.[27] Notice the hail in verse 17. It is one of the last plagues of the Day of the Lord.[28]

Some believe that verses 18-21 are about the siege of Jerusalem by Assyria, but they do not seem to apply since Jerusalem was spared. They could refer to the destruction of Jerusalem under Nebuchadnezzar, but there is no evidence of the Lord rising up as at Perazim, or the valley of Gibeon. It has been suggested that the work of the enemy is the Lord "rising up," however, this does not appear to be consistent with the examples the prophet gives, since it is God zealously fighting for Israel. The "strange work" likely refers to the sifting of Israel by foreign armies and could apply to either time. The overall context strongly suggests that these verses are about the surrounding of Jerusalem during the Day of the Lord Tribulation, and the Lord fighting for Israel.[29] Notice the Sun will also be affected at this time.

Valley of Ayalon

Verses 22-29 warn the people to stop the scoffing or things will be even harder. For the prophet says he has heard of "decisive destruction" for the whole earth. They are reminded that the farmer won't continually plow and harrow the ground but will plant seeds and gather a harvest. This refers to Israel. God's judgment will come to an end, and He will establish her and bring forth fruit.

Chapter 29
Verses 1-4 are about the destruction of Jerusalem. Ariel (lion of God) is another name for Jerusalem.
Verses 5-8 prophesy judgment on all the nations who come against her. As always, this part seems to jump to the end of the age (verse 5).

Verse 8 is a picture of the deception of the nations who think they are doing well but are deceived. They think they are benefiting by attacking Jerusalem, but they are not.

Verses 9-16 return to the faithlessness of Judah and the blindness that has come on them from the Lord (Rom 11:25). No one can read or understand the words of the prophet; they are like a sealed book. This is how it is today. But the Lord will restore them, and they will

---
[27] Joshua 10:10-15
[28] Rev 16:21
[29] Zech 14

again understand (verses 17 & 24). The Lord will restore the "children," the remnant of Jacob.

Jesus refers to this passage in Mt 15:8-9 when addressing the leaders of the people.

Chapter 30:1-17

The people are warned not to look for refuge in Egypt or to look to Egypt for help, which they did, but to look to the Lord. They are told that in repentance and rest is their salvation, but they would not listen (verse 15). So, since they won't turn to God, they will not have any protection.

Verses 18-33 again speak of the restoration of Israel and the Day of The Lord. The Lord is going to shake the nations back and forth as in a sieve (verse 28). The people of Israel are reminded of the joy of their festivals and how they will be renewed as the Lord pours out judgment on their enemies. Notice the plague of Hail at the end of the Tribulation (Day of the Lord judgment - verse 30).

Verses 31-33 address the coming judgment of Assyria by the Lord, even though it is in the same context. It is all future to the prophet who sees Israel's enemies being destroyed.

Chapter 31

Verses 1-3 again warn of going to Egypt for help rather than the Lord. He says they will all fall together.

Verses 4 & 9

God will protect Jerusalem and fight for it. Though this is a promise that the Lord will help if they turn to Him, as is the exhortation of verse 6, yet it is a promise that looks to the end of the age (see verse 7).

When General Allenby took Jerusalem from the Turks in 1917 (World War 1), British planes circled Jerusalem dropping warning leaflets in Arabic aimed at frightening the Turks. It succeeded and they fled handing the city to the British. At the time it was considered as a fulfillment of verse 5, "Like flying birds the Lord will protect Jerusalem." Allenby entered the city dismounted to show respect for the Messiah. It is probably not the only fulfillment.

Verses 8-9 deal with the destruction of Assyria, which the Lord carried out in Jerusalem under Hezekiah. This is viewed as part of the whole scenario which includes God's judgment on the nations at the end of the age!

Chapter 32
Verses 1-8 are about the Millennial kingdom and how righteousness will prevail, and the people will live in peace.

However, in verses 9-14, the people are called upon to wail and weep for the destruction that is coming. Yet, they are to intercede for the time when the Spirit is poured out on them from on high (verses 15-20).

Verse 19 talks about the hail when the city is destroyed. Though it is speaking of the imminent destruction, the context is the end of the age when the Millennium comes (verse 15 – "the Spirit is poured out" and "the wilderness becomes a fertile field").

Chapter 33
Verses 1-4 pronounce judgment on those who destroy Israel. As soon as they finish destroying, they will be destroyed. This has been true for all the kingdoms.

Verse 2 contains a prayer for God's graciousness to Israel.

Verses 5-14 again speak of the coming judgment and the sin of the people. The nations round about are warned to take notice as "sinners tremble in Zion."

Verses 14-24
There is the question in verse 14, "Who among us can live with a consuming fire?"[30] Then the answer comes (verses 15 & 16) - the righteous can. These are the ones who will receive the kingdom and see the King in his beauty. The rest of the chapter speaks of the Millennial age. The people will be restored and forgiven when the Lord saves them (verses 22-24).

Chapter 34
Verses 1-8 are about the destruction of the armies of the nations that come against Jerusalem in the Day of the Lord. The fact that this is the end of the age can be clearly discerned from verse 4:

"And all the host of heaven will wear away, and the sky will be rolled up like a scroll; all their hosts will also wither away as a leaf withers from the vine, or as one withers from the fig tree." Isa 34:4 NASU (Compare with Mt 24:29.)

---
[30] Heb 12:29

Notice the connection with Edom and Bozrah. It appears that the remnant will flee there, and the Antichrist and his armies will pursue them. Then the Lord will come and execute vengeance on them. The rest of the chapter talks about Edom becoming a perpetual waste as a result. In Isaiah chapter 63, the prophet returns to this event and talks about the Messiah whose garments are dipped in blood because of His treading out the winepress of God's wrath on the nations.[31] I realize that the campaign of Armageddon is said to take place in Israel and Jerusalem, but it is here as well!

Chapter 35
This wonderful chapter is about the restoration of Israel and Jerusalem (Zion), and the Millennial age. It starts off with the Arabah (the desert of Judea) blossoming and becoming like Carmel in the north. What an amazing thing! It will be lush and green for streams will flow from the house of God on Zion and the Dead Sea will be teeming with life (verses 1-2). The fainthearted are to be encouraged with this (verse 3) as the Lord will come with vengeance and save His people (verse 4). Then the eyes of the blind will be opened, the deaf ears unstopped, the lame will leap like a deer, and the tongue of the dumb will shout for joy (Remember Jesus' words to John the Baptist – this was the proof that He was bringing the kingdom and fulfilling these words). In verse 8, the prophet speaks of the highway that will be there, called "the highway of holiness," where nothing unclean will travel on it (completely safe). Perhaps this is the same highway spoken of earlier (Is 11:16, 19:23) for the remaining remnant of Israel to come back from all the nations.

The Arabah

"And the ransomed of the LORD will return and come with joyful shouting to Zion, with everlasting joy upon their heads. They will find gladness and joy, and sorrow and sighing will flee away." Isa 35:10 NASU

Chapter 36
Sennacherib invades Judah. He took 46 of the fortified cities of Judah and finally came to Jerusalem. Hezekiah had been preparing for him. He had fortified the city with a new wall, and he had built the famous tunnel to redirect the water from the Gihon spring to the pool of Siloam inside the city. This chapter records the rantings of the Assyrian general Rabshakeh trying to intimidate the people of Jerusalem.

Chapter 37:1-7
Hezekiah went to the Temple to cry out to the Lord, and he sent delegates to Isaiah the prophet, asking him to pray to the Lord for the remnant of Judah, that God would intervene and save them and the city. Isaiah told them not to be afraid of the king of Assyria who would return to his own land and die there.

---
[31] Compare with Rev 19

Verses 8-13
Rabshakeh returns to taunt the people. Remember that this siege took some time. He sent another letter to Hezekiah with more threats which cause him to seek the Lord again (verses 14-20) and send to Isaiah for help.

Verses 21-35
Isaiah again prophesied that his attempt would fail, and he would die in his own land. He declared further that the remnant would survive and take root downward and bear fruit upward. This prophecy looks not just to the present but the distant future as well. God has determined to save a remnant for David's sake and establish them over his kingdom.

"Once more a remnant of the house of Judah will take root below and bear fruit above. For out of Jerusalem will come a remnant, and out of Mount Zion a band of survivors. The zeal of the LORD Almighty will accomplish this." Is 37:31-32 NIV

God makes it clear that He is personally involved with this plan and His zeal will accomplish it. He has not left it to the work of man. It is absolutely guaranteed!

Verses 36-38
Then the angel of the Lord went out and struck down 185,000 men of Assyria at nighttime causing them to flee the next day. Sennacherib departed and returned home and was killed by his own sons.

Chapter 38
Shortly after this Hezekiah became mortally ill. Isaiah came to him and prophesied that he was about to die and should set his house in order. Hezekiah cried out to the Lord and wept bitterly. While Isaiah was on his way out from visiting Hezekiah, God told him to go back and tell the king that his prayers had been answered and another 15 years had been added to his life. He also told his attendants to apply a cake of figs to the boil and he would recover. This was obviously a prophetic activation. Hezekiah apparently asked for a sign to test the word. The Lord told him that the shadow on the stairway of his father would go backwards, which it did. Time actually went backward.[32]

Verses 9-20 are the words of Hezekiah describing the distress of his illness and his joy and thanksgiving after his healing.

---

[32] There is much discussion and even scientific evidence of this miracle. Nevertheless, we don't need to have such data. God did it and nothing is too difficult for Him.

Hezekiah was a righteous king who walked in the way of his father David. However, after his illness he made a bad mistake.

Chapter 39
The son of the king of Babylon came to King Hezekiah to congratulate him on his recovery, however, Hezekiah took him on a tour of all his treasures and showed him everything. He is then chastised by Isaiah who prophesied that all his treasures and the treasures of his fathers would be taken to Babylon, and that his sons also would be taken and become officials in Babylon. This of course happened during Zedekiah's reign. Showing all his treasures was probably an act of pride. He should have been more careful and boasted in the Lord. Hezekiah's reaction is selfish and should have been one of repentance.

Chapter 40
This beautiful chapter returns to the theme of the Day of the Lord.

Verses 1-2 exhort us to comfort the Jewish people and speak kindly to Jerusalem and tell her that her warfare has ended. She has received double from the Lord's hand and now is to be comforted. This is clearly our mandate today. Now is the time to comfort Israel.

Verses 3-8 have been interpreted by the Gospels as referring to John the Baptist,[33] however, the Day of The Lord is also in mind as we can see clearly in verses 5-8.

"The glory of the Lord will be revealed and all flesh will see it together."

Jesus' first coming has parallels to His second and the Day of The Lord. John the Baptist was a type of Elijah who is still coming. "All flesh" is a broader fulfillment. John is the voice who is calling out in verses 3 and 6. Verses 3-8 are a good description of John's message (see Luke 3:4-20).

Verses 9-11 are about Messiah's first and second comings. Remember the prophet sees both as the future Messianic era and the Day of The Lord. Notice the Lord coming in might with His ruling arm outstretched in judgment and power, yet He is like a shepherd gathering the lambs.

Verses 12-31
The prophet goes on to speak of the Lord's power and inscrutable wisdom, who created the universe and numbers all the stars. How foolish is idolatry (verses 18-20)?

---
[33] Mt 3:3, Luke 3:4-6

Notice the earth is referred to as a circle in verse 22, long before man knew it was so.

Israel is chastised to trust in the Lord who does not become weary or tired. And that those who hope in the Lord will gain new strength and sprout wings and pinions like eagles.

Chapter 41:1-7
These verses warn that it is the Lord who delivers up nations and subdues kings. He is the First and the Last. Jesus used this verse to describe Himself and assert His deity.[34]

Verses 8-14
Israel is encouraged to trust in the Lord who will help them. This is the remnant brought back from all the nations ("remotest part of the earth," verse 9). This is the State of Israel today. Notice, how they are told not to "look anxiously about them" - looking for help. What a great description of the attitude of the present-day nation, looking everywhere for help rather than to the Lord. All the nations are against them. The Lord reassures them He will help them.

Verses 15-20 are about the destruction of the nations by the Lord, who will use Israel to pulverize them. It is clearly a reference to Armageddon and the Millennial reign. The Lord promises to make rivers run in the desert.

Verses 21-29 are about the situation at the time of the writing, the idolatry of the people trusting in idols and the coming destruction from the north (Babylon).

Chapter 42
This chapter speaks of God's servant Israel and the Messiah.

Verses 1-17 are about the Messiah's coming and reign. Notice it includes His first coming (verses 1-3 & 7) and His second coming, during which He will establish righteousness (verses 4, & 13-17). Idols will be completely destroyed.

Verses 1-4 are applied to Jesus by Matthew[35] speaking of His healing and benevolent grace and mercy.

Verses 18-25 are about Israel the servant of the Lord. There is a deliberate contrast here, and in the chapters to come, regarding Israel as God's servant and the Messiah. Israel God's servant is spoken of as blind and unable to see or hear. Therefore, the Lord pours out His anger on them and gives them up to plunderers.

Chapter 43
This is a continuation of chapter 42 ("but now").

---
[34] Rev 1:8
[35] Mt 12:17-21

Verses 1-7
Israel is encouraged that the Lord will watch over them and protect them no matter what they go through (verse 2) because they are His and He loves them. Then He promises to bring them back from all the lands, North, South, East and West. This has been literally fulfilled since the middle of the 20th Century. Great numbers of Russians have returned as the Lord sovereignly released them from the former Soviet Union.

Verses 8-13 are addressed to the nation that is blind and deaf. The Lord affirms that He is the Savior, the one who has delivered them. There is no savior besides Him, and no one can deliver out of His hand. The nations are challenged to present their witnesses as to how these things happened. Israel is exhorted that they are His witnesses and His servant who are to know that He alone is God and no one else can save. Oh, how they need to remember this!

Verses 14-21 speak of the destruction of Babylon but are also likely referring to the last days Babylon, since it also talks about the restoration of Israel.

Verses 22-28 return to the theme of Israel's unfaithfulness and destruction.

Chapter 44
This chapter is a continuation.

Verses 1-8 return to the Millennial reign. God encourages Israel not to fear. He will redeem them and pour out His Spirit on them (verse 3) and pour out streams of water in the desert. The nations will speak of them with honor. Notice verse 6, "Thus says the Lord (Yahweh) and His Redeemer (the Messiah who redeems Israel) 'I am the first and I am the last, and there is no God besides Me'" (a definite affirmation of Christ's deity). Here it is used to assert that the Lord alone will deliver Israel, and they are His witnesses.

Verses 9-20 again discuss the blindness of Israel God's servant, and the extreme folly of idolatry. He makes an idol of part of a tree and cooks his food with the rest. Notice the hardening of Israel that continues to exist today, even though the Lord has delivered him.

"They do not know, nor do they understand, for He has smeared over their eyes so that they cannot see and their hearts so that they cannot comprehend." Isa 44:18 NASU

This is the hardening in part that has happened to Israel until the "full number of Gentiles comes into the church."[36]

Verses 21-23
Israel is encouraged to remember that they belong to the Lord and will not be forgotten. He says He has wiped out their sins, and they are impored to "return" to Him since He has redeemed them. This is a now word to Israel; the Lord has redeemed them from the nations. They are now being called to turn back to God, their deliverer. All the earth and creation are exhorted to rejoice as God shows forth His glory through Israel.

Chapter 44:24 - Chapter 45:13 are about the return of Judah from Babylon and the restoration of Jerusalem. Cyrus, the Persian king who set the exiles free and made a decree to rebuild the Temple is mentioned by name. What a remarkable prophecy. The Lord again declares that He is Yahweh the Savior, and that there is no God besides Him. Who else can do this? Who else can raise up a Cyrus and cause him to show such kindness to the Jews?

Verses 14-17 carry on this theme of Israel's salvation by God, and how the nations around them will serve them. This portion may look to the future kingdom.

Verses 18-25
Israel is reminded that the Lord has spoken these things from of old and has made them clear. He is the Lord the creator of the universe and there is no God besides Him. Those of Israel and the nations who carry the dumb idol, who cannot save, must answer this; Who has saved Israel and brought her back from the nations? All the nations are exhorted to turn to Him and be saved for the God of Israel is God and there is no other (verse 22). Then the Lord says: "Every knee shall bow to Him."[37]

"I have sworn by Myself, the word has gone forth from My mouth in righteousness and will not turn back, that to Me every knee will bow, every tongue will swear allegiance." Isa 45:23 NASU

In verses 24-25, - All will know that only in the Lord is righteousness and strength. In the Lord all the offspring of Israel will be justified and all who were angry at Him will be put to shame.

---

[36] Rom 11:25
[37] Rom 14:11, Phil 2:10

Chapter 46
Bel and Nebo were Babylonian gods who are pictured as stooping over. There is a contrast given of the nations (in this case Babylon) carrying about these stooped idols on animals. They are useless and burdensome to carry. The Lord reminds Israel that He has carried them from birth and will carry them in their old age. Would they compare Him to an idol? God affirms that He will grant salvation to Zion (Jerusalem) and glory to Israel.

Chapter 47
This chapter is about the destruction of Babylon, her enslavement, and the loss of her kingdom. The Lord said He was angry with His people Israel, His heritage, and gave them into the hands of the Chaldeans, but they had shown no mercy. Notice how their attitude is contrasted with what the Lord has repeatedly been speaking about Himself; "I am and there is no one beside me" (verse 8).

Though this chapter is about the overthrow of Babylon by the Medes and Persians, like all the other passages, it has its final fulfillment at the end of the age. The last great empire under Antichrist (with 7 heads and 10 horns), the 10 nation or regional alliance, is also pictured as Babylon. Remember Daniel's visions of the 4 great empires to dominate Israel. Now consider these verses together with the Book of Revelation, Chapters 17 & 18.

Compare Is 47:7-8 with Rev 18:7, and Is 47:9-11 with Rev 18:8, and Is 47:8 (sensual) with Rev 17:5 & 18:9, and Is 47:15 with Rev 18:9.

Chapter 48:1-16
The same theme is continued. The Lord is the deliverer of Israel. He says that from the beginning she has been a rebel, the sinews in her neck like iron, and her forehead bronze. In other words, they are very stubborn. So, the Lord says that He has proclaimed what will happen to them from the beginning, so that they will know it is He who does it and not an idol. He promised to try them in the furnace of affliction. Then the Lord says He will do it for His name's sake, and He will not allow His Name to be continually profaned among the nations. The Lord says He will act because He loves Israel (verse 14), and His arm will be against the Chaldeans (Babylon).

Verses 17-22
The Lord grieves as a father for Israel; "If only (18) you had listened to me all of this could have been avoided." However, He promises to deliver them in the same way as He did from Egypt. Verse 22 is often misquoted today as saying "There is no rest for the weary" but God is saying that Israel's wicked oppressors will have no rest.

Chapter 49:1-13
The islands and people from afar (US included) are told to "listen up." God is the one who has formed Israel from the womb and made him an arrow in His quiver. Israel is the Lord's

servant through whom He will show His glory. "But I said (Israel - verse 4), I have toiled in vain." Israel complains, saying that all she is going through is in vain. Then she says, "Yet, surely the justice due me is with the Lord."

As we have seen already, though Israel is God's servant, the Messiah also appears as God's servant who will save Israel throughout these passages. Verses 5-8 hint of someone from Israel - the Messiah.

Then the Lord says that they will not only be His servant but a light to the nations. All who have abhorred them will bow down to them and serve them. The Lord will restore them to the land and make them inherit the desolate heritages (verse 8). He will bring them from afar and lead them from all the nations.

Verses 14-21
"Zion says, 'The Lord has forsaken me.'" The Lord asks, "Can a woman forget her nursing child and have no compassion on the son of her womb?" (verse 15). The answer is clearly, no! But even if she should, the Lord says He will not forget Israel. He said He has inscribed Israel on the palm of His hands and her walls (Jerusalem) are continually before Him. These are powerful and passionate words. Thus the Lord promises to restore them and bring them back and rebuild the ruins. He says the land that was barren will be cramped for them, because of the number of children. This was not fulfilled after the return from Babylon. Here God says they will be numerous and prosperous in the land!

Verses 22-26
The Lord says that He will lift up His hand to the nations and they will bring the Jews from afar. Their sons and daughters will be carried on the shoulders. This has been and continues to be fulfilled. All the nations and kings will bow down to them. Can the prey be snatched from the mighty man? Yes! God will snatch them and save them, and their oppressors will be given their own flesh to eat. And all the earth will know that the Lord is the Savior of Israel (verse 26). Amen! Wake up church - wake up nations!

Chapter 50
Verses 1-3
The Lord says that He had to divorce Israel and sell her as a slave. Verses 2-3 seem to be asking why there was no one to intercede and cry out to the Lord to save them.

Verses 4-10 are about the Messiah. Notice verse 6, which speaks of His suffering before the council and His flogging.[38] The Messiah is the servant of the Lord and the Savior of Israel. All the nations are to walk in His light.

---
[38] Mt 26:67

Verse 11
This verse is saying that the one who makes his own light and walks in it will receive torment!

Chapter 51:1-5
The people are exhorted to seek righteousness by returning to the faith of Abraham and Sarah. Then the Lord promises to restore Israel and comfort all her waste places.

Verses 4-5 likely refer to the ministry of the Messiah who is pictured throughout these chapters. The Lord will judge the peoples in righteousness and for His judgments the coastlands (distant nations) will wait expectantly.

Verse 6 - the cosmic signs of the Day of The Lord.

Verse 7-10
The people are told not to fear the nations. I believe these verses are spoken to the recovered remnant (the current state of Israel) not to be afraid since the Lord will deal with them. They are reminded of the destruction of Egypt (Rahab) and Pharoah (dragon in the Nile). Rahab here is not the same as Rahab the prostitute; the spelling is different in Hebrew. It is a symbolic reference to Egypt (see Ps 87:4).

Verses 11-16 - The Lord will bring back the exiles to Zion with a great deliverance, similar to when He brought them out of Egypt, and everlasting joy will be theirs. Notice verse 13, how the people fear all day long because of the fury of the oppressor. This is the current situation. They are told to look to the Lord who will deal with the oppressors.

Verses 17– 23
Jerusalem is told to rouse herself - she who has no one to lead her among all her sons (the current remnant). The Lord says that the cup of His anger is removed from Jerusalem, and He will pour it out on all who trample on her.[39]

Chapter 52:1-10
This is a continuation of chapter 51. Jerusalem is told to rouse or awake! These verses are fulfilled in the Millennium when Jerusalem is restored and Messiah reigns from there. The Lord will rescue Jerusalem and bare His holy arm in the sight of all the nations (Day of The Lord).

Verses 11-12 are telling the people, especially the priests, to go out and touch nothing unclean. These verses seem to be talking about the people coming back from captivity with God leading them.

---
[39] Luke 21:24

Verses 13-15 together with **Chapter 53** are about the Yeshua, the suffering servant. The ancient Jewish rabbis believed that these passages were about the Messiah; however, after the destruction of Jerusalem in 70 AD, the surviving scholars changed the meaning to Israel rather than Messiah to counter Christianity.

These are the most marvelous prophecies about Jesus.

52:14 - His appearance was marred due to His beating.
52:15 - He will sprinkle many nations
53:2 - The tender shoot or branch
53:3 - No stately form, i.e., humble in appearance, despised and rejected
53:4 - He bore our sicknesses and pains
53:5 - Pierced for our transgressions and crushed for our iniquities - by His stripes we are healed
53:7 - He did not open His mouth but is led like a lamb to slaughter (didn't defend Himself)
53:8 - He was cut off for the transgression of the people - rejected
53:9 - Crucified with the wicked and with a rich man in His death (two thieves - Joseph of Arimathea)

Verses 10-12
As a result of Messiah's suffering for the sin of the people He will justify the many and the good pleasure of the Lord will prosper in His hand.

Chapter 54
The prosperity of Zion after she is redeemed. She will spread out to the left and to the right and possess nations and resettle the desolate cities. The Lord in His anger forsook them for a moment, but with great compassion He will gather them. The Lord promises never to forsake them or be angry with them again. God promises to set the stones of the city in antimony (rare metal) and precious stones (compare to New Jerusalem in Rev 21). Notice the reference to terror in verse 14.

Chapter 55:1-5
All who are thirsty are encouraged to come to the Lord and find food and drink without cost. Listen carefully to Him and delight in abundance. For the Lord will make an everlasting covenant with them as He did with David, and other nations will come to them to seek the Lord because of the way the Lord will glorify them.

Verses 6-9 are a now word. The people are exhorted to seek the Lord while He may be found – to call on Him while He is near. The wicked should forsake his way and the unrighteous their thoughts and return to the Lord; then He will have compassion on them. For His ways and thoughts are so much higher than ours. Nevertheless, He wants us to have His ways and thoughts.

Verses 10-13

The Lord promises to watch over His word to perform it. It will not come back to Him without accomplishing what He desires. The exiles will return! They will go out with joy and be led forth in peace. The mountains and the hills of Israel will break forth with joy before them. This word is sure!

Chapter 56:1-2

The justice of the Lord and His righteousness are about to come. Blessed are those who do right regardless of their social class or position. This is the kingdom to come - the Millennial Reign.

Verses 3-8 hold out a promise to foreigners (Gentiles) who join themselves to the Lord to love Him and minister to Him. They will be blessed and will be brought to the house of the Lord in Jerusalem (Temple). This is clearly a reference to the Millennial Temple. Their burnt offerings and sacrifices will be accepted. Then there is the verse quoted by Jesus when He drove out the moneychangers,[40] "My house will be called a house of prayer for all the nations." Today we often hear this verse being used of the church; this usage is based on Replacement Theology. Please note also, John 2:17 where it is said that Jesus was very zealous for the Temple. He will restore the Temple during the Millennial period and all the nations will come up to worship. Remember Isaiah Chapter 2.

Verses 9-12 are a contrast to the beginning of the chapter and pronounce condemnation on the wicked. They return to the theme of Israel's unfaithfulness - the problem facing the nation at the time of the revelation.

Chapter 57:1-13

continue the theme begun in the end of chapter 56. Israel's adultery is spoken about in great detail.

Then in the middle of verse 13, it changes back to the future restoration and blessing. Those who take refuge in the Lord will possess the holy mountain (the surviving remnant).

---

[40] Mt:21-13

Verses 14-15 speak of building up, but yet it is speaking of repentance. There must be repentance first. The Lord lives in a high and holy place, yet He also lives with the contrite and lowly of spirit (verse 15).

Verses 16-19 - The Lord will heal the righteous who turn to Him, and verses **20-21** declare that the wicked can never know peace.

Chapter 58:1-7
These verses are an indictment against Israel. They act religiously as though they were a righteous nation, and they wonder why God doesn't hear them. They fast, but it is only a religious exercise ("bowing one's head like a reed"). God is not pleased because they oppress the poor and needy and all their workers. The fast that the Lord wants is to take care of the poor and needy, loose slaves, undo the bonds of wickedness, let the oppressed go free, take care of widows and orphans, and not to abandon their needy relatives (own flesh). It is not that the Lord does not want them to fast, but rather that they do righteousness and then their fast will be heard.

Verses 8-14 are the promise of the Lord to the ones who repent and come to Him. Again, these verses, although they apply to the time of the writing, are fulfilled in the Millennial period. Their light will break out as the dawn. Their righteousness will go before them and the glory of the Lord behind them. When they call He will hear them. They will be blessed of the Lord and will rebuild the ancient ruins.

Verses 13-14 are a call to current repentance and restoration.

Chapter 59:1-8
The Lord's hand is not too short that it cannot save them, yet they are full of iniquity and will not turn to Him. Their iniquity is described in great detail. It seems to affect every area. Notice how involved the tongue is (verse 3).

Verses 9-15 declare that this is the reason there is no justice or righteousness, and though they look for light, there is only darkness and blindness. Their transgressions separate them from God.

Verses 15-21
In the middle of verse 15, the theme changes to the destruction and judgment of the Day of The Lord (Tribulation). This is the wrath of the Lord poured out on the nations who come against Jerusalem. Notice how the Lord is astonished that there is no one to intercede and stand with Him (verse 16). This is repeated in chapter 63. Also, notice the references to the coastlands and the West. The Lord will come (verse 19) like a rushing stream, and a Redeemer will come to Zion (Jerusalem), to the repentant remnant of Jacob. The promise of the Spirit which is upon Isaiah will be poured out on them.

Chapter 60
Chapter 60 is a continuation of the restoration begun in chapter 59 with Messiah's return. It is a most wonderful chapter. The Jewish people will rise and shine. The glory of the Lord will be upon them. The nations will bring back all the exiles in their arms as a mother carries a nursing child. All the nations will bring their glory into Jerusalem for the building up of the city and the Temple. It is a picture of what happened when they left Egypt only much greater. The Lord plans to make the Temple glorious! All the nations will serve them and bow down to them, which means; there will be remnants from the nations who survive the Tribulation (14).[41] The sons of those who despised Jerusalem (Jewish Jerusalem) will come and bow down, calling it the City of the Lord - the Zion of the holy One of Israel. Everyone will be a Zionist in that day! The presence of the sun and the moon will not be needed because the glory of the Lord will be so bright there. This is a repeat of what has been said before. Then the people will be righteous and possess the land forever!

Chapter 61
Verses 1-3 are the ministry of the Messiah.[42] When Jesus quoted this in the synagogue in Nazareth, He stopped midway in the second verse, because the rest would be fulfilled at His second coming and the Millennial reign.

Verses 4-11
They will rebuild the ancient ruins and cities. They will be priests of the Lord and will reign with Him - a kingdom of priests. Israel will fulfill her ancient call and destiny to the nations.

The nations (Gentiles) will be their servants.

---
[41] Mt 25:41-46
[42] Luke 4:18-19

Chapter 62
This is the glory of Jerusalem in the Millennial reign. She will be like a royal crown in the hand of the Lord. The land will no longer be forsaken but will be married to the Lord. The Lord will never allow them to be plundered again. They will drink wine in the courts of the Temple and praise the Lord.

Verse 10 is a call to preparation for the Messiah's appearing - a similar call to that of John the Baptist.

Verse 11
Messiah comes to the daughter of Zion and His reward is with Him.

Note the call to intercede in verse 1, and 6-7, until the Lord establishes His righteousness in Jerusalem and makes her a praise in the earth!

Chapter 63:1-6
The Messiah comes from the eastern desert (Bozrah) bringing the remnant with Him. This is the day of vengeance. He has trampled the nations in His wrath (the armies that have come to destroy Jerusalem) and His garment has become stained with their blood.[43]

Notice that there is no nation to stand with Him or the Jewish people (verses 3-5).

Verses 7-19 switch to thanksgiving and prayer. Isaiah makes remembrance of how the Lord saved Israel before, and how He has again shown such great mercy. In verses 15-17, there is a prayer to save Jerusalem and the Temple and to have mercy on the remnant.

Verses 18-19 end with the astonishing prophecy of the destruction of the Temple.

Chapter 64
The prayer continues and gets more intense, asking for God to rend the heavens and come down. The prophet remembers how the Lord saved the people in the past. There is a reference to Sinai when the mountains quaked. The Lord was angry because they sinned and continued in sin a long time, and all their righteous deeds are as a filthy garment (verse 6). No one calls on the Lord or arouses himself to take hold of Him (verse 7). The Lord is beseeched not to be angry beyond measure. Then the prophet looks at all the cities of Judah becoming a ruin and the beautiful Temple destroyed by fire (verse 11). This was fulfilled in 586 BC and again in 70 AD.

---
[43] See Rev 19:11-19

Chapter 65:1-7

God says that He permitted Himself to be found by a nation that did not seek Him (a reference to Gentiles coming to Messiah.[44] But all day long He has stretched out his hands to Israel, to a disobedient and obstinate people. And He goes on to describe their idolatry again.

Verses 8-16 - The Lord promises to not destroy the whole of Israel but to restore a remnant. These He refers to as His chosen ones who will inherit the mountains of Judah and all of Israel. These are His servants. But those who forsake the Lord and who forget His Holy Mountain (the nation going into exile) are destined for the sword and will bow down to slaughter.

Verses 13-16 contrast the blessings of the remnant with those who were rebellious.

Verses 16-25 are about the Millennium. The former troubles will be forgotten because the Lord will create a new (renewed) heaven and a new (renewed) earth. He will create Jerusalem for rejoicing and her people for gladness (18). Whoever does not reach the age of 100 will be thought accursed. In other words, everyone will live very long; but there will still be death until the end of the Millennium. They will be greatly blessed and outlive the work of their own hands (verse 22). And while they are still speaking, God will answer them. All shall live in peace and harmony, including the animals, and there will be no evildoing (verse 25).

Chapter 66:1-2

Heaven is the Lord's throne, and the earth is His footstool. "Where then is the house you can build for Me?" God is declaring how majestic He is, and there is no house that can contain Him, because He has made everything. Incidentally, though the Lord placed His presence in the Temple, it did not contain Him. The Jews understood this, and Solomon declared it when he dedicated the Temple. However, the Lord is not talking about the Temple here. He is saying that even though there cannot be a house built to contain Him, He will come to the one who is contrite of spirit and trembles at His word.

Verse 3 compares all those who bring offerings to the Lord as those who do evil. Their sacrifice is compared to something despicable in God's sight because of their hypocrisy and sin. God says they have chosen their own ways, so He has chosen His way to punish them (verse 4).

---

[44] See Rom 10:19-21

Verse 4-6
The Lord says He will punish them, because when He called, they would not listen, and when He spoke, they just ignored Him.

Verses 7-9 skip to Israel's labor pains at the end of the age (Day of the Lord - Tribulation). As is typical with the prophecies, both good and bad, because they are all future to the prophet, they seem to run into one another without distinguishing the time period.

Notice how Zion gives birth to a baby boy before the Tribulation begins. This is the manchild of Rev 12 and Micah 5:3. It is the body of Messiah - the Bride. Then notice "as soon as Zion travailed, she brought forth sons." This is the repentant remnant nation that comes to Him as soon as the Tribulation begins.

"Who has heard such a thing? Who has seen such things? Can a land be born in one day? Can a nation be brought forth all at once?"

This passage in verse 8 has been used to refer to the nation that was re-established in 1948. This application is totally valid. However, the context would seem to also suggest that it is the remnant nation that is born again during the Tribulation.

Verses 10-14
All are told to be joyful with Jerusalem and be satisfied with her. The Lord is going to give her peace like a river and the glory of the nations like an overflowing stream. Again, there is the promise that they will be glad and comforted in her.

Verses 14-17 are about the wrath of the Lord being poured out with fire on the armies of the nations.

Hinnom Valley

Verses 18-24
All the nations will come to see the glory of the Lord in Jerusalem. And they will bring back all the remaining Jews to Jerusalem and God will make some of them priests. And just as the new heavens and the new earth will endure before God, so will the offspring of Israel forever! Verse 24 says that all will be able to go and look on the corpses of those who have rebelled against Him. Their worm will not die, and their fire will not be quenched. This is a picture of the garbage heap in the Hinnom Valley in Jerusalem, where things were perpetually burning and being eaten by worms. Jesus used this metaphor when speaking of hell (Mark 9:48). The word Gehenna comes from the Valley of Hinnom.

Notes

Jeremiah (The Weeping Prophet)

Author: Jeremiah the prophet dictated it to his scribe Baruch.

Place: Judah

Time: 627-580 B.C.

Jeremiah's Call
Jeremiah's life and ministry were very difficult indeed. He was called from the womb to warn the people of God regarding the impending doom coming upon them if they did not repent. He was destined to be misunderstood and mistreated for trying to save the nation from destruction. His heart was as the heart of God, broken for the people whom He loved and who were unwilling to listen to Him. The word of God was like a burning fire within him which he could not hold in, and yet, it was that same word which brought him continual rejection. Living through Judah's last five kings, he saw the nation go into bondage in Babylon. He did not merely bring a message to the people who rejected it, but he ministered out of the broken heart of the Father.

False Prophets
Jeremiah's mission was made all the more difficult by the numerous "prophets" who were prophesying falsely in the name of the Lord. One of those prophecies, brought by Hananiah, is recorded in chapter 28. In fact, when you listen to the words of Hananiah they sound good enough. *"Thus says the Lord God of Israel, 'I have broken the yoke of the king of Babylon.'"*

In the past this would always have been the right word. God always defended Israel against her enemies and wanted His people to be victorious. So now all the prophets are declaring this. They are saying peace and prosperity to the people of Judah, which, of course, was the desired will of God. However, Judah is in a state of rebellion at this time and God has had enough. They must now face discipline. Thus, the prophets are speaking falsely, giving false visions and divination and the deception of their own minds. They have not sought the Lord on this matter but are led astray by their own agenda. Their lack of consecration and fear of Yahweh has led them to smugness and a false sense of security, much like the Harlot church of our day.

The Day of the Lord
Throughout the book the people of Judah are warned about the army from the north that is coming to destroy the city of Jerusalem and the Temple of God and carry off the people as captives. But as with most of the prophets there is a dual message here. One has to do with the immediate situation, and the king of Babylon coming against Jerusalem, and the other has to do with the nations coming against Jerusalem in the Day of The Lord at the end of the age. This theme of The Day of the Lord begins in chapter 4, *"I looked on the earth and behold, it was formless and void; and to the heavens and they had no light."*

Many have thought these verses referred to the beginning of creation, but they actually refer to the end of the age when the luminaries dwindle (Zech 14:6). The next verse makes this clear, *"I looked upon the mountains, and behold, they were quaking, and the hills moved to and fro."* This is a reference to the Day of God's Wrath at the end of the age. We also see this theme in chapters 25 and 30, and throughout the rest of the book.

Promise of Restoration
Despite the judgment God is forced to pour out on His people, the mercy and love in His heart come across very clearly in the promise of restoration, which begins even as early as chapter 3:11-19. It appears again in chapters 23, 30, 31, 32, & 33. God promises to bring the people back from all the nations to which they have been scattered and restore them to Himself in Messiah, who is the "Righteous Branch."

The book of Jeremiah ends with specific prophecies for the Gentile nations around Jerusalem. It also records the persecution of Jeremiah, the fall of Jerusalem, and the subsequent exile of Jeremiah in Egypt where he died.

Chapter 1:1-3 describe the book as the words of Jeremiah, the son of Hilkiah, of the priests of Anathoth in the land of Benjamin. It covers the span of his ministry from the thirteenth year of Josiah, son of Amon, until the eleventh year of Zedekiah and the exile of Jerusalem in the fifth month.

Verses 4-10
The Lord told Jeremiah that he was consecrated in the womb as a prophet to the nations. Nevertheless, he complains that he is just a youth and does not know how to speak. But the Lord admonished him not to say that, because He is sending him, giving him the words to speak. Therefore, he is not to be afraid because God will be with him to deliver him. Then the Lord stretched out His hand and touched the prophet's mouth and said: *"Behold I have put My words in your mouth."*

Jeremiah is appointed over the nations and over the kingdoms to "pluck up and to break down, to destroy and overthrow, and also to build and to plant."

What incredible authority the Lord has given to the prophet. But please notice that much of what he is called to speak is going to "pluck up and break down," to "destroy and overthrow." This is not consistent with the attitude prevalent in the church today, where everything the servant of the Lord says is supposed to be uplifting and encouraging only. Nevertheless, even though the word of God is ultimately uplifting, it is sometimes necessary for it to pluck things up and tear things down in order to build and plant. Indeed, when this flowery, "everything is positive" and "God just wants you to be blessed" message, is lined up with all the prophets, including the Messiah Himself, it is found woefully wanting.

Verses 11-12 - What do you see?
Jeremiah is shown a rod of an almond tree and the message is that God is watching over His word to perform it.

The almond tree blossoms in January, thus it is "awake" when the other trees are sleeping. The rod, of course, is an implement of discipline. Therefore, the Lord is saying that He is ready and looking for an opportunity to begin His work of judging Judah and that He will carry out His word swiftly.

Verses 13-19
Jeremiah is given a second vision and asked, *"What do you see?"* This time he sees a boiling pot facing away from the north. The boiling water, which is God's judgment, is facing the land of Judah and Jerusalem. God says He is going to bring all the families of the kingdoms of the north against Judah and Jerusalem to punish the people for their idolatry and unfaithfulness to Him. Then Jeremiah is told that he is to be strong, like a fortified city and a pillar of iron against the kings of Judah, its princes, and priests, because they are going to fight against his words and try to kill him. Yet, the Lord promises that if he will stand firm, he will be delivered.

<u>Chapter 2 & Chapter 3:1-10</u>
From the beginning of the book the theme of impending judgment from the northern kingdom of Babylon is evident. But judgment is clearly not the heart of the message. Judgment is coming because of the continual spiritual harlotry of the people. God's heart is broken over their refusal to turn back to Him fully and love Him like they did in the beginning. He starts reminiscing on those days in Chapter 2, and then asks; *"What injustice did your fathers find in me, that they went far from Me and walked after emptiness and became empty."* Can you hear His heart? God is saying, what was wrong with Me? Why was I not good enough for you? He is portrayed as a husband whose heart is broken over the repeated adulteries of His wife. *"Have you seen what faithless Israel did? She went up on every high hill and under every green tree, and she was a harlot there."* He even talks about how He gave Israel (Northern Kingdom) a certificate of divorce, and He wonders

why Judah didn't take it to heart when Israel was taken into captivity by the Assyrians but continued in harlotry and even got worse. It is clear God has had enough and even the repentance of the godly king Josiah, cannot save the people from the coming judgment. Yet, He appeals to them, that even now, if they would come back to Him with <u>all their heart,</u> He would give them another chance. From this we can deduce that, despite the sweeping reforms of Josiah, the people did not come back to God with a whole heart. The Lord knew that as soon as Josiah was gone, they would be back at it again.

Notice the language of harlotry and adultery throughout the book of Jeremiah and all the prophets for that matter. What a sad story it is? It is filled with raw emotion and passionate love. It is not God's desire to bring judgment, but there are times when it is the only remedy. No wonder Jeremiah is called the "Weeping Prophet."

Verses 11-18
The Lord said to Jeremiah that "faithless Israel" has proved herself more righteous than "treacherous Judah." This is to say that Judah has even become more faithless and even treacherous to God. But then the Lord speaks of kindness and restoration to both Israel and Judah. The prophet is told to speak to the north and tell the people to return. This is the promise of restoration at the end of the age.

"'Return, O faithless sons,' declares the Lord; 'for I am a master to you, and I will take you one from a city and two from a family, and I will bring you to Zion.'"

Notice that this is the restoration of a remnant at the end of the age, from all the places where they have been scattered, back to Zion. The Lord is the ultimate Zionist. Both Israel and Judah were taken initially to the north. The Lord promises to bring them both back together as one nation and establish His throne in Jerusalem.

Some would say that the Northern 10 tribes were lost, but this is not the case. A remnant from these 10 tribes had already become part of Judah prior to the Babylonian exile! And both are back together as one nation today, in their own land, and their eternal city of Jerusalem. Since this is true, we are now awaiting the Messiah to establish the Throne of the Lord and His Millennial reign, which is spoken of in verses 15-17. He will give them shepherds after His heart, and they will no longer think about the Ark of the Covenant because God's presence in Messiah will dwell among them in Jerusalem, and all the nations will come to worship there.

Verses 19-20
The Lord grieves over the nation - His sons. He wanted so much to bless them and make them beautiful among the nations of the earth, and be a Father to them. Yet, like a woman who acts treacherously toward her husband, they have acted treacherously toward Him.

Verses 21-25 & Chapter 4:1-2

There is a cry of repentance heard on the bare heights – in the places where they have committed adultery. This appears to be the cry of Israel repenting and realizing that they have forgotten the Lord and that He alone is their salvation. They realize that their high places are a deception and that they are covered with shame and humiliation. Perhaps this is the cry of the remnant that is left in the land, or else it is about their return and repentance at the end of the age, since at this time the Northern Kingdom has been exiled. The Lord says return "faithless sons" and promises to heal their faithlessness. But notice He says, it is not enough to just come back to the land, but they must come back to Him with sincerity. Verses 1 & 2 seem to be speaking to the exiled nation or the small remnant that is left, that even now if they are serious about coming back and will make a commitment to put away their idolatry from them, and not waver, He can still restore them.

Another possibility is that these verses are addressing all the sons of Jacob as Israel, because Judah is now told to repent, or she too will be judged. It is not uncommon for the prophets to address Judah as Israel, since they are the children of Jacob, and all the tribes were represented in their number.

Verses 3-6 - Repent

Judah and Jerusalem are warned to repent – to "break up their fallow ground" and not to sow among thorns. The fallow ground is hard ground where nothing can be planted. This is a picture of hardness of heart where the plough must come and break it up. Notice that we can break it up ourselves, but if not, God will send the plough or the rototiller to break it up.

Sowing among thorns is putting the seed into hearts where it will be choked out with other pursuits and pleasures. See the parable of the sower (Mt 13).

They are told to circumcise their hearts to the Lord, or His wrath will go forth with fire and burn with none to quench it. They are to call out, blow the trumpet, and assemble the people in all of the cities of Judah toward Zion (Jerusalem).

Verses 7-18 – Judgment from the North

Then He says that the lion has gone forth from his thicket. This is Babylon coming from the north to devastate the land.

The hearts of the king and the princes will fail, and the priests will be appalled, and the prophets astounded. Jeremiah says that the Lord has deceived the people by allowing the false prophets to proclaim "Peace," when the sword was actually coming. Because of the rebellion of their hearts the Lord put a lying spirit in the mouths of their prophets, giving them what they wanted to hear, even though He raised up Jeremiah to speak the truth.

Then He says that the judgment coming is like a wind that is too strong for winnowing and cleansing, but instead will bring destruction and blow them away.

Again, there is the call to repentance, and a reminder that this judgment is because of their deeds. It is their evil that they brought on themselves, and it is bitter!

Verses 19-31
The Lord laments the disaster coming and says He has anguish in His soul. The whole land is devastated and is a waste.

The Lord says that His people are foolish and stupid and learn nothing. They are shrewd when it comes to doing evil but know nothing about doing good.

Though the passage is about the destruction that is coming on Judah and Jerusalem, it now begins to speak of the Day of the Lord at the end of the age. We have seen this with all the prophets. It's as though they see all the judgment that is coming on Jerusalem, right to the end. We know this from some of the language used, such as, the whole land was devastated, the heavens had no light, and the mountains were quaking and the hills moving to and fro (23 & 24). The "Cosmic Signs" at the end of the age are mentioned again in verse 28 and in verse 31 we are told about Zion's labor pains. Nevertheless, in spite of the devastating judgment that is coming, the Lord promises not to execute a complete destruction.

Chapter 5:1-6
The Lord says that there is no one in Jerusalem who does justice and who seeks truth. He smote them, yet they did not weaken (become humble); He consumed them, but they refused to take correction. They have made their faces harder than rock and have refused to repent. Presumably this is speaking of the various judgments God has already brought on them.

Then Jeremiah says that it must be just the poor because they don't know the ways of God. He says he will go to the great and speak to them because they surely know. But then he retorts that they too have broken the yoke and burst the bonds, meaning they have shaken off the Lord's leadership and guidance. Therefore, the lion, the wolf, and the leopard, will tear them to pieces.

Verses 7-13
The Lord asks why He should pardon them and goes on to explain that He cannot. Even though He fed them well and took good care of them, they committed adultery and "trooped to the harlot's house." They are compared to well fed lusty horses, "each one neighing after his neighbor's wife." This is the way they treated the Lord their husband with their lusting after idols.

Israel and Judah have dealt treacherously with the Lord and have lied about Him. They have said that no misfortune will come on them, and that the Lord is not speaking that. Their prophets are as wind (blowing hot air) and the word is not in them. Thus the judgment will come.

However, again the Lord offers hope that it will not be a complete destruction!

Verses 14-17
The Lord says that He is making the words of Jeremiah fire and the people wood. He is bringing a nation from afar against them. He goes on to speak of Babylon as an ancient nation whose language they do not know. All of them are mighty men and their quiver is an open grave – suggesting a dual meaning, that they have many arrows, and they bring certain death.

Then He lists the things they will devour:
Their harvest, their food, their sons and daughters, their flocks and herds, their vines and fig trees and the fortified cities – essentially everything.

Verses 18-31
In the midst of this prediction of doom, again the Lord promises to spare a remnant (verse 18). And Jeremiah is told that when they ask why God has done this, he is to tell them that since they have forsaken the Lord, and served foreign gods in their own land, they will now serve strangers in a land that is not theirs.

Then the prophet is told to declare the word he is given in the house of Judah, to a foolish and senseless people who have eyes but see not and ears but hear not. This is reminiscent of Isaiah 6:9-13.

The Lord asks, *"Do you not fear me? Do you not tremble in My presence."* Obviously, the people have become so insensitive, so callous that they think the Lord will put up with them no matter what. They cannot imagine that the Lord would ever allow judgment to come against them.

The Lord reminds them of the boundaries He has placed for the mighty sea. Though the waves roar they cannot cross them, yet this people are stubborn and rebellious and do not seem to understand that it is the Lord who takes care of them. It is He who gives them rain in its season, and a harvest. Unlike the sea which knows its boundaries, they never seem to learn that the Lord is their provider. And wicked men among them have become rich and fat and sleek by preying on them. They live for themselves and for their own prosperity and do not plead the case of the orphan or defend the poor. Then the Lord asks again, "Shall I not punish these people?"

In verses 30 and 31 we are told that an appalling thing has happened in the land. The prophets are prophesying falsely, the priests rule on their own authority, and the people love it!

Chapter 6:1-15

Benjamin and Tekoa and those close to Jerusalem are told to get out because evil is coming from the north (Babylon). They will attack and lay siege to Jerusalem. The daughter of Zion will be cut off. Jerusalem is the city to be punished. As a well keeps its water fresh, so Jerusalem keeps wickedness fresh within her. It is a scathing rebuke and warning from the Lord that He is about to be alienated from them and to make their land uninhabited. The Babylonians will glean them as the vine and leave nothing remaining. Though as always it carries with it the hope of repentance, the die seems to be cast. There is no hope for the people. All of them are greedy for gain from the least to the greatest. And the leaders heal the wound superficially. In other words, they put a "band-aid" on it. They make it all good, and positive, saying, "peace, peace," when there is no peace. Just like leaders in the church today, they didn't want to hear anything "negative." "It's all good, they say, there is no judgment coming." God is too nice, and they are too special, for them to be concerned. They have no shame over their sin and abominations and don't even know how to blush. (What a sad description of the people of Judah and how perfectly it fits the modern, sinner-friendly, progressive church?) What is the use in even warning them since their ears are stopped and they cannot hear, and the word of the Lord has become a reproach to them? The prophet says he is full of the wrath of the Lord and is tired of holding it in. It is now going to be poured out on all, old and young, husband and wife, prophets and priests, houses, and fields, and all the inhabitants of the land.

Verses 16-21

The Lord asks them to stand by the way and look for the ancient paths; the paths of righteousness and goodness that have been walked in from the beginning, that give rest and peace to the soul. But they said, "We will not walk in it." He set watchmen over them blowing the trumpet, but they would not heed the warning. Therefore, the earth is warned, God is bringing disaster upon them because they would not listen to His words and have rejected His law. But of course, they continue with the incense that comes from Arabia (Sheba) and offer sacrifices to Him in their rebellion. Therefore, the Lord is putting stumbling blocks before them, and they will stumble.

Verses 22-26

Once again, they are told that Babylon is coming from the north. The army of the Chaldeans is coming, and they will have no mercy. There is nowhere to go for terror is on every side.

They are told to mourn and weep bitterly in sackcloth and ashes for suddenly the destroyer will come.

Verses 26-30
God says that He has made Jeremiah an assayer of the people, as one who assays silver. But there is no point, He says, since they are so rebellious. They are bronze and iron and all are corrupt. Even though the bellows blow fierce and make the fire very hot, the impurities (the wicked) are not drawn out. Therefore, the whole thing is as rejected silver and the Lord has rejected them.

Chapter 7:1-16
Jeremiah is told to stand at the gate of the Lord's house and proclaim the word given to him. We do not know which gate this was, but it was likely one of the inside gates and at a time when there were many people there. The message is simple; amend your ways, and I will let you dwell here.

"Amend your ways and your deeds, and I will let you dwell in this place. Do not trust in deceptive words, saying, 'This is the temple of the LORD, the temple of the LORD, the temple of the LORD.' For if you truly amend your ways and your deeds, if you truly practice justice between a man and his neighbor, if you do not oppress the alien,[45] the orphan, or the widow, and do not shed innocent blood in this place, nor walk after other gods to your own ruin, then I will let you dwell in this place, in the land that I gave to your fathers forever and ever."

The word of the Lord confronts the idolatry of Judah and their sin of injustice toward one another, particularly the oppression of widows and orphans and aliens among them. They disobey Torah, which is the rejection of God and His Word, and yet they think that because the Temple of the Lord is among them, they are protected from judgment. They found it impossible to believe that God would allow Jerusalem to be destroyed since His House was there and they are faithful to offer sacrifices. It is just religious activity for them, and they have brought their wickedness and thirst for unjust gain into the Temple itself and have made it a den of robbers (verse 11). The Messiah Himself would address this same issue on more than one occasion.[46] Nevertheless, Jeremiah tells them to go look at the ruins of Shiloh, the first place that the Lord put His Name, and what He did to it because of the wickedness of Israel. Thus, the Lord says He will do the same to Jerusalem and His Holy Temple unless they repent, and He will scatter them as He did the northern kingdom of Israel.

---
[45] The "alien" refers to gentiles who want to live among them and obey Torah, and not just people pouring in from other countries.
[46] Mt 21:13

Verses 21-27
Jeremiah is told by the Lord not to pray for Judah, because He will not hear him. They are committing idolatry in the streets of Jerusalem and making cakes for the Queen of Heaven.[47] Thus the Lord's anger is kindled and will be poured out on them. Interestingly, this same Queen of heaven is worshiped today, by many who claim to be Christians albeit in a different form.

Though God gave Israel much instruction concerning sacrifices and offerings, His covenant with them was not based on these. He told them to obey His voice and walk in the way He commanded them, and He would be their God and they would be His people. But they have not inclined their ear or listened to the voice of the Lord and refused to hear His Word spoken by the prophets. Thus, they will not listen to Jeremiah either. Truth has perished from their mouth.

Verses 28-34
Jeremiah is told to cut off his hair in mourning and take up a lamentation on the bare heights for his voice to be heard because the Lord has rejected and forsaken this generation of His wrath and they are cut off. Again, we are told how they have defiled the House of God with idols and set up high places in Topheth or the valley of Ben Hinnom which is immediately south of the city. Here they offered their children in the fire to Baal and Moloch, which are essentially the same. Then we are told that the Lord Himself will change the name of the place to 'the Valley of Slaughter,' because they will be slaughtered and buried there in the coming destruction. It seems clear, that this is also a reference to the judgment that takes place here at the end of the age.

The valley of Hinnom was also the place where the thrash was burned, which is why Jesus used it to speak of Hell or Gehenna (Mk 9:43-44).

Chapter 8:1-3
These verses are a continuation of the previous prophecy in Chapter 7. In the coming destruction of the Chaldeans, they will take out the bones of the kings, priests, and prophets, and scatter them on the ground in desecration. In this way, they will be strewn on the ground and spread before the sun, moon and stars, and the host of heaven, which they worshipped and served. Verse 3 tells us that the remnant of Judah will choose death and not life, not only in their rebellion against Babylon, but it also seems to be referring to their slavery in the coming exile.

---

[47] This Queen of Heaven had many names in the ancient world. For them she was Ashtoreth the mother of Tammuz whom she had by Baal.

Verses 4-17

This passage is similar to chapter 6 and in some places identical. It's as if the Lord is simply flabbergasted at their lack of repentance – their stubbornness and stiff necks. The birds know the seasons of their migration, but they do not know the ordinance of their God. Their leaders are liars, and they heal the wound superficially, and the "lying pen" of the scribes twists and distorts God's Word and makes it into a lie. They have no shame as they run headlong into destruction. Therefore, the Lord has sent the sorting horses of the Babylonians from the North, which is why they are coming "from Dan." They will devour the land and its inhabitants. They are coming among them like deadly snakes that cannot be charmed.

Verses 18-22, Chapter 9:1-11

In these passages, the Lord mourns over the destruction and exile of His people. He mourns over their sin and refusal to repent so that He could not heal or restore them.

"My sorrow is beyond healing, my heart is faint within me! Behold, listen! The cry of the daughter of my people from a distant land: 'Is the LORD not in Zion? Is her King not within her?' Why have they provoked Me with their graven images, with foreign idols?"

There is a balm in Gilead. The Lord is in Zion. They could have been healed. They could have been reconciled. But they refused to listen and provoked the Lord to anger. Now they cry from a distant land.

"Oh that my head were waters and my eyes a fountain of tears, that I might weep day and night for the slain of the daughter of my people!"

These are words of pain. They are the words of God who is brokenhearted over the adultery of His people and the destruction He must bring on them.

Therefore thus says the LORD of hosts, 'Behold, I will refine them and assay them; for what else can I do, because of the daughter of My people?

Again, the Lord says He will refine them as silver for the sake of a remnant because there is no other option. The destruction is coming. The city will be a heap of ruins – a haunt of jackals without inhabitant.

Verses 12-16

A lament for the land that is laid waste like a desert, and no one passes through because of the sin of Judah and their idolatry with the Baals. Thus, the Lord says He will feed them wormwood and give them poison to drink; obviously, a metaphor for the bitter destruction that is coming. He will scatter them to the nations and draw out a sword after them until they are annihilated (Lev 26:33). The language is passionate and seems to be total, yet God always promises to restore a remnant.

Verses 17-22
Judah is told to call on the professional mourners to come and wail for Zion, because of the death and destruction. The event is pictured as having happened already. Death has entered the houses and palaces. The young men and the children are cut down in the streets. The corpses of men fall like dung in the open field, and no one gathers them.

Verses 23-26 – The Lord is Righteous
Let not the wise man boast in his wisdom or the mighty man in his might or the rich man in his riches. Let him who boasts, boast of this, that he knows Yahweh and understands that He is the one who exercises lovingkindness, justice, and righteousness in the earth, for He delights in these things (2 Cor 10:17).

The Lord says that the day is coming when He will punish all the uncircumcised (Gentiles) who are in the surrounding lands, Egypt, Ammon, Moab and Edom, who shave their faces, and also Judah is included, even though they are circumcised in the flesh they are uncircumcised in heart.

Chapter 10 – The Stupidity of Idols
Jeremiah confronts them on their fear of the idols of the nations whose customs are a delusion. The Lord mocks their idols that are just hunks of wood from the forest, and that can't stand or walk or see or hear. A craftsman decorates it with gold and silver and then props it up with pieces of wood and nails, so it won't fall down. How stupid?

"Like a scarecrow in a cucumber field are they, and they cannot speak; they must be carried, because they cannot walk! Do not fear them, for they can do no harm, nor can they do any good."

However, Yahweh is the true and living God – the everlasting King. At His wrath the earth quakes and the nations cannot endure His indignation. It

Canaanite god

is He who made the earth by His power and established the world by His wisdom. He is the portion of Jacob and not these hunks of wood. He is the maker of all, Yahweh of armies is His name and Israel is the tribe of His inheritance. Nevertheless, now they are to be slung from the land. Their shepherds (leaders) have not sought the Lord, so their flock is scattered. A great commotion is coming from the land of the north (Babylon), to make the cities of Judah a desolation and a haunt of jackals.

The chapter ends with a prayer for mercy. A cry for the Lord to correct them in justice and not just with anger lest they be destroyed completely. Also, a plea for justice to be visited on the nations who do not know Him or who have not called on His name. Let there be wrath on those who have persecuted Jacob and especially on the Babylonians who will make Judah a desolation.

Chapter 11:1-17

The Lord tells Jeremiah to remind the people, that, when He brought them out of Egypt, He proclaimed a curse on them if they would not obey His voice and keep His covenant which He made with them. These are the curses spoken by Moses in Deuteronomy 27, that were again spoken by Joshua on Mt Ebal in the promised land (Josh 8:30-35). The Lord told Jeremiah to speak all these words in the cities of Judah and the streets of Jerusalem. These are undoubtedly the words spoken by the Lord to Jeremiah, but perhaps he is also told to speak and remind Israel of all the words spoken by Moses and Joshua. Nevertheless, though he is to speak, it is to no avail, because they have conspired to go back to the sins of their ancestors, who refused to listen to the Lord and have worshiped other gods and broken the covenant. Thus, the Lord is bringing disaster on them which they will not be able to escape, and though they cry to Him He will not answer them. Then they will cry out to the idols that cannot save them.

Again, the Lord tells Jeremiah not to pray for them in the day of their disaster because He will not listen. And He asks what right they have to be in His House since they have done so many vile deeds. His broken heart is clearly expressed as He calls them "His beloved" and reminisces about how they were a beautiful green olive tree when He called them, but now He has pronounced evil against them because of what they have done to provoke Him by offering sacrifices to Baal.

Verses 18-21

Though there were many plots against Jeremiah, we are here told that the Lord revealed to him plots devised on his life, which in this case, seem to be coming from the men of Anathoth (his hometown) who want to stop his prophesying. Jeremiah says that he did not know of these plots and was like a lamb led to the slaughter. Then he prays for God's judgment to fall on them for what they have done. The Lord answers him and says that He is about to punish them. Their young men will die with the sword, and their sons and daughters by famine, and no remnant will be left to them.

Chapter 12:1-6 – Jeremiah's Question

Jeremiah pleads his case to the Lord, and he wants to know why the wicked prosper. Though the question could be viewed as general, it seems that it is a continuation of the discussion of the previous chapter. Jeremiah wants to know why all the wicked, and the men of Anathoth that plot against him, are prospering while the land mourns. Why has the Lord blessed them and yet he must go through such adversity and want? It's a question that many of us ask today as well. Why are those who distort God's Word and lead His people astray so prosperous and popular, and those who preach the truth suffering hardship and adversity. "You know me," he says. "You know what's in my heart." He cries out for their punishment and for God to drag them off like sheep for slaughter and to set them apart for a day of carnage.

In verse 4, the people seem to be saying that Jeremiah will not see their end days, or in other words, they will outlive him because his prophesies are false. However, the Septuagint has them saying, "God will not see our ways." In either case, those who are doing evil think what they are doing will not be punished by God and Jeremiah is all hot air.

Verses 5-17 – God's Answer
To Jeremiah directly God answers,

"If you have run with footmen and they have tired you out, then how can you compete with horses? If you fall down in a land of peace, how will you do in the thicket of the Jordan?"

It seems that Jeremiah is being warned that if he is having a hard time now, what will he do when the Babylonians come? If he is finding it hard to hang on when the country is in peace, what will he do when the desolation starts? The Lord also warns him that his brothers, and his father's house, have cried aloud against him and, even if they say nice things to him, he is not to listen or be taken in by them. Then the Lord addresses the issue of judgment on the unrighteous nation; in a rather lengthy response, He says that He has forsaken His house, abandoned His inheritance, and given the beloved of His soul into the hand of her enemies. The sword of the Lord will make the land a desolation and there will be no more peace for anyone.

The Lord also makes it clear that the nations who have persecuted Judah and tried to steal their inheritance will be dealt with. He will uproot them as He uproots Judah from among them. But He also promises to have compassion and bring those nations all back to their lands. And if, when they come back, those who taught Israel to follow Baal, will learn the ways of Israel and follow the Lord, then He will establish them together with His people. But if any nation does not listen, He will completely destroy it!

Chapter 13:1-11 – Linen Waistband
Jeremiah was told by the Lord to buy a linen waistband and put it around him. This waistband, or sash, was primarily for appearance and beauty rather than functionality. It was expensive and not something Jeremiah was used to wearing. Some believe that with his humble clothing this would have really stood out since it was a garment of the rich. Therefore, it would be really noticed by the people and surely became the talk of the town. Then the Lord appeared to him a second time and told him to bring it to the Euphrates and hide it in

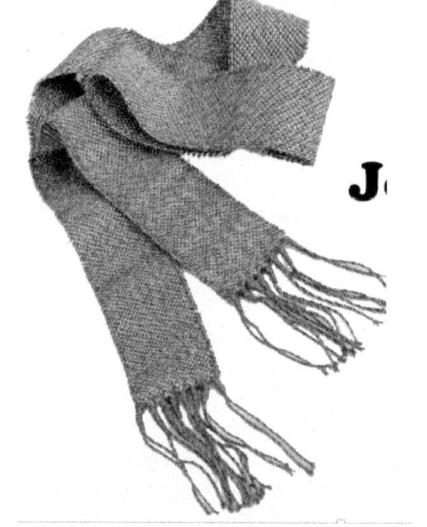

a crevice of the rock. Then after many days the Lord told him to go and get it, and it had become completely worthless.

This was a prophetic picture for Judah. The prophet was giving them a visual, a sort of video of the time, or what we would call 'a prophetic activation.' The sash represented Israel whom the Lord had caused to cling to Him, as His special people for renown and glory, but instead they went after other gods. Therefore, the army coming from the North (Euphrates) will destroy their pride and glory and make them worthless like the waistband.

Verses 12-14 - Drunkenness
Jeremiah is told to speak to the people and tell them that all the jugs are to be filled with wine. The response is predicted. They will say, "We know all the jugs have to be filled with wine." Then the prophet will say that God is going to fill all of them, prophets (false ones), priests, and kings, with drunkenness and smash them against each other, both sons and fathers. He will no longer have pity or show compassion toward them.

Verses 15-27 – Exile Coming
Here is another woeful warning to repent from their adultery, because God is about to expose their nakedness and harlotry and scatter them to the wind. Though it is a strong warning, it is filled with tenderness and compassion.

"But if you will not listen to it, My soul will sob in secret for such pride; and my eyes will bitterly weep and flow down with tears, because the flock of the LORD has been taken captive."

Alas, expecting them to change is like asking the Egyptian to change his skin or the leopard to change his spots. They will be taken captive and carried off into exile by the army coming from the North.

<u>Chapter 14:1-10 – Drought</u>
These verses speak about a great drought that has come upon the land and all Judah is in mourning. There is no water in the cisterns and the land is cracked. The farmers cover their heads in shame. There is no grass in the field, and the donkeys cry out like jackals.

It is not known when this drought took place, but it is evidently during the ministry of Jeremiah. It is the result of God's curse that has come on them because of their sin and harlotry with Baal, who was supposedly able to bless them with rain for their crops. Nevertheless, they cry out to the Lord because they are desperate and they confess their sin and apostasies, yet it is too late. The Lord is not listening and will not save them because their repentance is not real. They only want to get out of their calamity. In verse 11, Jeremiah is told again not to pray for them, because, when they fast, the Lord will not listen to them, or when they offer sacrifices, He will not receive them. Instead, because of their stubborn and unrepentant heart, He will make an end of them with the sword, famine, and pestilence.

Verses 13-16 - False Prophets
The false prophets of Judah, and apparently there were many, are declaring peace and prosperity to the people of Judah, which, of course, was the desired will of God. However, Judah is in a state of rebellion at this time and God has had enough. They must now face discipline. Thus, the prophets are speaking falsely, giving false visions and divination and the deception of their own minds. They have not sought the Lord on this matter but are led astray by their own agenda.

It is easy then to see how unpopular Jeremiah's message was. *"Bring your necks under the yoke of the king of Babylon and serve him and his people, and live" (Jer 27:12).* This was, of course, a good message, but it was not what the people wanted to hear or what they would have expected to hear. Thus, the prophets who prophesy falsely and say there is no sword or famine coming, will meet their end with sword and famine, and those who eat up this false message will be thrown out into the streets, and no one will bury them.

Verses 17-22
These verses seem to be connected with the beginning of the chapter because of verse 22; except they depict the condition of the people after the destruction. This time the weeping and praying seems genuine, like they finally get it. But, alas, it is too late. They cry out in despair and are sorely wounded. "Have You completely rejected Judah?" they ask. They plead for His covenant with them not to be annulled and acknowledge that He alone is the true God and the one who has done these things. Therefore, they can still hope in Him.

<u>Chapter 15:1-14 – Words of Grief</u>
These words express the grief in the heart of God over the sin of His people and the judgment that must be brought. Even if Moses and Samuel were to stand before Him, His heart would not be with them. And then the sad words, *"Send them away from My Presence."*

The Lord says He is tired of relenting over their sin. And when they ask where they should go, Jeremiah is to inform them of the four kinds of doom that they are destined for; death, the sword, famine, and exile in a foreign land. Though this exile to Babylon is temporary, it becomes the beginning of the long dispersion known as the Diaspora (verse 4). And all this is to come upon them because of their evil deeds, but even more specifically the sin of the wicked king, Manasseh (2Kings 21:1-9).

Verses 12-14 speak of the nation from the north, that cannot be beaten back, taking the treasures of Judah and Jerusalem, particularly of the Temple, back to a land they do not know (Babylon).

Verses 15-21- Jeremiah Pours Out His Complaint
This passage is similar to chapter 12. Jeremiah cries out to the Lord for protection and healing from his suffering and justice against his oppressors. It seems he is having one of those moments of doubt, like John the Baptist. He appears to have become somewhat angry and bitter of soul from all the rejection and abuse and injustice he has had to suffer. He is not having a "crisis of faith," though he sounds like he is resentful. The feelings he is expressing have been shared by many servants of God, who have had to stand up to their generation and say the difficult things that no one wants to hear. True prophets are generally misunderstood, rejected, and abused, not only by the world, but by God's people who prefer prosperity and "positive" words of destiny more than the truth they need to hear. And it can become very discouraging when all those who are speaking falsehood and lies are so popular and prosperous, while you struggle and suffer doing the right thing. Indeed, when we consider the sheer weight of the word alone, that Jeremiah had to bear, and then add to it the continual abuse, imprisonment in dungeons and cisterns, it is easy to understand His question. "Lord what about me? What happens to me?

It does appear that the Lord rebuked Jeremiah when He said, "If you return, then I will restore you." If he turns from his attitude and trusts the Lord fully in His dealings with him, God promises to restore him and protect him and deliver him and make him a fortified wall. If he will extract the precious from the worthless, the Lord will make him His spokesman. This is clearly about his speech. If he is to be the Lord's mouthpiece, he cannot speak things that grieve the Lord or misrepresent Him. He is also warned that, although some of the people may turn to him, he is not to turn to them or follow them.

Chapter 16:1-10
The Lord told Jeremiah not to take a wife for himself or have children because they would be slain with all the others, and this would be unbearable for him. Again, there is a vivid description of all that is going to happen to the people through famine, disease, and the sword. They will be prey for birds and animals and no one will lament or mourn for them in any way. Jeremiah is told not to mourn for them. He is also told not to rejoice with anyone because of a wedding, or any feast, since the Lord is about to eliminate from the land the voice of rejoicing and gladness and the voice of the groom and the bride.

All these things Jeremiah had to tell the people, and when they ask why the Lord will do this, he is to tell them it is because they and their forefathers forsook the Lord and did not keep His Law but worshipped other gods. Furthermore, they refuse to listen and continue to walk in the stubbornness of their own heart. Thus, the Lord says, He will hurl them out of the land into a land they have not known, where they will serve other gods day and night, and He will not spare them.

Verses 14-21- Restoration Promised
In the midst of the coming dark gloom, where God promises to pay them back doubly for their sin (verse 18), is found this beautiful promise of restoration. The Lord says He will bring them back from the land of the North and all the countries to which they have been

banished. However, this is not just the restoration from Babylon; it also speaks of the restoration at the end of the age, when the restoration of Israel to the land will overshadow the deliverance from Egypt. God unconditionally promises to restore them to the land of their fathers. This incredible end-time restoration took place in the 20th Century and the Jewish people are still going home. However, it came with a heavy price. First fishermen would come and fish for them. This happened in the latter part of the 19th Century and the early part of the 20th. Men like Theodor Herzl were the fisherman that pleaded with them to come back and settle the ancient homeland, but the majority refused. Then came the Nazi hunters who murdered them in vast numbers until the survivors of this unspeakable Holocaust had no choice but to board ships heading for the Holy Land. As difficult as it is to accept that this was the hand of God, it is nevertheless, clearly stated in the text, and was apparently necessary to fulfill God's promise.

Though I was not alive during the Holocaust, I vividly remember the planeloads of people coming from around the world to make Aliyah (return to the Land). Throughout the 80's we prayed for the Christians and Jews trapped behind the Iron Curtain of the Soviet Union, only to see it crumple at the end of the decade. Then they came, planeload after planeload, as an army of good Samaritans helped them to return home. How fortunate we are to live in the time of the Biblical restoration signaling the soon return of the Messiah.

Chapter 17:1-4 – The Heart is Deceitful

"The sin of Judah is written with an iron stylus and with a diamond it is engraved upon the tablet of their heart and on the horns of their altars."

The sin of Judah is so serious and so deep that it is written on their hearts with an iron stylus or pen. Their hearts are hard and stony, and their sin is deeply etched into them. It is also etched into the horns of their altars which they have built on every high hill. When they think of their children, they think of their altars. This is obviously a reference to the child sacrifices which they have made to Baal and the Asherim. Thus, God's anger burns against them and He will give them to their enemies, and they will serve them in a land they do not know.

Verses 5-13
A contrast is made between the one who trusts in man and the one who trusts in the Lord. Cursed is the one who trusts in mankind and makes human flesh his strength. He is like a bush in the desert that is trying to survive in stony places without water. But the one who trusts in the Lord is like the tree planted by the water, as in Psalm 1. He will not wither and is not fearful of heat or drought. Instead, he will be blessed and always bear fruit.

Then comes the verse that is so widely used with regard to the state of the human heart or spirit. It is deceitful above all else and desperately sick. This addresses the potential for evil motives and self-deception that dwells in each of us. The proverbs warn us to watch over our heart and cultivate it like a garden, for from it flow the springs of life (Prov 4:23). The Lord says that He searches the heart and tests the minds, and He will give to each man according to his ways (motives) and the result (outcome) of his deeds. This theme runs throughout the Bible. God promises to judge mankind not only on the basis of deeds, but on motives as well (1 Cor 4:5).

Despite the fact that verse 9 speaks about the condition of the human spirit and its tendency toward evil, it cannot be removed from its context and its relationship to verse 1. The heart of Judah is desperately sick and who can understand it? Nevertheless, the curse is coming on them because their heart has turned away from God. As the partridge hatches eggs that it did not lay, so too, those who attain wealth unjustly will lose everything in the end and be fools. Thus, also will Judah, that has forsaken the Lord and lived for dishonest gain, lose everything to the Babylonians, even the glorious Temple in Jerusalem.

Verses 14-18
Jeremiah cries out to the Lord to heal him and deliver him from his enemies who keep mocking and persecuting him. He reminds the Lord that he has been a faithful shepherd and has not longed for the calamity to come. He says that all the words of his lips have been spoken in God's presence. He pleads for justice and shame to come on them and not on him since he has made the Lord his refuge.

Verses 19-27
Jeremiah is told to go and stand in the gates of Jerusalem through which the kings and the people go in and out and warn them that they must keep the Sabbath holy and carry no load through the gates, and do no work on the Sabbath. If they do this, as their forefathers were commanded, then there will be kings on the throne, and many people going in and out of the gates, and the city will be inhabited forever. People will come in from all over the land bringing their sacrifices to the House of the Lord. But if they fail to heed the word and are disobedient toward the Sabbath, then the Lord will kindle a fire, and the city and its palaces will be consumed.

Chapter 18:1-12 – The Potter
Jeremiah is told to go down to the Potter's house and watch him at work and there the Lord will speak to him. So, he went down, and the Potter was making a vessel on the wheel, but the vessel was flawed in his hand, so he reshaped it into another vessel as it pleased him. Then the word of the Lord came to Jeremiah to speak to the people of Judah. The word was essentially, "If the potter can change his plans, then the Lord can change His plans also, since He is the Potter (Rom 9:21)." If He plans to uproot a nation and destroy it, and they repent of their sins and turn from evil, then surely, He can change His plan and bless them. Furthermore, if a nation that He has purposed to do good to, turns away from good

and does evil, and refuses to listen to His voice, then He can change His mind about the good He had planned to do to it. Thus, the Lord is about to bring calamity on Judah because they refuse to turn from their evil ways and are flawed and broken like the vessel of the Potter. They will continue to follow their own plans and the stubbornness of their evil heart.

Verses 13-17
The virgin of Israel has become a harlot and committed harlotry with the idols of the Canaanites. "Ask now among the nations. Who has heard of such a thing?" None of the nations have forsaken their own gods to follow the gods of other nations. Yet Israel has forsaken Yahweh their God, to burn incense to worthless idols. They have stumbled from their ancient path to walk in a bypath or byway. Rather than walking on the clear and obvious road before them, they go off the road onto bypaths and trails that lead to ruin. This is such an appalling and unnatural thing they have done. Does the snow of the mountains of Lebanon (Hermon) not water the fields for the farmers? Do the cool mountain springs from the same source, get snatched away? Of course not! Then how can they do such an evil thing? Thus, God will make their land a desolation and an object of hissing. He will scatter them to the wind and show them His back (cold shoulder) rather than His face (blessing).

Verses 18-23
Jeremiah's enemies plot against him and determine to attack him with their tongue and denounce his prophecies. "The Law won't be lost to the priest or counsel to the sage or the divine word to the prophet," they say, in defiance of the words of Jeremiah. Thus, they tell Judah to pay no attention to his words.

On account of the assaults of his enemies, Jeremiah again cries out to God. He asks Yahweh to give heed to the words they are speaking against the prophet, and reminds Him of how he had originally prayed for them and asked that God's wrath be turned away from them. Now however, he prays for the promised judgments to come swiftly on them because of their evil designs and treachery.

Chapter 19 – The Broken Jar
Jeremiah is told to buy an earthenware jar, take some of the elders and the people and some of the senior priests with him, and go down to the valley of Hinnom by the potsherd gate, and proclaim the words the Lord will give him.

Hinnom Valley

Then Jeremiah proclaims the word of the Lord in the Valley of Hinnom. The Lord says He is about to bring disaster upon this place, because of the sin they have committed in the Valley of Hinnom. They have forsaken the Lord and made this an alien place and offered sacrifices to foreign gods that they or their forefathers had never known. They filled the place with the blood of the innocent by offering their sons in the fire to Baal. Therefore, it will no longer be known as Topheth (place of burning) or the Valley of Hinnom, but rather the Valley of Slaughter, because the Lord will allow them to be slain here by their enemies and the birds of the air will eat their flesh. He will also bring desolation to Jerusalem, and it will become an object of horror to everyone who passes by. Jeremiah also prophesied the siege that was coming and the famine that would cause them to eat their sons and daughters. All this was fulfilled by the Babylon invasion.

Then Jeremiah is told to break the jar in the presence of the people he has brought with him and declare that God is going to break this people, and the city, as one shatters an earthen vessel which cannot be repaired, and they will bury them in this valley, because there is nowhere else. And the city will be as Topheth, and all the houses will be defiled as Topheth, because of all the sacrifices that were burned on their rooftops to the heavenly host.

Then Jeremiah came from Topheth and stood in the court of the Temple. Again, he declared that the Lord is going to bring on Jerusalem, and all its towns, the entire calamity He has declared against it, because they have not repented at the hearing of His words but stiffened their necks and hardened their hearts.

It is important to note that even though verse 11 seems to suggest that Jerusalem will not be rebuilt, this is not the case. The point is that the destruction will be so total so as to be like the broken jar. Yet God can redeem and restore the fortunes of His holy city Zion.

Chapter 20:1-6
Pashhur the priest, the son of Immer, was the chief officer in charge of the house of the Lord and was also, apparently, a false prophet (verse 6). He heard about Jeremiah's words and had him beaten and put in the stocks by the Benjamin Gate, close to the Temple. This was not merely an arrest but torture as well, not only from the beating, but the stocks which were also designed to cause pain and discomfort. The next day he released Jeremiah who proceeded to declare to him a change of name and a not very pleasant future. The name Pashhur seems to mean "peace" or "tranquility," but Jeremiah says God no longer calls him Pashhur, but Magor-missabib, which means "terror on every side." Then he tells him God will make him a terror to all his friends whom he will see with his own eyes, slaughtered by the sword, and the city and the Temple destroyed, and the rest of the people taken to Babylon with him, where he will die. It is not clear if this Pashhur, who was obviously a powerful person in Jerusalem, is the same Pashhur who was father of Gedaliah (Jer 38:1) or the one whose descendants came back with Zerubbabel (Ezra 2:38), but it is likely.

Verses 7-18 – Jeremiah's Complaint
These verses are a mixture of bitter complaint, cursing, and confidence of God's presence and deliverance. We do not know if they were uttered at this time or earlier in the prophet's life. It is also possible that they are uttered while Jeremiah is suffering in the stocks and that is why they are recorded here. In either case, they are clearly on account of the betrayal

and rejection the prophet receives from those he thought were his friends (verse 10) and from the suffering that comes on account of the word of God. When he says that God has deceived him, he is likely saying something like, "God why did you do this to me. I didn't sign up for this. Why am I going through this when I am the one speaking the truth?" He goes on to say that if he doesn't speak God's word and just "dials it down," and many want him to do, it becomes a fire that is shut up in his heart and bones, and he cannot bear it. Thus, he must speak. Yet, he hears the whispers of those around him who mock him, thinking he is crazy and who are looking for an opportunity to kill him.

Then in verses 11-13, the prophet proclaims God's protection and righteousness. The Almighty who examines the heart and mind will put his enemies to shame and their disgrace will not be forgotten. He prays for God's vengeance on them since he has committed his cause to the Lord and is doing what is right before Him. He breaks out into praise of the Lord who rescues the needy from the hands of the wicked.

Then in the last portion of the chapter, Jeremiah breaks into bitter cursing of the day he was born, and even the person who brought his father the news. Why did he come out of the womb to see nothing but trouble and sorrow and end his days in shame? Though these are sad words and bitter words, they are understandable considering the suffering of the prophet. He is rejected, beaten, and imprisoned, for bringing the unpopular and hated truth, while the majority speak "positive" lies in the name of the Lord and prosper. This is the lot of all who spoke the word of the Lord in days past, and it is again in our day. Nevertheless, though we cannot judge this great servant of God, whose life and ministry still convict us today, it was not good for him to curse himself as he did.

Chapter 21 - Verses 1-10
Zedekiah, king of Judah, sent two messengers (Pashhur & Zephaniah) to Jeremiah asking for God to save them from the Babylonians and do a miracle. They have hardened themselves to the word of the Lord. They presume God wants to save them as always and are unwilling to listen to anything else. Jeremiah continues to bring the word of the Lord, that the city will be burned with fire, and they should submit to the Babylonians and not rebel against them. If they had listened and humbled themselves, they would have been safe, and the city would not have been destroyed and they would not be exiled. But Jeremiah knew they would not listen.

Verses 11-14 & Chapter 22: 1-30
King Zedekiah is told that if he and his house will turn back to the Lord and repent of injustice and robbery of the poor, orphans, widows, and strangers, He will spare them, and the city and the kingdom of Judah will carry on. However, if they do not obey the Lord, his house will become a desolation and the city will be destroyed. The Lord says that, though the city is like Gilead to Him or a summit in Lebanon (beautiful and strong), He will tear it down and destroy it, and all who pass by will know it was destroyed because of the sin of Judah in forsaking the covenant of the Lord.

Verses 10-11 - Jehoahaz will never return from Egypt but will die there.

Verses 18-19 - Jehoiakim will not be mourned.

Verses 24-30 - Jehoiachin (Coniah) will be exiled to Babylon and die there. He will not prosper and have no descendant on the throne of David.

Chapter 23 - Verses 1-4 – Promise of Restoration

God says He will deal with the shepherds (leaders) of Judah who have not cared for His flock. He also promises to restore the remnant of Israel and bring them back from all the countries where He will scatter them, and He will raise up shepherds for them after His heart.

Verses 5-6 - The promise of Messiah, the Good Shepherd, the righteous Branch of David who will reign as king and bring righteousness to the people. *"In His days Judah will be saved and Israel will dwell securely."*

Verses 7-8 - The Lord says that days are coming when they will no longer say,

"As the Lord lives who brought up the sons of Israel from the land of Egypt," but will instead say, *"As the Lord lives who brought up and led back the descendants of the house of Israel from the north land and from all the countries where I had driven them."*

Verses 9-40 condemn the false prophets of the land who prophesy falsely and whom the Lord has not sent. They prophesy a false dream and lead the people astray. The Lord promises to cast them away from His presence along with the city which He gave them and their fathers.

The words spoken of the false prophets in these verses are a vivid description, not only of the deception of the prophets of ancient Jerusalem, but of the prophetic movement in the church today. They also prophesy out of the deception of their hearts, and their imagination, lying words regarding revival and world peace, when the wrath of the Lord is about to be released on the earth.[48]

Chapter 24 – Basket of Figs

Jeremiah is shown 2 baskets of figs. One contains very good figs and the other very rotten figs. The good figs are the exiles who were taken with Jehoiachin (Jeconiah or Coniah); among them were Daniel and Ezekiel. The bad figs are Zedekiah and the ones who remain in Judah that are to be cast out and scattered throughout the lands. The good figs will be the remnant that the Lord will bring back to the land from the good basket and plant them again in the land. Since the remnant of Israel is likened to figs in this chapter, we deduct that when Jesus spoke about the fig tree blossoming, He was referring to the remnant of Israel being restored at the end of the age (Mt 24:32).

---

[48] Verse 20

Chapter 25:1-30 – 70 years

These are the words that came to Jeremiah in the 4th year of Jehoiakim concerning all the people of Judah. He told them that from the 13th year of Josiah, he had spoken to them again and again and they had not listened. His message was for them to turn from their evil deeds, and idolatry, and dwell in the land God gave to their forefathers. But the Lord says they have not listened and have provoked Him to anger with the work of their hands. Because they have not listened, the Lord says, He will bring Nebuchadnezzar, king of Babylon, against them and all the nations round about, and they will all serve the king of Babylon 70 years. This is the amount of time the exiles will be in Babylon (see Daniel 9:2). Then the Lord says He will punish the land of the Babylonians (they will be taken over by the Medes and Persians).

Fresco of a basket of figs at Villa Poppaea, Oplontis, Italy.

Verses 31-38

Then, as is typical in the prophets, the prophet jumps from the plunder of Jerusalem and the nations round about (entire Middle East including Babylon) to the Day of the Lord at the end of the age. The Lord has a controversy with the nations concerning Israel and Jerusalem and how they have treated them, and He will enter into judgment with all flesh. "A great storm is being stirred up from the remotest parts of the earth, and those slain by the Lord on that Day shall be from one end of the earth to the other." This storm is being stirred up now and all the nations are setting their faces against Israel.

Chapter 26 – Jeremiah Seized

In the beginning of the reign of Jehoiakim king of Judah, the Lord told Jeremiah to stand in the court of the Lord's House (Temple) and speak His words to the people, in the hope that they will listen and repent, and He will not have to bring the calamity on them. If they will not listen to the word, then the Lord says He will make the Temple like Shiloh (where the Tabernacle used to be - meaning it will be in ruins) and the city He will make a curse. All the priests and prophets heard Jeremiah speaking all these words. Then they seized him and wanted to kill him. Interestingly, Jesus spoke the same word to His generation in the restored Temple and they rejected Him as well.

The royal officials of Judah came and sat in the entrance to the Temple at the New Gate, and the priests and prophets came to them seeking for the death of Jeremiah. But Jeremiah repeated his words to them, and they were unwilling to put him to death because they were afraid of his words. Then others stood up and reminded them about what Micah had prophesied in the days of Hezekiah, that Jerusalem would be plowed as a field, and they had repented and not harmed Micah. Also, there is the mention of a certain Uriah, a contemporary of Jeremiah who had brought the same word and had to flee to Egypt.

Apparently, Jehoiakim sent to Egypt and brought him back and killed him. However, Ahikam son of Shaphan (apparently a royal official), protected Jeremiah.

Chapter 27 – Serve the King of Babylon

In the beginning of the reign of Zedekiah the Lord gave Jeremiah these words to speak to Judah, and all the surrounding nations, by the messengers who apparently came to Zedekiah from these kings. He is told to make yokes and put them around his neck and prophesy to them that they must all serve the king of Babylon, and it will be well with them. But the nation that will not submit to Babylon will be destroyed. Jeremiah spoke all the words that God gave him to the people, and priests, and to the royal officials, and also the messengers from the other nations. He warned Judah not to listen to their prophets who were lying to them, saying that Babylon would not come against them, and that the vessels of the Lord's house, that had already been taken, would be returned. On the contrary, Jeremiah told them that the rest of the vessels that remained, would also be taken to Babylon, and would not be returned until the people returned.

Chapter 28 – Hananiah's Demise

In the same year, in the beginning of the reign of Zedekiah, Hananiah the prophet who was from Gibeon, spoke to Jeremiah in the Temple area in the hearing of all the priests and the people, saying, that in two years the yoke of Babylon would be broken and the vessels of the Temple, which were in Babylon, would be returned. He also said that God was going to bring back Jehoiachin and the exiles at the same time. Jeremiah responded by saying in essence, that He hoped the Lord would do that. However, he said that all the prophets who had spoken before them, had spoken against many nations. Yet, the prophet whose words come to pass is the one the Lord has sent.

Then Hananiah took the yoke from Jeremiah's neck, broke it, and said that in two full years the Lord would break the yoke of Nebuchadnezzar from off the neck of all the nations. Jeremiah just went home.

Then the Lord spoke to Jeremiah, apparently on his way home, and told him to go back and tell Hananiah that he had broken a yoke of wood but now the Lord would put a yoke of iron on all the nations. Furthermore, since the Lord had not sent Hananiah, and he was making the people trust in a lie, He would remove him from the face of the earth. Hananiah died the same year in the 7th month.

Chapter 29 – Build Houses and Settle in Exile

Jeremiah wrote to all the exiles who were taken into Babylon with Jehoiachin and told them to settle down and build houses and raise families. He told them to seek the peace and welfare of the place where God had sent them, and the Lord would prosper them. Then in 70 years the Lord would visit them and bring them back to their own land.

"For thus says the LORD, 'When seventy years have been completed for Babylon, I will visit you and fulfill My good word to you, to bring you back to this place. For I know the plans that I have for you,' declares the LORD, "plans for welfare and not for calamity to give you a future and a hope. Then you will call upon Me and come and pray to Me, and I will listen to you. You will seek Me and find Me when you search for Me with all your heart. I will be found by you,' declares the LORD, "and I will restore your fortunes and will gather you from all the nations and from all the places where I have driven you,' declares the LORD, and I will bring you back to the place from where I sent you into exile.'" Jer 29:10-14 NASU

He also told them that their brothers who were still in Judah and Jerusalem would soon join them and that the Lord was going to drive them out with the sword and famine. He also pronounced judgment on the false prophets who were among the people in Babylon, who were prophesying false and speaking against Jeremiah. He spoke of a prophet named Ahab and another named Zedekiah (not king Zedekiah), who were false prophets and whom Nebuchadnezzar would roast in the fire. He then pronounced judgment on a certain false prophet named Shemaiah, who had been sending letters to the priests in Jerusalem prophesying falsely and trying to conspire against Jeremiah to have him thrown in prison. *"Behold, I am about to punish Shemaiah the Nehelamite and his descendants; he will not have anyone living among this people, and he will not see the good that I am about to do to My people," declares the LORD, "because he has preached rebellion against the LORD." Jer 29:32 NASU*

Chapter 30:1-3 - Jacob's Distress
Now begins in earnest, long and lengthy prophecies concerning the end of the age and the restoration of the Jewish people - the Day of the Lord (Tribulation period and the Millennial reign of Messiah). God will bring them back to the land and restore their fortunes.

Verses 4-11
Immediately after verse 3, when the people are back in their land, comes the Tribulation period (Day of The Lord) referred to in verses 4-7 as the Birth Pains or Jacob's Distress. These birth pains are not the same as in Chapter 22:23, when the people are exiled to Babylon. These are the birth pains at the end of the age. The Day is great, and there is none like it. But the Lord will deliver Jacob this time and completely destroy the nations that are attacking them, all the places to which He scattered them. The remnant of Israel will be rescued and will live securely on the land with no one to make them afraid. They will finally realize the promised kingdom of David under the rule of the Messiah.

Verses 12-17

The Lord laments that He had no choice but to do this to them because their iniquity is so great and their wound is incurable. Yet He promises to punish their enemies who do these things and heal and restore them.

Verses 18-22

The Lord will restore the fortunes of the "tents" of Jacob and have compassion on his dwelling places. The Lord promises to restore the ruined cities, fill them with joy, and cause all the earth to honor them. Please note, the use of "tents" referring to the cities and dwelling places of Jacob and the city of Jerusalem. This is the same as the passage in Amos 9:11 which is so misused today.

"Their leader shall be one of them, and their ruler shall come forth from their midst; and I will bring him near and he shall approach Me; for who would dare to risk his life to approach Me?' declares the LORD." Jer 30:21

When it speaks of their leader coming from among them (verse 21), it might be a reference to the Messiah, who was mentioned earlier in the chapter. However, it is more likely referring to the Nasi or appointed leader in the Millennium.[49] Since the Messiah is the Lord it is unlikely that He is the one approaching the presence of God as described in the verse.

Verses 23-24 - are about the Day of the Lord at the end of the age (latter days) - today.

Chapter 31:1-14- Restoration to the Land & To God
These are famous verses about the regathering of Israel and her restoration at the end of the age.

"For thus says the LORD, 'Sing aloud with gladness for Jacob, and shout among the chief of the nations; Proclaim, give praise and say, "O LORD, save Your people, The remnant of Israel." Behold, I am bringing them from the north country, And I will gather them from the remote parts of the earth, Among them the blind and the lame, The woman with child and she who is in labor with child, together; a great company, they will return here. With weeping they will come, and by supplication I will lead them; I will make them walk by streams of waters, on a straight path in which they will not stumble; for I am a father to Israel, and Ephraim is My firstborn.'" Jer 31:7-9 NASU

"Hear the word of the LORD, O nations, and declare in the coastlands afar off, and say, 'He who scattered Israel will gather him and keep him as a shepherd keeps his flock. For the LORD has ransomed Jacob and redeemed him from the hand of him who was stronger than he. They will come and shout for joy on the height of Zion, and they will be radiant over the bounty of the LORD -- over the grain and the new wine and the oil, and over the young of the flock and the herd; and their life will be like a watered garden, and they will

---
[49] Ezek 45:7

never languish again. Then the virgin will rejoice in the dance, and the young men and the old, together, for I will turn their mourning into joy and will comfort them and give them joy for their sorrow. I will fill the soul of the priests with abundance, and My people will be satisfied with My goodness," declares the LORD.'" Jer 31:10-14 NASU

Verses 15-20
Verse 15 is a reference to the weeping in Bethlehem (where Rachel died - Mt 2:18). But it is also a picture of the continual mourning of the Jewish people. But they are told that the weeping will end. The Lord has heard their grieving and will restore them. They are repenting for their sin (verse 18).

"For after I turned back, I repented; and after I was instructed, I smote on my thigh; I was ashamed and also humiliated because I bore the reproach of my youth. Is Ephraim My dear son? Is he a delightful child? Indeed, as often as I have spoken against him, I certainly still remember him; therefore My heart yearns for him; I will surely have mercy on him," declares the LORD." Jer 31:19-20 NASU

Verses 21-40
The people will come back from all the lands and the Lord will establish again all their cities and the "Holy Hill." Just as the Lord watched over them to pluck up, break down, overthrow, and destroy, so now He will watch over them to build and to plant. This is a now word to which the nations and the church would do well to listen. After the Lord brings them back, He will establish a new covenant with them. This is the covenant which we believers in Messiah have already entered into.

"Behold, days are coming, declares the LORD, when I will make a new covenant with the house of Israel and with the house of Judah, not like the covenant which I made with their fathers in the day I took them by the hand to bring them out of the land of Egypt, My covenant which they broke, although I was a husband to them, declares the LORD. But this is the covenant which I will make with the house of Israel after those days, declares the LORD, I will put My law within them and on their heart I will write it; and I will be their God, and they shall be My people. They will not teach again, each man his neighbor and each man his brother, saying, 'Know the LORD,' for they will all know Me, from the least of them to the greatest of them, declares the LORD, for I will forgive their iniquity, and their sin I will remember no more." Jer 31:31-34 NASU

Another word the church would do well to understand, is that the Lord has promised that Israel will always be a nation before Him. They do not get swallowed up by the church. Their national identity as His chosen nation will always exist.

"Thus says the LORD, Who gives the sun for light by day and the fixed order of the moon and the stars for light by night, Who stirs up the sea so that its waves roar; the LORD of hosts is His name: if this fixed order departs from before Me," declares the LORD, then the offspring of Israel also will cease from being a nation before Me forever." Jer 31:35-36 NASU

Also, please note that God has promised to restore the city of David and rebuild it and establish it as the capital of the earth.

"Behold, days are coming, declares the LORD, when the city will be rebuilt for the LORD from the Tower of Hananel to the Corner Gate. The measuring line will go out farther straight ahead to the hill Gareb; then it will turn to Goah. And the whole valley of the dead bodies and of the ashes, (Hinom Valley) *and all the fields as far as the brook Kidron, to the corner of the Horse Gate toward the east, shall be holy to the LORD; it will not be plucked up or overthrown anymore forever." Jer 31:38-40 NASU*

Chapter 32:1-17
The word that came to Jeremiah in the 10th year of Zedekiah which was the 18th year of Nebuchadnezzar and he had laid siege to the city of Jerusalem. Jeremiah was imprisoned in the court of the guard which was in the king's house. Zedekiah had shut him up because of his prophesying against the city and telling them to surrender to Babylon. The Lord told Jeremiah that his first cousin would come to him asking him to buy his field from him which was at Anathoth (outside Jerusalem). Jeremiah had confirmation of the word of the Lord when his cousin Hanamel came to him asking him to buy the field. Jeremiah bought the field for 17 shekels of silver. The deed was signed in the presence of witnesses and the silver weighed out. Jeremiah then told Baruch, his scribe, to take it and seal it in an earthenware jar that it would last a long time. The message was; fields and vineyards would again be bought in the land.

Verses 16-25
Jeremiah prays to the Lord. He laments the sin of the people and the capture of the city and yet, in spite of this, he is buying a field.

Verses 26-44
The Lord responds to Jeremiah, reminding him why He had to bring all this calamity on the people and the city.

"Indeed the sons of Israel and the sons of Judah have been doing only evil in My sight from their youth; for the sons of Israel have been only provoking Me to anger by the work of their hands, declares the LORD. Indeed this city has been to Me a provocation of My anger and My wrath from the day that they built it, even to this day, so that it should be removed from before My face, because of all the evil of the sons of Israel and the sons of Judah which they have done to provoke Me to anger -- they, their kings, their leaders, their priests,

their prophets, the men of Judah and the inhabitants of Jerusalem. They have turned their back to Me and not their face; though I taught them, teaching again and again, they would not listen and receive instruction. But they put their detestable things in the house which is called by My name, to defile it. Jer 32:30-34 NASU

The Lord is here sharing His heart with the prophet. He also laments the burning of the city and the scattering of the people and assures the prophet that it is only temporary.

"Now therefore thus says the LORD God of Israel concerning this city of which you say, 'It is given into the hand of the king of Babylon by sword, by famine and by pestilence.' Behold, I will gather them out of all the lands to which I have driven them in My anger, in My wrath and in great indignation; and I will bring them back to this place and make them dwell in safety. They shall be My people, and I will be their God; and I will give them one heart and one way, that they may fear Me always, for their own good and for the good of their children after them. I will make an everlasting covenant with them that I will not turn away from them, to do them good; and I will put the fear of Me in their hearts so that they will not turn away from Me. I will rejoice over them to do them good and will faithfully plant them in this land with all My heart and with all My soul. For thus says the LORD, "Just as I brought all this great disaster on this people, so I am going to bring on them all the good that I am promising them. Fields will be bought in this land of which you say, "It is a desolation, without man or beast; it is given into the hand of the Chaldeans. Men will buy fields for money, sign and seal deeds, and call in witnesses in the land of Benjamin, in the environs of Jerusalem, in the cities of Judah, in the cities of the hill country, in the cities of the lowland and in the cities of the Negev; for I will restore their fortunes,' declares the LORD." Jer 32:36-44 NASU

Chapter 33 – Millennial Kingdom to Come

Verses 1-13
While he was still confined in the house of the guard, Jeremiah receives from the Lord this most amazing prophecy of restoration. God says that He will restore the fortunes of Judah and Jerusalem and make it as it was at first. He will also pardon and cleanse them of all their iniquities and transgressions. The land which will be desolate will be restored and the people will be restored with flocks and herds. Jerusalem will be restored from its desolation and ruins and in it will be heard again the voice of the bridegroom and the voice of the bride. Though this was fulfilled when the exiles returned, it seems also to be referring to the Messianic era and the Millennium. The city of Jerusalem is made glorious and is

renowned around the world and is given an abundance of peace. The temple will also be restored.[50]

Verses 14-26

In these verses the prophecy goes on to clearly talk about the Millennial reign. The righteous Branch of David, which refers to the Messiah, will spring forth and execute justice and righteousness in the earth. In those days Judah will be saved, and Jerusalem will dwell in safety, and it will be called Yahweh Tsidkenu (Zedek) or "Yahweh Our Righteousness." The Messiah Yeshua (Jesus) is a priest and king after the order of Melchizedek, and in Him both offices are united, and He will be king of Jerusalem.

The prophecy goes on to state categorically that unless we can break God's covenant with the day and night, so that they are not at their appointed time, David will not lack an heir to his throne and the Levitical priests to serve with him. Jesus who is the Son of David will rule on His Throne, and also the Levitical priests will be restored with Him. This reality is confirmed by other verses which show that the Third Temple will be cleansed and restored when Messiah comes (Ezek 40-48, Dan 9:27).

The prophecy goes on to make it clear that it is not just the Messiah, but that Israel will be restored and multiplied in the last days.

"Thus says the LORD, 'If My covenant for day and night stand not, and the fixed patterns of heaven and earth I have not established, then I would reject the descendants of Jacob and David My servant, not taking from his descendants rulers over the descendants of Abraham, Isaac, and Jacob. But I will restore their fortunes and will have mercy on them.'"

<u>Chapter 34:1-7 – Zedekiah to be Captured</u>

While Nebuchadnezzar, king of Babylon, had laid siege to Jerusalem and the other remaining fortified cities in Judah, Lachish and Azekah, Jeremiah was given a word for Zedekiah king of Judah. Jeremiah went to Zedekiah and declared the word he had received. The Lord had told him that the king of Babylon would burn the city and that Zedekiah would be taken prisoner to Babylon. Nevertheless, he would not die by the sword but would die in peace, and as spices were burned for his fathers, they would also be burned for him.

Verses 8-22

Apparently, king Zedekiah had made a covenant with the people of Jerusalem, a blood covenant (verses 18-19), to free all the Hebrew slaves in Jerusalem. But after making the covenant and setting the slaves free, they turned around and broke it enslaving them once again.

It is hard to understand why the king needed to make a covenant with the people concerning this, since it was already a command of Torah that the slaves were to be released every 7 years. Nevertheless, God spoke to Jeremiah that just as they, and their fathers, had been

---
[50] Verse 18

disobedient to His command to free the slaves, God was about to bring the Babylonians back against the city and they would burn it with fire, and the corpses of the people would be food for the birds of the air. Also, as the king and the officials of Judah had made a covenant to free the slaves and then reneged on it, King Nebuchadnezzar would carry them off into slavery in Babylon.

Chapter 35 – Jonadab's Sons
During the reign of Jehoiakim, Jeremiah was told to go to the Rechabites and bring them into a chamber in the Temple and lay pitchers of wine before them. But they refused to drink since they had obeyed the voice of Jonadab, the son of Recab their father, who told them not to drink wine, or own fields, or vineyards, or build houses, but to live in tents. Then the Lord asks the sons of Israel why Jonadab's sons could listen to him and obey him in such and extraordinary way, yet they would not listen to the voice of the Lord after he has sent so many messengers to them. Thus, He promised to hand them over to the Babylonians because of their refusal to obey.

The point here has nothing to do with wine or houses, but obedience. The Lord is pointing out the obedience of the sons of Jonadab and wondering why His people would not obey Him. Then Jeremiah commends the sons of Jonadab and tells them they will never lack a man of their family to stand before the Lord always.

Chapter 36:1-26 – Burning God's Word
In the 4th year of Jehoiakim, Jeremiah received instruction from the Lord to write down on a scroll all the words He had spoken to him from the beginning to the present. He was then to read it again in the hearing of the people, in hopes that they might repent, and God would not be forced to pour out His anger on them. Jeremiah dictated all the words to Baruch, his scribe, and asked him to go read it in the House of the Lord on a fast, which he did a year later. It apparently took a year to complete the work. When one of royal officials heard the words, he went and told all the others. Then they sent for Baruch and had him read the words to them. When they heard the words, they were fearful and asked if Jeremiah had dictated them. Then they brought the scroll to the king and told Baruch to go hide himself along with Jeremiah. When king Jehoiakim heard just a small portion of the scroll, he took a scribe's knife and cut the scroll and threw it in the fire, over the objections of some of his officials. It was winter at the time which is why he had a fire burning in his fireplace. Then he commanded that Jeremiah and Baruch be seized, but the Lord hid them from him.

Verses 27-32
Then Lord told Jeremiah to dictate all the words again and let Baruch write them on another scroll. We are also told that this time, many similar words were added. He was to tell Jehoiakim that he will have no one to sit on his throne and his dead body would be cast out to the heat of the day and the frost of night. The Lord would bring on him and his officials and all Jerusalem the things written in the scroll.

This incident illustrates once more the remarkable hardness of the hearts of Israel's leaders. They just wouldn't hear that God was going to bring judgment on Jerusalem – His holy city. Yet today, we see the same kind of hardness in the hearts of so many church leaders. They simply will not listen to the teaching of Scripture or tolerate the notion that His long-awaited end-time judgments are coming on the world. And just like King Jehoiakim they despise God's Word and will pay a heavy prince of condemnation. The Lord is slow to anger and abounding in lovingkindness, but His judgments eventually come.

Chapter 37:1-10 – Jeremiah Arrested
Zedekiah whom the king of Babylon had made king in place of Jehoiachin (also known as Jeconiah), did not listen or obey the words of the Lord any more than His brother Jehoiakim. However, when Pharaoh Necho II, King of Egypt, had come with his army to help Judah, and the Babylonians had lifted the siege on hearing this news, Zedekiah sends messengers to Jeremiah to seek prayer and help from the Lord. Jeremiah sent word back to him from the Lord that the siege would resume, and the city would be burned with fire. He said, even if the army of Nebuchadnezzar were to be defeated and only a few wounded soldiers left, they would burn the city.

Verses 11-21
When the siege was lifted Jeremiah went to Benjamin to buy property (likely the field the Lord told him to buy in chapter 32) and while in Benjamin he was arrested and accused of trying to escape to the Babylonians. They took him to Jerusalem and put him in a dungeon. He was there many days until Zedekiah sent for him. It appears that Zedekiah respected Jeremiah and didn't want to harm him, yet he would not believe the word or obey the Lord. But he did listen to Jeremiah's plea not to be put back in the cistern, Thus he had him brought to the guardhouse, and given a loaf of bread daily. It appears he stayed there, except for another brief stint in Jonathan's cistern, until the city was about to fall, since it says, the bread ran out.

Chapter 38 – The Cistern Again
When the royal officials heard all the words that Jeremiah was speaking to the people, that they should go and serve the king of Babylon and no harm would come to them, and not to remain in the city, they asked the king to put him to death. In their minds, he was not looking out for the welfare of the city and was scaring away the fighting men. So the king gave them permission to take him and they lowered him back into a cistern with ropes and

he sank down in the mud. One can see this cistern in the city of David today. I have seen it, and I can tell you, it is really small and very deep.

Then an official named Ebed-melech an Ethiopian, had mercy on Jeremiah and got permission from the king to have him taken out. So they got rags, and lowered them to Jeremiah with ropes to put under his arms, and they hauled him out and took him to the court of the guardhouse. Then Zedekiah sent for Jeremiah to ask him again what the Lord was saying. He swore to Jeremiah that he would not put him to death, regardless of what it was. However, he was not to tell any of the officials about the conversation. Jeremiah pleaded with him to surrender to the king of Babylon, and all would be well with him and the city would not be burned. Zedekiah was afraid of what they would do to him if he surrendered. Jeremiah told him they would not mistreat him. However, if he did not surrender, the city would be burned with fire, and he would not escape. They would abuse him and his family. Zedekiah kept his word to Jeremiah, and when the officials interrogated the prophet, they discovered nothing and left him alone in the guardhouse until the end came.

Chapter 39 – The Final Siege
In the 9th year of Zedekiah, in the 10th month, Nebuchadnezzar's army laid siege to Jerusalem. The siege lasted until his 11th year, and the 4th month and the 9th day (9th of Av) Then the Babylonians broke through the wall. When Zedekiah saw this, he tried to escape in the night with all his men. But the Chaldeans followed them and captured them in the plains of Jericho. They brought them to Nebuchadnezzar at Riblah and he passed sentence on them. He slew the sons of Zedekiah before his eyes and all the royal officials. Then they poked out Zedekiah's eyes and took him, and all the rest of the Jews, to Babylon. Some of the very poor they left behind in the land and gave them fields and vineyards. Nebuchadnezzar gave orders for Jeremiah to be taken care of and let do what he wished. He was allowed to stay in the land. Jeremiah had a word from the Lord for Ebed-melech the Ethiopian, while in the guardhouse, that he would be spared and let live in the land and not given over to the Chaldeans – undoubtedly for his kindness to the prophet.

Chapter 40:1-6 – Jeremiah Released
Nebuzardan the captain of the guard released Jeremiah and told him he could go with him to Babylon, and he would take care of him, or he could go back with the others to Gedaliah who had been put in charge of the remnant that was left. Jeremiah chose to go back and went to Gedaliah at Mizpah. Then all the exiles who had been scattered about came to Gedaliah at Mizpah. Many returned from other places where they had fled. Then Gedaliah told them to settle in the land and cities they had apparently taken over, and to gather in

wine and oil and summer fruit. It was essentially the same message that Jeremiah preached. Live in the land and serve the king of Babylon and it will go well with you![51]

However, Johanan told Gedaliah that there was a plot against him by Ishmael the son of Nethaniah, of the royal household of Judah, who apparently was aligned with the king of Ammon. Gedaliah would not listen to Johanan son of Kareah who warned him of the plot and asked to be allowed to go and kill Ishmael. Gedaliah thought it was a lie and would not permit him to go.

What incredible kindness the Chaldean ruler showed Jeremiah the prophet. It certainly seemed that he understood what the Lord had intended for the city and the people. This illustrates that God uses secular rulers to carry out His will. The captivity came in fulfillment of God's decrees and was ended by another Gentile ruler raised up by God.

Chapter 41 - Treachery
Ishmael, who was of the royal family, came to Gedaliah at Mizpah with a band of men. He sat down to eat and then slaughtered Gedaliah whom the Lord had put in charge of the land and all his men. He also slew the Babylonian soldiers who were there. The next day 80 men from Shechem and Shiloh came to Mizpah with their beards shaved and clothes torn, and their bodies gashed (apparently mourning) having grain offerings and incense to bring to the Temple (perhaps they had not heard it was destroyed). Ishmael slew them all and cast the bodies in a cistern. Then he gathered all the people that were left and determined to cross over to Ammon.

When Johanan the son of Kareah, and the men that were with him, heard what Ismael had done, they pursued them to fight with them. They caught up with them at the great pool in Gibeon, which is just northwest of Jerusalem. When the people with Ismael saw Johanan and his men coming, they ran to them. However, Ismael and eight men escaped from Johanan and went to Ammon. Then Johanan gathered all the people and went to stay near Bethlehem in preparation for a journey to Egypt, since they were afraid of the Chaldeans because of the murder of Gedaliah.

Chapter 42 – More Fake Repentance
Johanan and the commanders and all the people with them, pleaded with Jeremiah to seek God for a word of direction for them. Why they needed such a word is unimaginable since God clearly revealed His will to them through Gedaliah. Nevertheless, they persisted and as always promised to obey.

Then they said to Jeremiah, "May the LORD be a true and faithful witness against us if we do not act in accordance with the whole message with which the LORD your God will send you to us. Whether it is pleasant or unpleasant, we will listen to the voice of the LORD our

---
[51] 2 Kings 25:24

God to whom we are sending you, so that it may go well with us when we listen to the voice of the LORD our God." Jer 42:5-6

Jeremiah, who already knew what they should do, agreed to seek the Lord anyway on their behalf. Ten days later the Lord in His great love and kindness and patience, spoke to him. The word was the same as before. If they stay in the land and obey the king of Babylon, things will go well with them, and God will not bring any more calamity on them. But if they rebel and go to Egypt the Lord will bring on them the sword and famine which they are afraid of and they will die there with no survivors.

Chapter 43:1-7
Jeremiah knew of course that they were insincere in their request to know God's will for them. They obviously have not repented from their evil ways and now reject the final opportunity to save their lives and live in peace. No sooner is Jeremiah finished speaking, than they accuse him of lying to them and that he has not heard from the Lord. This is the standard response of those who want to hear pleasant messages rather than what God has to say. They attack the messenger and accuse him or her of lying, and refuse to believe what they are hearing, or reading, is what God said. Thus they bring a curse upon themselves by altering and disobeying His Word. In this way, the commanders and leaders arose and took all the people, including Jeremiah and Baruch who was still with him, into the land of Egypt as far as Tahpanhes.

It seems that the remnant that was left in the land was sifted once again by the Lord. There was treachery against Gedaliah, and even Johanan and his men who tried to prevent this, refused to listen to the words of Jeremiah because they were afraid of the king of Babylon. It seems impossible that anyone would refuse the word of the Lord from Jeremiah at this stage, yet they did. But it is also clear that God is carrying out His judgments already pronounced, and that the land was to remain idle for the 70 years that the nation was in exile.

Verses 8-13 – Babylon Will Come
Then God spoke to Jeremiah in Tahpanhes to take some stones and place them in the brick terrace in the entrance to Pharaoh's palace and prophecy in the presence of the Jews that were there. The prophet declared to them the following word:

"Thus says the LORD of hosts, the God of Israel, 'Behold, I am going to send and get Nebuchadnezzar the king of Babylon, My servant, and I am going to set his throne right over these stones that I have hidden; and he will spread his canopy over them. He will also come and strike the land of Egypt; those who are meant for death will be given over to death, and those for captivity to captivity, and those for the sword to the sword. And I shall set fire to the temples of the gods of Egypt,

and he will burn them and take them captive. So he will wrap himself with the land of Egypt as a shepherd wraps himself with his garment, and he will depart from there safely. He will also shatter the obelisks of Heliopolis,[52] which is in the land of Egypt; and the temples of the gods of Egypt he will burn with fire.'"

Chapter 44 – Refugees Still Rebels

Jeremiah confronts the remnant that now reside in Egypt. It seems that God's mercy knows no bounds in warning these people again and again. Jeremiah recalls their abominable deeds and idolatries in the land of Judah that brought such calamity on them. He specifically mentions the detestable worship of the Queen of Heaven.[53] He warns them that if they do not repent and turn to the Lord that they will not escape in Egypt. Yet, in a most despicable fashion, they collectively respond to Jeremiah, saying that they will continue with their idolatry and even insinuating that, while they were doing it in Judah and Jerusalem, they were well off and prosperous. Thus, their fate is sealed – they will die by the sword and famine, with only a tiny remnant to survive. Jeremiah also proclaims that Pharoah Hophra will be given over to his enemies. This happened in 568BC when his general Amasis, who had deposed him and defeated him in battle, handed him over to his enemies among the Egyptians who strangled him. In 567BC, Nebuchadnezzar invaded Egypt.

Chapter 45 – Prophecy to Baruch

This short chapter records what Jeremiah had told Baruch his scribe previously, during the 4th year of Jehoiakim king of Judah. Baruch, who is obviously distraught over the things that are coming upon Judah, is encouraged not to not seek anything for himself since God is about to uproot the whole land. He is comforted that his life will be spared wherever he goes!

As God's people have been punished for their rebellion against Him, the nations round about need not rejoice in their demise. The next five chapters detail the punishment God will also bring on them for their rebellion and mistreatment of Israel! Though they are collected here under a heading and identity given by the scribe, they were predicted well before they were to take place.

Chapter 46: 1-12 – Carchemish 605BC

Pharoah Necho of Egypt had an alliance with the Assyrians against the Babylonians. He was on his way to fight there in 609BC when the good king Josiah met him and was slain. Judah then became a vassal kingdom of Egypt. In 605BC, Necho with all his forces joined

---

[52] One of these obelisks now sits in Vatican square.
[53] This Queen of Heaven had many names in the ancient world. For them she was Ashtoreth the mother of Tammuz whom she had by Baal. Sadly, many who claim to be Christians today are worshipping the same pagan idol whom they think is Mary the mother of Jesus.

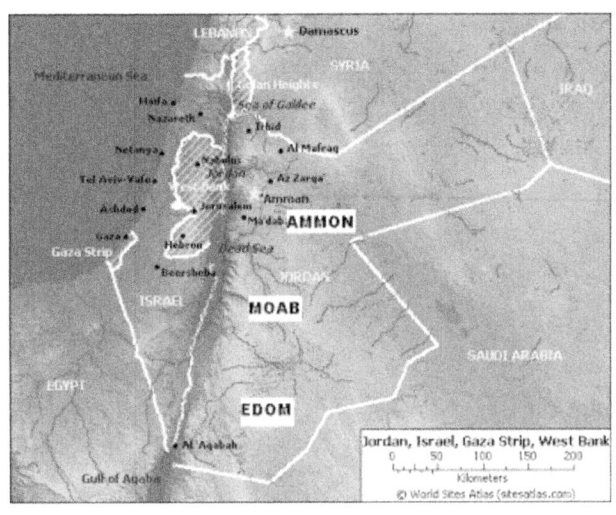

the Assyrians against Nebuchadnezzar at Carchemish where they are both soundly defeated. This was the end of the Assyrian Empire and Egypt was in retreat having lost all its territory, including Judah.

Verses 13-26
These verses predict the invasion and destruction of Egypt by Nebuchadnezzar. God used the Babylonians to bring destruction upon Egypt and its gods. Also, this was to fulfill Jeremiah's warnings to the exiles of Judah that had entered there and refused to repent of their idolatry. Though Egypt suffered destruction and plunder under the Babylonians, it did recover (verse 26).

Verses 27-28
The last two verses proclaim once again, the promise of God to have compassion on Jacob and restore Israel to its homeland. Though they will be disciplined severely, they will be restored. God promises to make a full end of those nations to where he had driven them. Though the return from Babylon was part of this restoration, it seems clear that a greater restoration from all the nations, such as we have seen in our day, was also implied.

Chapter 47 – Prophecy Against Philistia
In verse 1, we are told that this prophecy was given before Pharaoh conquered Gaza. That was Pharaoh Necho II who conquered it in 609 BC. Ashkelon was destroyed by the Babylonians in 604BC. The Philistines were descendants of Ham and appear to have come from Caphtor which is likely modern-day Crete. Gaza was rebuilt and destroyed again by Alexander the great in 332BC and most of its inhabitants killed. Though it is possible that a tiny remnant of Philistines could have survived, after the Babylonian conquest they disappear from the pages of history.

Chapter 48 – Destruction of Moab
Moab was the nation to the southeast of Israel, descendant from Lot and his older daughter. They have been very arrogant against the people of Israel throughout their history and against the Lord. Their day of judgment comes in 582BC under the Babylonians. Their cities and their gods are destroyed. They are taken away as exiles and are no longer a people. There is great mourning and weeping in Moab. The Lord grieves over them because He has to destroy them. It saddens His heart, since they are the children of Lot, the nephew of Abraham.

At the end of the chapter there is a promise to restore Moab in the latter days. This is the period we are living in today. Moab is part of the Hashemite Kingdom of Jordan today!

Chapter 49:1-6 – Prophecy Against Ammon

Ammon was a nation on the northeast of Israel that was also descended from Lot, through his younger daughter. Ammon oppressed the Israelites throughout its history just as Moab had done. It had also taken advantage after the exile of Israel to occupy the territory of Gad just as Moab had done with the cities of Heshbon, Kiriathaim and Nebo which had belonged to Reuben. Their capital Rabbah would become a mound of ruins and they would suffer the same fate as Moab. The city referred to as Ai, is not the same as the one conquered by Joshua.

As with Moab, there is a promise of restoration. Ammon today is part of Jordan and it's capital Amman is situated where Rabbah had been.

Verses 7-22 – Prophecy Against Edom

Edom was the nation to the south and east of the Dead Sea. Though they were family, being the descendants of Esau, Jacob's twin brother, they were always cruel to Israel, even refusing them passage through their territory on the return from Egypt. When the Babylonians conquered Judah, it appears that the Edomites invaded in the south and began to move into cities in the Negev, especially Hebron. When Nebuchadnezzar destroyed Jerusalem and the Temple, it appears that the Edomites were helping him. This is referenced in many Bible passages. It is believed by some that Babylon destroyed Edom, at least the original kingdom around 500BC. Then we are told that the Nabateans occupied their territory. This is precisely what we find at the time of Jesus. Idumea, the remnant of Edom, occupies the Negev and Nabatea, the area that was once Edom.

This prophecy of Jeremiah is extremely similar to the prophecy of Obadiah (see pg. 6). Edom was to become a perpetual ruin. It is part of the territory in Jordan today.

Verses 23-27 – Against Damascus

Damascus was destroyed by Tiglath-Pileser in 722 BC. It was to be rebuilt and apparently destroyed again by Nebuchadnezzar. The city was rebuilt many times since but that does not necessarily mean there is a future fulfillment of this passage or Isaiah 17. Hamath and Arpad are coastal towns in ancient Syria.

Verses 28-33 – Against Kedar and Hazor

These verses detail the destruction of the kingdoms of Kedar and Hazor in the east, which was carried out by Nebuchadnezzar. The Hazor mentioned, is not the Hazor in Northern Israel, but both places were in Ancient Arabia.

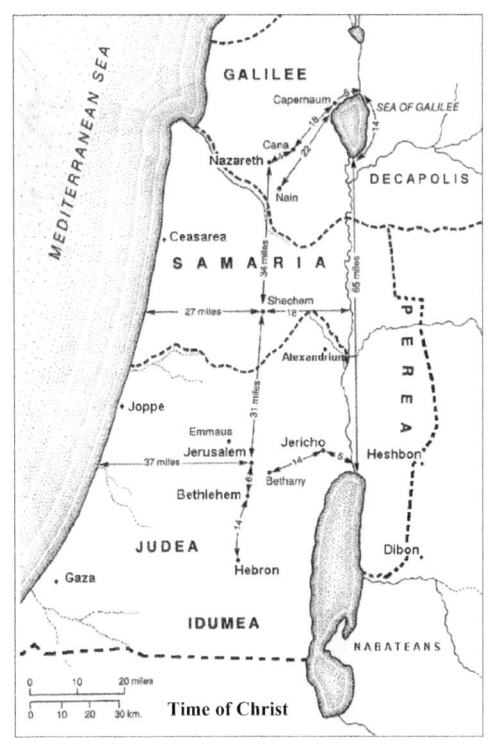

119

Verses 34-39 – Against Elam
Elam is the territory of Ancient Persia and is known today as Iran. We are told that they were excellent archers and thus the phrase, "break the bow" means their strength and army will be destroyed.

Iran today is under very evil rule. It is mentioned in Ezekiel 38 & 39 as a participant in the Gog Magog invasion of Israel. God Himself will rain down a future destruction on the armies of Iran. Yet despite all that, there is a future restoration promised in the last days!

Chapter 50 & 51 – Fall of Babylon
These chapters prophesy in great detail the destruction of Babylon by the armies of the Medes and the Persians from the north. This took place in 539BC. Babylon will no longer be inhabited. It will be a haunt of jacals and a heap of ruins. It's gods Marduk and Bel have been put to shame.

There is so much is written about the fall of Babylon and her destruction. This empire brutalized the people of Judah, taking them captive and destroying the Temple (51:28). Because of these actions the vengeance of the Lord will be taken out on her. Even though God used Babylon to punish His people, the time will come for her punishment, and she will not be spared. God says to pay her back for all that she has done.

Another theme in chapter 51 besides the fall of Babylon is the restoration of Zion and the Temple. God has promised to bring back His people Israel to her land and restore His "heritage." Babylon has held them fast, but God will let them go and they are told to return to Zion. Babylon and Rome will be judged for what they have done to God's people and the Temple.[54]

"Come forth from her midst, My people, and each of you save yourselves from the fierce anger of the LORD."

Though Babylon was invaded, taken over, and later abandoned becoming a heap of ruins as it is to this day, all the punishments and violence that was spoken does not appear to have occurred in ancient time. When we analyze that and put it together with the revelations of Daniel and the Book of Revelation, we begin to see that from God's perspective, Babylon is not just the Chaldean kingdom of old, but the representation of the subsequent empires that would dominate the land of Israel and its people. From Nebuchadnezzar's dream in Daniel chapter two, we see that Babylon is the head of gold and thus it is the name

---
[54] Jer 50:28, 51:11

given to all of the kingdoms mentioned in the prophecy. The fourth kingdom is Rome which destroyed Jerusalem and scattered the Jewish people throughout the earth. Then in Revelation chapters 13 and 17, we see the revival of the Roman Empire from Daniel chapter 2, 7 & 8 depicted as the city of Rome (Rev 17:18). It is a political system with a harlot religious system riding on top of it. This system which is centered in Rome today and rides atop the EU, is easily discernable. It is the Harlot system, the prostitute church which mixes a false Christianity with all the false Babylonian worship of the world. Thus, it is the culmination and amalgamation of all the empires and their religious systems that persecuted God's people.

In the same way that Babylon fell apart, Rome fell apart and was scattered, but it's capital never received the judgment pronounced. And just like Babylon that destroyed Jerusalem and its Temple, Rome has yet to receive the wrath of God. The coliseum and the arch of Titus were built from the spoils of Jerusalem and the Temple, and they are still standing. Therefore, there is a specific judgment for this city known as Babylon that is spelled out in Revelation chapter 18. In one hour, her judgment comes, and it is total. Also, just as there was a remnant of Jews that came out of Babylon while the vast throng remained, there is a remnant church today that has come out of this Harlot and will not participate with her. And thus the cry goes out again, even today, "Come out of her My people

Similarities between Jeremiah chapter 50 & 51 with Revelation 17 & 18

"Repay her according to her work; according to all that she has done, so do to her; for she has become arrogant against the LORD, against the Holy One of Israel." Jer 50:29

"Pay her back even as she has paid, and give back to her double according to her deeds; in the cup which she has mixed, mix twice as much for her.: Rev 18:6

"Flee from the midst of Babylon, and each of you save his life! Do not be destroyed in her punishment, for this is the LORD'S time of vengeance; He is going to render recompense to her." Jer 51:6

"Come forth from her midst, My people, and each of you save yourselves from the fierce anger of the LORD." Jer 51:45

"I heard another voice from heaven, saying, 'Come out of her, my people, so that you will not participate in her sins and receive of her plagues; for her sins have piled up as high as heaven, and God has remembered her iniquities.'" Rev 18:4-5

"Babylon has been a golden cup in the hand of the LORD, intoxicating all the earth. The nations have drunk of her wine; therefore the nations are going mad." Jer 51:7

"The woman was clothed in purple and scarlet, and adorned with gold and precious stones and pearls, having in her hand a gold cup full of abominations and of the unclean things of her immorality...." Rev 17:4

"For all the nations have drunk of the wine of the passion of her immorality, and the kings of the earth have committed acts of immorality with her, and the merchants of the earth have become rich by the wealth of her sensuality." Rev 18:3

"O you who dwell by many waters, abundant in treasures, your end has come, the measure of your end." Jer 51:13

"Come here, I will show you the judgment of the great harlot who sits on many waters, with whom the kings of the earth committed acts of immorality, and those who dwell on the earth were made drunk with the wine of her immorality." Rev 17:1-2

Also, Isaiah in his prophecy against Babylon:

"Now, then, hear this, you sensual one, who dwells securely, who says in your heart, 'I am, and there is no one besides me. I will not sit as a widow, nor know loss of children.' Isaiah 47:8

"To the degree that she glorified herself and lived sensuously, to the same degree give her torment and mourning; for she says in her heart, 'I SIT as A QUEEN AND I AM NOT A WIDOW, and will never see mourning.'" Rev 18:7

Jeremiah 51:59-64
In these verses Jeremiah recorded that he gave to Seraiah the single scroll containing all these words against Babylon and told him to read it out loud after he got there. Then he was to tie a stone to it and throw it in the Euphrates and proclaim that Babylon will sink down as this stone and never rise again. Seraiah the son of Neriah went to Babylon along with Zedekiah. Then we are told that the words of Jeremiah end. Thus we assume that chapter 52 was added by someone else.

Chapter 52 – The Fall of Jerusalem
This chapter records the sad story of the fall of Jerusalem. It mirrors 2 Kings 25. It is self-explanatory and needs no interpretation. It begins with Zedekiah who did evil in the sight of the Lord and how he rebelled against the king of Babylon. It records that in his ninth year, Babylon laid siege to Jerusalem which lasted two years until the city walls were breached in 586BC. King Zedekiah and his men tried to escape to the Arabah but were captured at Jericho. They were taken to the king of Babylon at Riblah in the land of Hamath in Syria. Nebuchadnezzar had Zedekiah's sons slaughtered before his eyes and his own

eyes poked out. He was put in bronze fetters and taken to Babylon where he was imprisoned until his death. Also, as we have seen, only the poorest of the land were left behind.

We are also told how Nebuzaradan the captain of the guard burned the city and the Temple on the 9th of Av,[55] and we are given a detailed list of all the treasures that he took. However, there is no mention of the Ark which would have been the greatest. It is believed, according to Jewish sources, that Jeremiah hid the Ark somewhere under the Temple Mount. Another possibility is that it was hidden in Qumran as the Copper Scroll[56] seems to suggest. It has not been seen since.

Francois Xavier Fabre, 1766-1837.

Then the chapter ends with the story of Jehoiachin being released from prison in Babylon by Evil-Merodach son of Nebuchadnezzar, after many years in captivity. He is shown grace and favor and had his meals in the king's presence the rest of his life.

---

[55] The second Temple was also destroyed by the Romans on the 9th of Av. Many other tragedies have afflicted Israel on this day!
[56] The Copper Scroll was found in Qumran. It is ancient and contains a list of where Temple Treasuries including the Ark are hidden.

Notes

Lamentations

Lamentations was likely written by Jeremiah. It is a very sad book and for this reason it is usually ignored. Indeed, many regular Bible readers have never read it. Some probably wonder why it is even in the Bible. Yet it is a testimony to the broken heart of God, and the prophet, over Jerusalem and all the destruction that has come to the holy people. It is written as poetry and each chapter is broken into 22 verses, except for chapter 3 which has 66 verses – 3x22. Also, it is an acrostic. The Hebrew alphabet has 22 letters and each of the 22 verses begins with a different letter in the alphabet.

Chapter 1 & 2 - Mourning for Jerusalem

Jerusalem is pictured as a woman sitting on the ground in extreme pain of grief and loneliness. She who was once great among the nations sits like a widow bereft of all her children. She weeps bitterly in the night. She has none to comfort her among all her lovers and no one cares about her. All her friends dealt treacherously and have become her enemies. Judah has gone into exile under affliction and harsh servitude. The roads of Zion (Jerusalem) are in mourning because no one is coming to the appointed feasts.

Horace Vernet, Jeremiah on the ruins of Jerusalem (1844)

These verses clearly illustrate the Biblical teaching regarding Israel and the land, and Israel and Jerusalem. It is not just a piece of land. It is not just an ancient city. It is their city – God's city. The people and Jerusalem are inextricably linked. They must not be separated, and those who separate them, such as Babylon and Rome and the modern nations of the earth will pay a heavy price for their sin.

Jerusalem who was once the perfection of beauty is now a heap of ruins. All who pass by hiss and shake their heads. They gloat over the destruction of Zion saying, "We have swallowed her up. This is the day for which we have waited." As she weeps and wails for the young men and virgins, she asks that the Lord bring upon them the day of which He has spoken and make them like her.

As the prophet weeps and cries out, Jerusalem's tears run down her cheeks all day long. It is hard to know if it is the prophet that cries out in pain or the city itself. Such is the bond between the two.

Repeatedly there is lamentation over all that Jerusalem has done - her princes, priests and prophets who spoke lying visions. The Lord is truly justified to bring all this calamity on her.

Chapter 3 – God Wounds and Heals

The chapter begins with Jeremiah describing his own pain and suffering. His whole life has been bitterness of soul. He laments over what the Lord has caused him to go through. He has not had any happiness. The Lord has torn him in pieces and made him desolate. Then we find these beautiful verses as he cries to the Lord for mercy. His hope is restored as he remembers the goodness of the Lord.

"The LORD'S lovingkindnesses indeed never cease, for His compassions never fail. They are new every morning; great is Your faithfulness." Vs 22-23

Then he begins to encourage the suffering with hope, telling them to wait on the Lord for He is good to those who seek Him.

In the midst of God's fierce judgment upon Judah and Jerusalem comes the hope of restoration.

God will not reject forever. If He causes grief, He will have compassion according to His abundant lovingkindness. He does not afflict the sons of men willingly but will by no means leave the guilty unpunished. Who is there who speaks, and it comes to pass unless the Lord has commanded it? Then he reaffirms that both good and ill come from the mouth of the Lord. Many modern teachers take issue with this and declare that God never causes harm or sickness or destruction. But they argue not only with Jeremiah, but with the Lord Himself who brought all these calamities upon His people.

Then the prophet calls for repentance. "Let us examine and probe our ways and return to the Lord." He again recalls all that the Lord has done and how He has not listened to their prayer. Then he remembers how he cried to the Lord from the lowest pit. Perhaps he is speaking of the cistern. The Lord heard his cry and drew near to him and told him not to fear. Then he pleads with the Lord to hear His case and deal justly with his oppressors and recompense them according to the work of their hands.

It is likely that as Jeremiah cries to the Lord and laments over the destruction of Jerusalem and the exile of the people and all that he has personally suffered, he begins to prophesy concerning the suffering of the Messiah on the same hill of Zion. This is very similar to the way David cried out to the Lord and ended up foretelling the future of the suffering Christ (Psalm 22). Consider the following:

'Is it nothing to all you who pass this way? Look and see if there is any pain like my pain.." 1:12

"All who pass along the way clap their hands in derision at you; they hiss and shake their heads..." 2:15

This mirrors what happened to Jesus while He hung on the cross and those who were watching mocked Him.

"I have become a laughingstock to all my people, their mocking song all the day. He has filled me with bitterness, He has made me drunk with wormwood."

Jesus was laughed at all day on the cross and given gall to drink.

"Let him give his cheek to the smiter, let him be filled with reproach." 3:30
When Jesus was taken before Caiaphas and also when He was flogged, His beard was pulled out.

Chapter 4 – The Horror of the Siege
The siege of Jerusalem by the Babylonians lasted two years. This chapter laments the horror and personal pain of it.

The gold has become dark, and the sacred stones have been poured out on the corner of every street. The stones are Jerusalem's unique golden stones, that are now on every street. The young men of Zion were once worth their weight in gold, now they are as valuable as earthen vessels.

Even the jackal nurses it's young but the daughters of Jerusalem have become cruel. The tongue of the infant cleaves to its mouth and the little ones cry for bread, but no one breaks it for them. The famine is so severe and there is nothing to eat. And the wealthy who are used to eating delicacies, are desolate in the streets. Those raised in purple (nobility) are in ash pits. Because the iniquity of the people is worse than Sodom that was overthrown in a moment and there is no one to help. The consecrated ones were white like snow and milk. They were like polished stones. Now they are as soot. Their skin is shriveled on their bones. It is withered and has become as wood. What a description of the agony of starvation? It is better to be slain with the sword than to die of hunger. Then comes the most horrific part. The women boiling their dead children to eat.

The Lord has accomplished His wrath. He poured out His fierce anger and kindled a fire in Zion that has consumed its foundations. The kings and the nations around could not believe that the enemy could enter the gates of Jerusalem - the city of God with the Holy Temple. No one believed that this could ever take place – yet it did, because of the sin of God's people, the prophets and the priests who shed the blood of the righteous. And all the help they sought was to no avail. No one came to their aid. The Lord has scattered them.

The prophet goes on to talk about the sin of Judah and how God has punished them for their iniquity. However, he reminds Edom who is rejoicing over Judah, that the cup will come around to them as well. They will also drink of the Lord's wrath. Then comes a word of comfort and a promise of restoration. Judah has received her punishment and her time of exile will end.

Chapter 5 – Have Mercy Oh Lord

This chapter laments the plight of the exiles and assumably the few that remain. Their inheritance is gone. Their houses are occupied by aliens. They are like orphans without a father. They have to pay for everything now and slaves rule over them and there is no one to deliver. Life is very difficult indeed. They are now suffering for the sins of their fathers.

Once again, the destruction of Zion is recalled. The women were ravished, and the princes were hung by the hands. No mercy was shown to anyone. Now all are gone. There are no elders at the gate – no young men playing music. Joy is gone from their hearts and their dancing has been turned into mourning. The crown is gone from the head of Zion because of her sin. The city is desolate and foxes prowl in it. Because of this sadness has gripped her people and their eyes are dim.

Then comes the cry for mercy - the pain of the prophet's heart.

"You, O LORD, rule forever; Your throne is from generation to generation. Why do You forget us forever? Why do You forsake us so long? Restore us to You, O LORD, that we may be restored; renew our days as of old, unless You have utterly rejected us and are exceedingly angry with us." Lamentations 5:19-22

Notes

Daniel

Daniel and his three friends were extraordinary Jews. They would not tolerate any disloyalty to the God of Israel, regardless of the cost. They prospered among the heathen and Daniel, who was highly esteemed in heaven, received in visions and revelations the whole history of his people. This future history which was revealed to him takes up most of the book. Indeed, that which is revealed to him is the backbone of all eschatology[57] and it is about the Jewish people. The book of Daniel is considered the Revelation of the Old Testament, and without an unfolding of its secrets, there is no understanding of the latter days.

Chapter 1 – Keeping Kosher

In 606BC Nebuchadnezzar of Babylon attacked Judah and took Jehoiakim captive along with about 10,000 of the nobility of the land. Daniel and his friends were part of this captivity. He also took with Him some of the vessels from the house of God and brought them to the land of Shinar.

Daniel and his three friends, Hananiah, Mishael, and Azariah, were taken into the king's court where they were to be taught the language and customs of Babylon. They also got a name change and were given a portion of the king's choice food and wine. This presented a big problem for them, as much of it was likely non-Kosher, meaning it was not prepared and or included ingredients that would be contrary to Torah. Daniel pleaded with the official to release them from eating the king's food. The official was greatly concerned and told him that he would lose his head if they should begin to look skinny or haggard. Then Daniel requested that they be given only vegetables and water for ten days and then the official would be able to see that they were fine and had no ill effects from their diet. So he continued to give them vegetables only. God intervened on behalf of Daniel and his friends and blessed them with knowledge and wisdom. Daniel was also gifted with an understanding of visions and dreams. This of course, was a divine set up similar to that of Joseph in Egypt. These four young men were interviewed by the king and taken into his personal service. Then we are told that Daniel continued in this capacity until Cyrus the king.

Chapter Two – The Statue

Then Nebuchadnezzar had a dream that greatly alarmed him. He sought an interpretation from his wise men, but they were unable to give any, especially since he asked that they

---

[57] The study of end-times.

tell him the dream first. In this way, God eliminated their noise and not only prepared the way for Daniel to interpret the dream, but for him to become the second in command in all of Babylon.

This is the beginning of the prophetic revelation in the book of Daniel that will encompass the whole of history as it relates to the Jews. The vision is of a statue which represented four kingdoms that would come. These four kingdoms would each govern Israel and enslave them. But out of the last would come a final kingdom which would appear in the last days when Israel was restored.

Through a series of visions and angelic visitations, the prophet Daniel received the future history of the Gentile nations as it relates to Israel. It is very important to understand however, that when Israel is not in the land, the Gentile history is not pertinent to them and is ignored by the prophecies. This is a most important point. Failure to see this has resulted in mass confusion in eschatological teaching.

The revelations that Daniel received in Chapters 2, 7, and 8, are different details on the same events. They must be put together to be understood. The dream of Nebuchadnezzar, which is covered in Chapter 2, summarizes the future of the four Gentile empires which will directly control Israel. They are explained again in Chapter 7 with more detail. Then Chapter 8 focuses in on two of them, namely Media Persia and Greece. The future wicked king Antiochus Epiphanes comes out of Greece. He is a type of the End-Time Antichrist.

The following is an illustration of this:
➤ **Head of Gold** represents **Babylon** the first kingdom to rule over Israel
➤ **Breast and Arms of Silver** represent **Media-Persia** the second to rule over Israel
➤ **Belly and Thighs of Bronze** represent **Greece**
➤ **Legs of Iron** represent **Rome**
➤ **Feet of Iron and Clay** represent the **Revived Roman Empire (EU)** to emerge at the end of the age

The Roman Empire destroyed Jerusalem in 70AD and scattered Israel to the ends of the earth. The subsequent empires that conquered the land are irrelevant to the prophecy because the nation of Israel was in exile and separated from the land - AD70 – 1948
➤ **Represented by the Black Line**
➤ **Feet of Iron and Clay – West & East**
➤ **Alliance (Iron & Clay) – Revived Roman Empire**

> **THE FEET OF IRON & CLAY** represent the area ruled by the roman empire since that period. Notice, there have been many empires in that region all fighting against each other, but none were able to put the empire back together (Humpty Dumpty). However, it has now happened without force to fulfill the prophecies, and it began the same time Israel came back into the land.

Note: The feet of Iron and clay come together in the end as 10 Toes to fulfill the purpose of the Beast (See Rev 13, 17 & 18).

Can you tell which period we are living in?

THE EUROPEAN UNION, which began with the **WEU** and the **Treaty of Brussels in 1948**, is the final Empire which is the embodiment of all the others (Rev 13:1-6).

Notice the stone cut out of the mountain without hands (Kingdom of God) strikes the statue on the toes and it (Kingdom of God) fills the whole earth.

Chapter 3 - The Fiery Furnace

Instead of thanking the God of heaven and accepting the revelation given him, Nebuchadnezzar turns to worship the dream itself, thinking that the statue revealed is a god that must be worshipped. He ordered the statue he saw in the dream to be built in the plain of Dura and for all the peoples to worship it. Of course, Daniel and his three friends would not bow down to an idol. As a result, the Chaldeans brought charges to the king against Shadrach, Meshach and Abednego. Daniel appears to have escaped this likely because he had a higher rank and was not with the other three. When the king heard that they would not bow he was furious and had them brought before him. Once again, he commanded them to bow down to the idol or be thrown into the fiery furnace. The response of these three godly Jews has resounded throughout history as a rallying cry for those who face persecution.

"O Nebuchadnezzar, we do not need to give you an answer concerning this matter. If it be so, our God whom we serve is able to deliver us from the furnace of blazing fire; and He will deliver us out of your hand, O king. But even if He does not, let it be known to you, O king, that we are not going to serve your gods or worship the golden image that you have set up." Daniel 3:16-18

Then the king's blood boiled with anger, and he ordered the furnace heated seven times more and had the three men bound and thrown into the fire which was so hot that even some of those throwing them in died. Nevertheless, when Nebuchadnezzar looked in the fire, he not only saw Shadrach, Meshach and Abednego walking around in the fire but there was a fourth person with them which he said looked like a "son of the gods." Because of this statement many believers assume that the fourth person was the "preincarnate Christ." However, there is no reason to make such an assumption and build theology on it. The fourth person was likely the angel of the Lord. Indeed, in verse 28, Nebuchadnezzar said that God sent His angel to deliver them. Perhaps he got this from the men themselves. In any event, they were not harmed, and their clothes were not singed and didn't even smell of smoke. The king marvels at this great miracle and praises the God of Shadrach, Meshach and Abednego even making a decree that anyone who speaks against their God should be torn limb from limb. He also blessed them and made them to prosper in Babylon together with Daniel the prophet.

Chapter 4 – King Goes Crazy

This chapter begins with the words of Nebuchadnezzar the king giving glory to the God of heaven as he tells the story of his second dream interpreted by Daniel and what happened to him.

In the dream the king saw a tree in the midst of the earth. It grew exceedingly great and the whole earth nested in its shade. Then an angel came and commanded that it be cut down and its stump left in place but with a band of iron and bronze around it. Then it says that he was to be drenched with the dew of heaven and his mind changed from that of a man to that of a beast for seven periods of time (7 years).

The tree of course represented the kingdom of Nebuchadnezzar. It was to be cut down and the king was to lose his mind and eat grass like an ox for a period of 7 years and then the kingdom would be restored to him. This would happen because of his pride and to teach him that the Most-High God is king over the realm of mankind and bestows it on whom He wishes.

Twelve months later the king was walking on the rooftop of his palace and bragging about all that he had done, when the vision was fulfilled. He was driven away from his palace and made to eat grass like an ox and his hair grew like eagle's feathers and his nails like those of a bird.

The chapter ends with the king returned to his senses and praising the God of heaven for humbling him and for teaching him such an important lesson.

"At that time my reason returned to me. And my majesty and splendor were restored to me for the glory of my kingdom, and my counselors and my nobles began seeking me out; so I was reestablished in my sovereignty, and surpassing greatness was added to me. Now I, Nebuchadnezzar, praise, exalt and honor the King of heaven, for all His works are true and His ways just, and He is able to humble those who walk in pride." Daniel 4:36-37

Chapter 5 – Belshazzar's Feast

Belshazzar, also known as Evil-Merodach, was the son of Nebuchadnezzar. He gave a feast for a thousand of his nobles and gave orders that the vessels of gold that were taken by his father from the Temple in Jerusalem, were to be brought to him and used for the consumption of wine. This was clearly mocking the God of Israel and it cost him dearly. Immediately after he had done this a human hand appeared writing a message on the wall. The king was so frightened that his knees knocked together. As usual, none of his wise men and magicians could tell him what the message meant. The queen however remembered Daniel and what he had done for Nebuchadnezzar. Interestingly, even though Daniel's name was changed to Belteshazzar in his youth, he is known as Daniel. This speaks volumes regarding his character and relationship with God.

The king summons Daniel and relays to him all that he has heard about his fame. He promises him that he will be clothed in purple and have a gold necklace around his neck and be third ruler in the kingdom. Daniel, who is old now and has had all that before, is clearly not interested. It is also clear that he is not afraid of the king since he tells him to keep his gifts. Nevertheless, he interprets the message for him.

"Now this is the inscription that was written out: 'MENE, MENE, TEKEL, UPHARSIN.' This is the interpretation of the message: 'MENE'— *God has numbered your kingdom and put an end to it.* 'TEKEL'— *you have*

been weighed on the scales and found deficient. 'PERES'— your kingdom has been divided and given over to the Medes and Persians."

It was just that simple. Belshazzar went too far and now he is finished. His rule is done. He is about to die, and his kingdom given to the Medes and Persians. Today we use the expression, "The handwriting is on the wall," to suggest the end of a matter is coming. This expression comes from this passage.

Belshazzar goes through the ritual of rewarding Daniel and then we are told that the same night he was slain, and the kingdom was taken over by Darius the Mede at the age of sixty-two.

Chapter 6 – Daniel Escapes a Plot

King Darius had appointed 120 satraps (provincial governors) over his kingdom and 3 satraps over them of which Daniel was one. However, because of the blessing of God on him, Daniel began to distinguish himself above all the others and Darius was intending to put him in charge of all his kingdom. Upon discovering this, the other satraps became jealous and conspired against Daniel to do him harm. But because of his impeccable character and integrity they were unable to find any accusation. Thus they convinced the king to make a law that they knew Daniel could not obey. They enticed they king, by appealing to his pride, that he should sign a document into law that for a period of thirty days any person who made a petition to a god other than the king, should be thrown into the lion's den. They knew this would trap Daniel since he would not be able to disobey God or stop his daily prayer.

When Daniel found out the letter was signed, he didn't cower or change his routine. On the contrary, he went into his house and to his place of prayer, with the windows open toward Jerusalem, and continued praying and giving thanks to God three times a day as he had always done. Then these men came upon him praying and making petition to God and they brought the matter to the king. They reminded the king of the decree he had made and how it could not be revoked. The king agreed. Then they revealed that Daniel had been violating the kings decree and was petitioning his God three times a day. Thus, they declared that Daniel had no respect for the king and his edict and was to be thrown into the lion's den. Darius was greatly distressed when he heard this and wanted very much to save Daniel. But because of the finality of his decree, he had to carry out the order. Daniel was thrown into the lion's den and a stone was placed before the entrance which was sealed by the king's signet ring and those of his nobles so it could not be disturbed.

Though Darius was deeply troubled, he began to believe that God would deliver Daniel. In fact, he even told him so. Then he went home and fasted all night and was not able to sleep. Perhaps he prayed to the God of Daniel, we don't know. But in any event when he arose the next day and went to the lion's den, he found Daniel safe and sound. Darius called to Daniel, "Daniel, servant of the living God, has your God, whom you constantly serve, been able to deliver you from the lions?" Daniel replied that since he was innocent before his God and before the king, the Lord had sent his angel and shut the mount of the lions and he was not harmed. Darius was very pleased and gave orders for Daniel to be taken out of the den and the ones who had conspired against him to be thrown in instead. The lions immediately tore them to pieces. Then the king made a decree and sent it out to his kingdom that all were to fear and tremble before the God of Daniel. Then we are given what appears to be the conclusions of Darius regarding the God of Daniel which are written in the decree.

"For He is the living God and enduring forever, and His kingdom is one which will not be destroyed, and His dominion will be forever. He delivers and rescues and performs signs and wonders in heaven and on earth, who has also delivered Daniel from the power of the lions."

When we consider the courage and character of this man Daniel and his love for God and His purposes, it is not surprising that he is highly esteemed in heaven (Dan 10:11). Would that the leaders of God's people today had one-half of his backbone. He outlived kings and kingdoms and always rose to the top because his life was pleasing to God Almighty.

"So this Daniel enjoyed success in the reign of Darius and in the reign of Cyrus the Persian."

Chapter 7 - Vision #2 - The Four Beasts

Daniel had a dream and visions in his mind as he lay on his bed. In the dream he saw four great beasts coming up out of the sea, which for any Jew of that day, was the Mediterranean. These four beasts are empires that arise and rule over Israel. They don't just rule over the land when Israel is no longer there, as other empires have done. They rule over the land and the people.

4 Empires Again – corresponds with Daniel Chapter 2

This is essentially the same message as the statue of Nebuchadnezzar only with more detail. The vision presents the same four kingdoms that will arise on the earth and persecute the Holy People (the Jews). As in the first vision, the Roman Empire and the Empire of Antichrist at the end of the age are pictured as one.

"I was looking in my vision by night, and behold, the four winds of heaven were stirring up the great sea (Mediterranean). And four great Beasts were coming up from the sea, different from one another." Daniel 7:2-3

The Beast of the Revelation is the same as that of Daniel. That is why John gives so little explanation. Students of Scripture were expected to know these things. The book of Daniel was and is the "Revelation" of the "Old Testament" (Mt 24:15).

Rev 13:1 And he stood on the sand of the seashore. And I saw a beast coming up out of the sea, having ten horns and seven heads, and on his horns {were} ten diadems, and on his heads {were} blasphemous names. (NAS)

FOUR GREAT BEASTS
- **Four Kingdoms that will arise from the earth (vs 17)**

1. **LION** - WINGS OF AN EAGLE - ***BABYLON (NEBUCHADNEZZAR)***

2. **BEAR** - RAISED UP ON ONE SIDE - ***MEDIA/PERSIA***

3. **LEOPARD** - 4 WINGS - 4 HEADS - ***GREECE*** (THE KINGDOM DIVIDED INTO 4)

4. **DIFF THAN ALL OTHERS** – it's a conglomeration of all 4 (vs 12) – ***ROME & THE REVIVED ROMAN EMPIRE (TEN HORNS)***

And the ten horns which you saw are ten kings, who have not yet received a kingdom, but they receive authority as kings with the beast for one hour. These have one purpose and they give their power and authority to the beast. "These will wage war against the Lamb, and the Lamb will overcome them, because He is Lord of lords and King of kings, and those who

are with Him are the called and chosen and faithful. Rev 17:12-14 NAS

The European Union
In Nebuchadnezzar's dream of a statue (chapter 2) the feet of iron and clay came together in the end as 10 Toes to fulfill the purpose of the Beast. The European Union, which began with the WEU and the Treaty of Brussels in 1948, will become this final Empire, which is the embodiment of all the others.[58] In addition, the stone cut out of the mountain without hands is the Messianic Kingdom, which strikes the statue on the toes, shattering it. Then the kingdom of Christ fills the whole earth!

"The Brussels Treaty was signed on 17 March 1948 by Belgium, France, Luxembourg, the Netherlands, and the United Kingdom. The Brussels Treaty Organization, as it was then called, provided for collective self-defense and economic, social, and cultural collaboration between its signatories. On 23 October 1954, the Brussels Treaty was modified to include the Federal Republic of Germany and Italy, thus creating the Western European Union. In November 1988, a Protocol of Accession was signed by the WEU Member States with Portugal and Spain. The ratification process was completed in March 1990. Greece followed a similar process in 1992 and 1995 thus bringing the total WEU membership to 10."

In June 2000 the WEU created the post of High Representative and Common Foreign Security Policy Chief, giving him or her a 5-year term. This person filling this office is the representative of the EU and eager to broker a treaty with Israel. Though the WEU has disbanded or submerged, it is easy for these ten nations to re-emerge for a purpose, such as brokering a treaty with Israel. One or more of these nations could drop out, but others can take their place. Since this has already happened once, it is not difficult for it to happen again.

---

[58] Rev 13:1-2

EU SYMBOLS

The 'Mid-East Beast' Myth

For more than a century, and especially since 1948, the majority of premillennial[59] scholars have understood that the last empire spoken of in Daniel Chapters 2 and 7 was the Revived Roman Empire. This was not dreamed up because they were located in the West, or because they had a Western mindset, as is suggested by the proponents of this new "Mid-East Beast" theory. On the contrary it is solidly based on the visions given to Daniel and their fulfillment in history. Why then are some wanting to take us back to a Middle Ages understanding? Actually, the answer is quite simple, and it is one I have been preaching for the last twenty-five years. They fail to understand that the prophecies of Daniel have to

---

[59] Those who believe Christ is coming and will reign for 1000 years.

do with Israel and not just the land. These prophecies predict the occupation and domination of Israel by Gentile empires. Once Israel was removed from the land by God through the Roman Empire in 70AD, the prophecies were no longer in operation until they were united as a nation with the land in 1947/48. This is a most essential understanding, and it is true for all Biblical prophecy regarding the end of the age. Without Israel in the land, the prophecy does not apply - period. This is also the primary proof we are at the end of the age, and the prophecies are once again being fulfilled, because Israel is back in her ancient homeland.

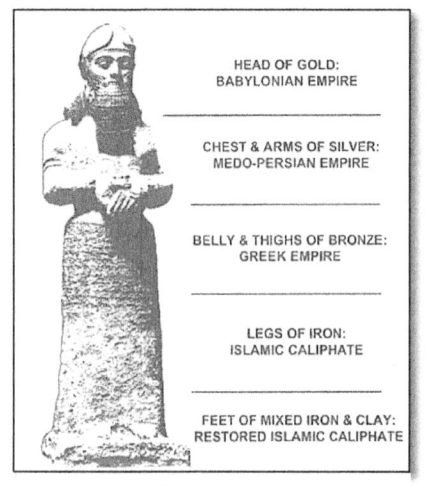

Chart from "Mid-East Beast" by Joel Richardson

Daniel's interpretation of Nebuchadnezzar's dream (Dan 2:36-45) makes it clear that the statue represents four consecutive kingdoms beginning with Babylon. These four kingdoms would govern the Middle East, and more importantly, Israel. Then there is a fifth kingdom that comes out of the fourth, represented by the feet and toes, but it is different than any kingdom that has gone before. It is a revival of the fourth but with very different characteristics since it is an alliance of nations and peoples who come together for a purpose but do not adhere – like iron and clay. In Daniel Chapter 7, the prophet is given another picture of these kingdoms as four great beasts. The first three are identified by name as Babylon, Media-Persia, and Greece. The last one is not identified since it is so different, and the prophet was unable to compare it to anything. This last beast takes up where Greece left off and ends out the age as the Antichrist kingdom with ten horns. It is very clear from history, and even the New Testament, that Rome conquered Greece, dominated Israel, crucified the Messiah, destroyed the Temple, and banished the nation to exile in 70AD. This destruction under Rome was prophesied throughout Israel's history. To suggest that this empire was not the fourth beast, because it came from the West rather than the East, is truly absurd. But even worse is the claim that the fourth beast was an Islamic Caliphate, which came on the scene nearly six hundred years later, when Israel no longer occupied the land. To ignore the Roman Empire, which conquered Greece and terrorized Israel more than any other, fulfilling a host of biblical prophecies, is not only absurd, it is irrational. It is hard to imagine how any biblical scholar can take this seriously. Yet many of them do because they have not been able to understand the role of the Middle East empires that have come and gone after Rome. Now someone comes along and gives them an alternative that seems to fit the current situation and they are all ears. Since they have not been able to understand the mystery of the toes, they are ready to abandon Rome as the fourth kingdom and jump ahead to an Islamic Caliphate that began in the seventh century. However, besides the glaring omission of the Roman Empire in this scenario, and even if we assume that all the various Islamic Caliphates throughout history were one entity, what do we do with the Crusader Kingdom and the British Empire?

There are many other problems with the Antichrist Kingdom being an Eastern Islamic Caliphate, such as the fact that it is an alliance (Dan 2:41-43, Rev 17:12-13), and the Book of Daniel clearly connects the Antichrist with the Roman Empire (Dan 9:26, Rev 17:9-13, 18). Yet, the foundation of this theory is the notion that Rome was not the fourth kingdom. On this it stands or falls to the ground. There can be no doubt that Rome is the fourth beast, a revival of which began the same year Israel became a nation once again in her own land –1948. The emergence of the EU and its development into the United States of Europe, with a goal to swallow up Israel and bring peace to the Middle East, is the obvious fulfillment of these prophecies. It came out of the Roman Empire and encompasses the same territory. It is not committed to the destruction of Israel as the Islamists, but desires to swallow it up with a treaty and EU membership. This is now put on hold until the situation changes on the ground, and on the Temple Mount in Jerusalem, and Israel is willing to consecrate the Holy Place. Then they will all be back in the peace mood. After much pain and sorrow, the Final Status Agreement or Peace Treaty will be signed, and Israel will likely become part of the EU, which will complete the beast's seventh head. This will be the time of peace and security which ends abruptly beginning the Tribulation period (1Thess 5:2-3).

The other scenario, being presented by the Islamic Caliphate Theory, requires Israel and the whole Middle East, including much of Europe, to be dominated by a brutal Islamic regime the likes of ISIS. However, what would this mean for Israel? And what would happen to Christians? You see, not only have they modified biblical history to exclude Rome as an important player, they have also written off the future time of peace and security taught by Daniel and Paul (Dan 9:27, 1Thess 5:2-3).Yes the Antichrist is a man of war, but before he is revealed as the Antichrist he is a man of peace who will amaze the whole world, and sadly even many in the church.

It seems to me that those who accept this Islamic Caliphate theory have written off the West as a major player in the days to come. They see Islam on the rise and ready to take over the world. However, while it is true that Islam has its sights set on world conquest, it would be very foolish to rule out the Western nations that God used to scatter Israel and bring them back again. Islam may be on the warpath against the West, but it is a house seriously divided. How many Caliphates are there? How many barbaric factions? How many Jihadists warring against each other? Indeed, about the only thing they agree on is the destruction of Israel. And my friends, that is not going to happen now or ever. Make no mistake about it, no Islamic Caliphate will take over Israel or usher in Daniel's 70th Week. This will be a smooth, slick politician who is given authority by the EU to carry out his mission of "Peace and Security."

Little Horn

Verse 8 – <u>**Another Little Horn**</u> *(Antichrist)* came up among them and subdued 3 Horns (Kings) – Mouth uttering Great Boasts

In Daniel Chapter 7, verse 8, a Little Horn rises up and subdues three of the 10 kings. At this time, we can only speculate as to who and what these three kingdoms are that are subdued by the Antichrist. Perhaps they are the Benelux Union countries of Belgium, the Netherlands, and Luxembourg. These countries between them share the European Union headquarters and government as well as the home of the UN's International Court of Justice. Also, since Switzerland is the only European country not a member of the EU, and the capital of the banking system, perhaps the Antichrist will operate from Switzerland and take over the Benelux countries which would also be part of his capital.

Corresponding Prophecies of Revelation 13, 17 & 18

There are two beasts that emerge in Revelation Chapter 13. The first is the political system which is the Revived Roman Empire under Antichrist.

*"And the beast which I saw was <u>**like a leopard**</u>, and his <u>**feet were like {those} of a bear**</u>, and <u>**his mouth like the mouth of a lion**</u>. And the dragon gave him his power and his throne and great authority. And {I saw} one of his heads as if it had been slain, and his fatal wound was healed. And the whole earth was amazed {and followed} after the beast; and they worshiped the dragon, because he gave his authority to the beast; and they worshiped the beast, saying, "Who is like the beast, and who is able to wage war with him? And there was given to him a mouth speaking arrogant words and blasphemies; and authority to act <u>for forty-two months</u> (3½ YEARS) was given to him. And he opened his mouth in blasphemies against God, to blaspheme His name and His tabernacle, {that is}, those who dwell in heaven. And it was given to him to make war with the saints and to overcome them; and authority over every tribe and people and tongue and nation was given to him. And all who dwell on the earth will worship him, {everyone} whose name has not been written from the foundation of the world in the book of life of the Lamb who has been slain." Rev 13:2-8 NAS*

Then there is a second beast called the False Prophet which represents a religious system that is pictured in Revelation Chapter 17 as the harlot riding the beast.

"And he carried me away in the Spirit into a wilderness; and I saw a woman sitting on a scarlet beast, full of blasphemous names, having seven heads and ten horns. And the woman was clothed in purple and scarlet, and adorned with gold and precious stones and

pearls, having in her hand a gold cup full of abominations and of the unclean things of her immorality, and upon her forehead a name was written, a mystery, "BABYLON THE GREAT, THE MOTHER OF HARLOTS AND OF THE ABOMINATIONS OF THE EARTH." And I saw the woman drunk with the blood of the saints, and with the blood of the witnesses of Jesus. And when I saw her, I wondered greatly." Rev 17:3-6

The apostle John wondered greatly when he saw this woman. But the angel admonished him saying, "Why do you wonder?" It's as though he expected John to know who she was.

The woman is a harlot and yet she represents Babylon where false religion began. The term "harlot" is used biblically to refer to spiritual apostasy and adultery. It is used that way throughout Scripture as the term "virgin" is used of spiritual purity. Thus, this woman represents a backslidden religious system - a world religious system full of abominations as it rides atop the political system that gives it prominence. However, we are given more information about the woman and the beast that carries her.

"Here is the mind which has wisdom. The seven heads are seven mountains on which the woman sits, and they are seven kings; five have fallen, one is, the other has not yet come; and when he comes, he must remain a little while. And the beast which was and is not, is himself also an eighth, and is one of the seven, and he goes to destruction. And the ten horns which you saw are ten kings, who have not yet received a kingdom, but they receive authority as kings with the beast for one hour. These have one purpose and they give their power and authority to the beast. These will wage war against the Lamb, and the Lamb will overcome them, because He is Lord of lords and King of kings, and those who are with Him are the called and chosen and faithful. And he said to me, 'The waters which you saw where the harlot sits, are peoples and multitudes and nations and tongues. And the ten horns which you saw, and the beast, these will hate the harlot and will make her desolate and naked, and will eat her flesh and will burn her up with fire. For God has put it in their hearts to execute His purpose by having a common purpose, and by giving their kingdom to the beast, until the words of God should be fulfilled. And the woman whom you saw is the great city, which reigns over the kings of the earth.'" Rev 17:9-18

We are told that the woman sits on seven hills. This of course is the city of Rome since it was built on seven hills and verse 18 is emphatic that the woman is the "great city which reigns over the kings of the earth." This can only be Rome at the time the book of Revelation was written. Therefore, there is no escaping the fact that the Vatican, a Roman city state in the heart of the EU at the end of the age, will lead the harlot religious system.

REV 17 - JUDGMENT OF BABYLON
- Great Harlot on Scarlet Beast - (Religious & Political) Babylon the Great the Mother of Harlots and the Abominations of the earth.
- Drunk with the Blood of the Saints
- **The Beast** that carries the Woman has Seven Heads and Ten Horns (Vs 7)
- The Beast **WAS** and is **NOT** and is **About to Come Out of the Abyss** and go to Destruction
- The **Seven Heads** are **Seven Mountains** on which the Woman sits (Rome is built on Seven Hills)
- And they are **Seven Kings** (or Kingdoms), **Five have fallen**, **One is**, the **Other has not yet come**
- When he comes, he must remain a **Little While** (Small time)
- The Beast which **WAS** and is **NOT, is Himself also an Eight, and is One of the Seven** and goes to destruction

~~~~~~~~~~

The Seven Heads

"Five have fallen, one is, and the other has not yet come. When he comes he must remain a little while (short time). The Beast which was and is not is himself also an eight and is one of the seven and goes to destruction."

We understand from our studies in Daniel that the ten horns are ten kingdoms or nations that empower the individual who represents them with a specific purpose for a short time. But now we understand that this beast has seven heads. The woman sits on seven hills, but she rides a beast (political system) with seven heads. If we try to understand the seven heads as kings or Roman Emperors that existed, it does not fit since there were many Emperors after this time. However, if we understand that kings may also mean kingdoms, as it does in Daniel 7, the meaning becomes clear. Thus, we conclude that the seven kings of Revelation 17 are seven kingdoms which have and will include Israel. One thing they all have in common is their control of Israel – the land and the people. These are Egypt, Assyria, Babylon, Media/Persia, Greece, Rome, and Antichrist's Kingdom (EU). At the time of John, five have come and gone (fallen from power). These are Egypt, Assyria, Babylon, Media/Persia, and Greece. One is left - Rome. One is yet to come which remains a little while (EU with Israel - very short – 3½ years) and then the eighth which is one of the seven (Antichrist's Kingdom).

The Seventh Head Forming
The seventh head is clearly the EU which is the embodiment of the Revived Roman Empire. However, until the EU incorporates Israel it is not the completed seventh head. The European Neighborhood Policy is the beginning of the process of bringing Israel into the EU with a treaty. Since all the nations are being aligned in regional unions, Israel will

also become part of this alignment and its only option is the EU. Thus, the covenant or treaty signed by Israel and the leader of the EU, together with the neighboring countries, will not only be a peace treaty but will also be an alignment of Israel with the EU. This will be the fulfillment of Daniel 9:27. Then the seventh head or kingdom will be complete, and it will remain for a *"little while"* (Rev 17:10). When this EU/world leader breaks the covenant three and a half years later, he is revealed as the Antichrist (man of lawlessness – 2Thess 2:8) and will take control of the world and usher in the eight kingdom which is really the seventh that has radically changed its dominion and character (Rev 17:11).

More on the Harlot

It is intriguing that the Vatican continues to be a state in Rome. It continues to dominate the city. The office of the Roman Catholic Pontiff seems tailored to lead a false religious system that will be aligned with the Beast. It will include all the "mainline" churches and false religions. It will also include the Emerging Church and many Evangelicals and Charismatics. The agenda of saving the planet and Western culture coupled with the universalist remake of God will lure them in. Also, dividing the land of Israel to bring world peace will be a high priority. All those who hold to the truth of Scripture will be hated by all.

Union for the Mediterranean

Towards the end of the Tribulation, the Antichrist and his ten supporting nations will burn the city of Rome and will attack the religious system headquartered there. The False Prophet will have also abandoned the city by then since he remains by the Antichrist's side (Rev 17:16-18).

This destruction of Rome will likely be the result of a nuclear bomb. This seems obvious from the description in Revelation 18:15-17. Also, consider the vast wealth of the Vatican and understand why the merchants are crying (Rev 18:9). This destruction comes from the hand of God, and it is for all the atrocities committed by the city under the Roman Empire and the Roman Church. Both are guilty of the blood of the saints – Jews and Christians (Rev 17:6). Consider the brutality of the Romans against the Jews and realize that it has not been punished. Also, consider the plans that were hatched in Rome and have a look at the Arch of Titus which mocks the Jews and the Holy Temple. What about the Colosseum itself and the brutality of Rome against Christians? Then add to that all the Christians who were murdered and tortured by the Catholic Church, throughout the centuries, and one can understand why Rome has a special judgment.

"And in her was found the blood of prophets and of saints and of all who have been slain on the earth." Rev 18:24

Babylon the Great

The name "Babylon the Great" is a mystery according to John because it does not actually refer to Babylon the ancient city, but the city of Rome, the Harlot, and the World Religious System. It also represents the kingdom of Antichrist, which is the embodiment of all the others that have gone before. Indeed, when we consider the statue of Nebuchadnezzar in Daniel 2, we understand that the stone cut out of the mountains (Messiah's kingdom) struck the statue on the feet (Antichrist's kingdom) and destroyed it. Thus, Antichrist's kingdom represents the whole statue of empires that persecuted God's people, and since the head is Babylon, it could be referred to as Babylon. This is borne out by the following verse corresponding to Isaiah 47:7 which refers to Babylon.

"...for she says in her heart, 'I SIT as A QUEEN AND I AM NOT A WIDOW, and will never see mourning.'" Rev 18:7

Now consider this passage concerning Babylon or the Daughter of Babylon:

"Come down and sit in the dust, O virgin daughter of Babylon; sit on the ground without a throne, O daughter of the Chaldeans! For you shall no longer be called tender and delicate...... I was angry with My people, I profaned My heritage and gave them into your hand. You did not show mercy to them, on the aged you made your yoke very heavy. Yet you said, 'I will be a queen forever.' These things you did not consider nor remember the outcome of them." Is 47:1-7

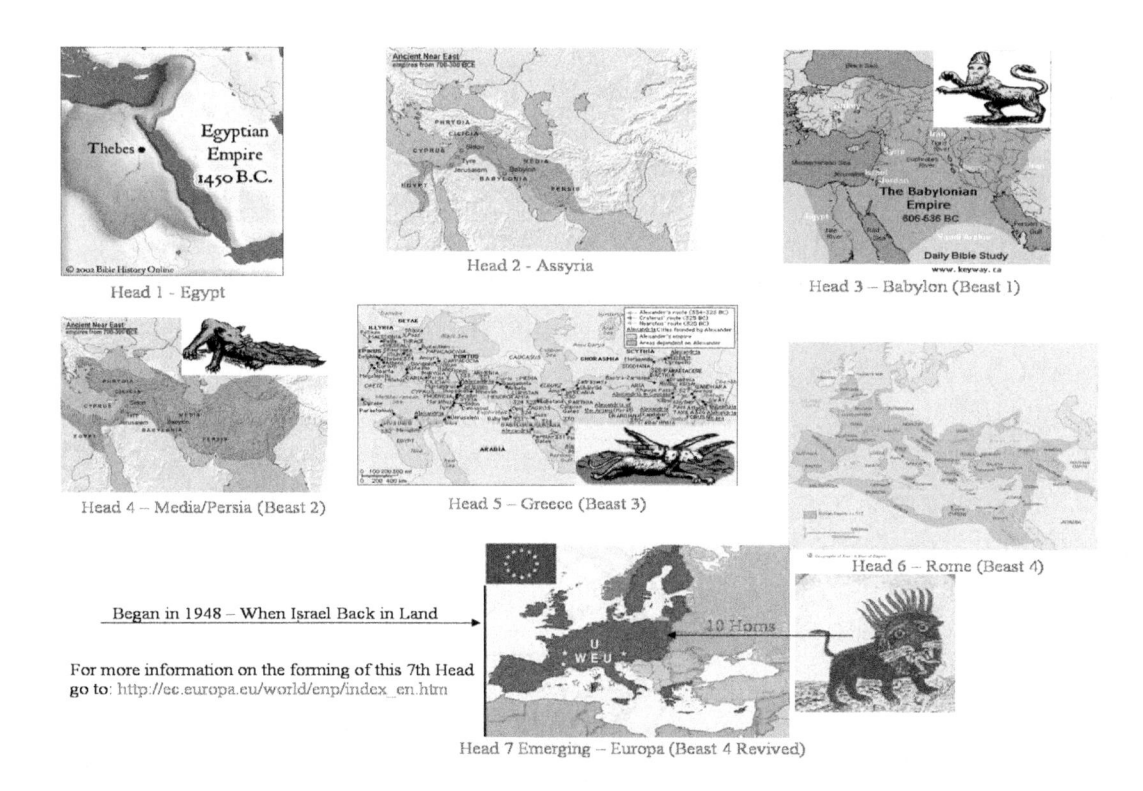

Head 1 – Egypt
Head 2 – Assyria
Head 3 – Babylon (Beast 1)
Head 4 – Media/Persia (Beast 2)
Head 5 – Greece (Beast 3)
Head 6 – Rome (Beast 4)

Began in 1948 – When Israel Back in Land

For more information on the forming of this 7th Head go to: http://ec.europa.eu/world/enp/index_en.htm

Head 7 Emerging – Europa (Beast 4 Revived)

148

The city of Rome was also referred to by the early church as Babylon (1Pet 5:13). In addition, the harlot religious system is the mother of harlots, because all idolatry and false religion has its origins in the land of Shinar. Therefore, Babylon as the city of Rome, and as the Antichrist Empire, and as the Harlot Religious System, is judged at the end of the Tribulation. But the city of Rome has a specific judgment which is illustrated in Revelation Chapter 18.

Will Ancient Babylon be Rebuilt?
There are some Bible prophecy experts who suggest that the judgment of Revelation 18 is intended for the ancient city of Babylon, which is today merely a ruin in Iraq. They speculate that it will be rebuilt and become a great international city once again. However, there is much to suggest that the ancient city of Babylon does not fit the description of the city mentioned in Revelation 17 and 18. For example:

• It is a center of commerce, enterprise and trade (Rev 18:3, 11-13).
• It is the city that shed the blood of the martyrs of Jesus (Rev 17:6). Ancient Babylon was in ruins long before Jesus came.
• It is a city on seven hills (Rev 17:9). Babylon cannot qualify for this, whereas, Rome has always been known as the city on seven hills.

The European Parliament building in Strasbourg, France. (Shutterstock) – patterned after the unfinished Tower of Babel

- Immoral and drunken (Rev 17:2). Rome wins this one also.
- City that rules over many nations (Rev 17:15-18).
- Sailors cross the sea to get there (Rev 18:17-18).
- An entertainment capital (Rev 18:22-23)

Perhaps the greatest reason why ancient Babylon cannot be the city spoken of in Rev 17 and 18 is because it was a ruin at the time of the writing of the book. Also, the only city at the time of the writing that could qualify for Rev 17:18 is the city of Rome!

"And I saw the beast and the kings of the earth and their armies, assembled to make war against Him who sat upon the horse, and against His army." Rev 19:19 NAS

Back to DANIEL 7

Throne Set Up – Ancient of Days – Judgment Passed

"A river of fire was flowing and coming out from before Him; thousands upon thousands were attending Him, and myriads upon myriads were standing before Him; the court sat, and the books were opened." Daniel 7:10 NAS

*"And the beast was seized, and with him the false prophet who performed the signs in his presence, by which he deceived those who had received the mark of the beast and those who worshiped his image; these two **were thrown alive into the lake of fire** which burns with brimstone." Rev 19:20 NAS*

Son of Man Comes (Erchomai not Parousia)

"I kept looking in the night visions, and behold, with the clouds of heaven One like a Son of Man was coming, and He came up to the Ancient of Days and was presented before Him. And to Him was given dominion, glory and a kingdom, that all the peoples, nations, and {men of every} language might serve Him. His dominion is an everlasting dominion which will not pass away; and His kingdom is one which will not be destroyed." Daniel 7:13-14 NAS

Messiah's Kingdom Destroys the Revived Roman Empire and reigns forever

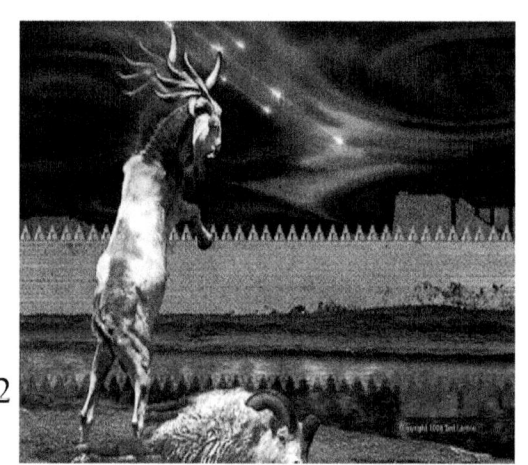

~~~~~~~~~~~~

Chapter 8 – Vision #3 - Ram, Goat & Little Horn

- **Ram with Two Horns** (one longer than the other) – **Media-Persia**)
- **Male Goat (Greece)** – Large Horn **(Alexander)**
- **Broken Horn** – Alexander dies at the age of 32 in Babylon
- **4 Horns Arise in its place** (Kingdom passed on to his 4 generals)

"And out of one of them (Seleucid - Syria - King of The North) came forth a rather small horn which grew exceedingly great toward the South, (Egypt) toward the East (Babylon - Persia), toward the Beautiful Land (Israel)

Read on to the end of the Chapter

Interpretation

- **Antiochus Epiphanes** ("God Manifest") who came at the end of the Seleucid Empire, and persecuted the Jews, was a type of Antichrist who will appear at the end of the age
- Latter period a King will arise insolent and skilled in intrigue
- His power will be mighty, but not of his own power (supernatural power from satan)
- He will destroy (or corrupt) mighty men and the holy people (Lit. the people of the saints- Jews)
- Causes deceit to succeed
- Opposes the Prince of Princes (God – High Priest – also Jesus)
- Broken without human agency (Lit. hand) – defeated by Judas Macabbee – defeated by Christ

2,300 Evenings and Mornings
Not 2,300 days – morning & evening sacrifice = 1150 days or 3.2 years – from Antiochus' desecration of the Holy Place to the rededication by Judas Maccabee - Hanukah

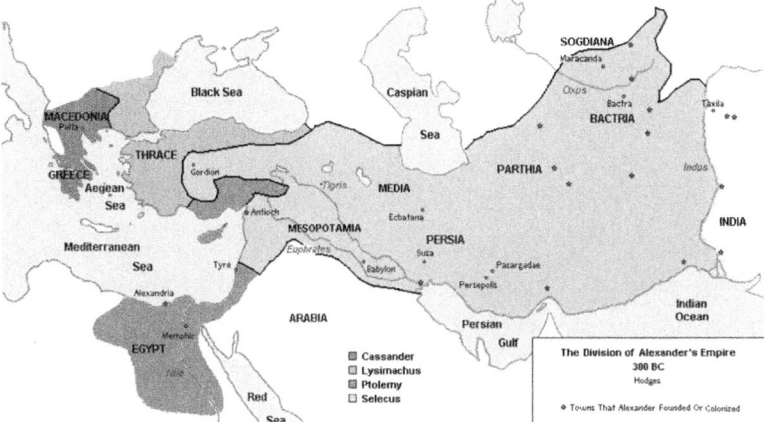

In a similar manner Antichrist will also desecrate the Holy Place and it will be rededicated by Jesus 3½ years later.

Chapter 9 – Daniel's Prayer & God's Answer

Verses 9: 1-23
Daniel's prayer for the Jewish people, the City, and the Sanctuary – repentance for sins of fathers.

It is extremely important to connect the focus of the prayer with the prophecy because the answer has to do with all three. Thus, when the people are out of the land the prophecy did not apply.

Daniel's 70th Week
"Seventy weeks (Lit. SEVENS) have been decreed for your people and your holy city, to finish the transgression, to make an end of sin, to make atonement for iniquity, to bring in everlasting righteousness, to seal up vision and prophecy, and to anoint the most holy place. So you are to know and discern {that} from the issuing of a decree to restore and rebuild Jerusalem until Messiah the Prince {there will be} seven weeks and sixty-two

weeks; it will be built again, with plaza and moat, even in times of distress. Then after the sixty-two weeks the Messiah will be cut off and have nothing, and the people of the prince who is to come will destroy the city and the sanctuary. And its end {will come} with a flood; even to the end there will be war; desolations are determined. And he will make a firm covenant with the many for one week, but in the middle of the week he will put a stop to sacrifice and grain offering; and on the wing of abominations {will come} one who makes desolate, even until a complete destruction, one that is decreed, is poured out on the one who makes desolate." Daniel 9:24-27 NAS

Seventy Sevens = 7 x 70 = 490 YEARS
(Sh'mittah periods Lev:25:8 - 7 x 7 =49 and the Year of Jubilee)

JEWISH PEOPLE HAVE 490 YEARS TO:
"...to finish the transgression, to make an end of sin, to make atonement for iniquity, to bring in everlasting righteousness, to seal up vision and prophecy, and to anoint the most holy place."

Please note that these are all themes of Yom Kippur and they will be fulfilled by Jesus the High Priest. The 490 years are completed on Yom Kippur in the Day of the Lord. This is the Day when Jesus is revealed as King in Jerusalem.

"So you are to know and discern {that} from the issuing of a decree to restore and rebuild Jerusalem until Messiah the there will be seven weeks and sixty-two weeks; it will be built again, with plaza and moat, even in times of distress. Then after the sixty-two weeks the Messiah (JESUS) will be cut off and have nothing, and the people of the prince who is to come (ANTICHRIST) will destroy the city and the sanctuary. And its end will come with a flood (ARMIES); even to the end there will be war; desolations are determined."

The Prophecy states that Jerusalem would be rebuilt within 49 years. It was!

Then it states that from the issuing of a word, command, or decree to restore and rebuild Jerusalem (not the Temple) until Messiah there would be 7 sevens and 62 sevens or 483 Biblical years at the end of which Messiah would be cut off or rejected.

Note the Biblical year is 360 days long (see Gen 7:11, 8:3-4 - 5 months = 150 days) following the Lunar calendar.

Robert Anderson's calculations in 1895 – Accepted by the majority

The issuing of a decree or word – Artaxerxes Longimanus "in the month of Nisan, in the twentieth year"

Neh 2:1, March 14, 445 BC

Date for the Messiah being "cut off" (from Israel) = April 6, AD 32
- 483 * 360 = 173, 880 Days
- Then add 24 days from March 14 to April 6, AD 32
- Then add 116 Leap Days computed by the Royal Observatory Greenwich as having occurred by the during that time.
- 173,740 + 24 + 116 = 173,880

This is apparently where the seventy sevens clock stops because Israel is not in the land and the Holy Place is defiled by Gentiles. There are seven years or one week left, known as Daniel's 70th Week. This week is the last seven years of this age. The clock starts with the initiation or confirming of a covenant (treaty) between the apostate Jewish leaders and the world leader who becomes the Antichrist that directly involves the Temple Mount.

*"And he will make a firm covenant with the many **for one week, but in the middle of the week** he will put a stop to sacrifice and grain offering; and on the wing of abominations {will come} one who makes desolate, even until a complete destruction, one that is decreed, is poured out on the one who makes desolate."*

The Seventy Weeks of Daniel

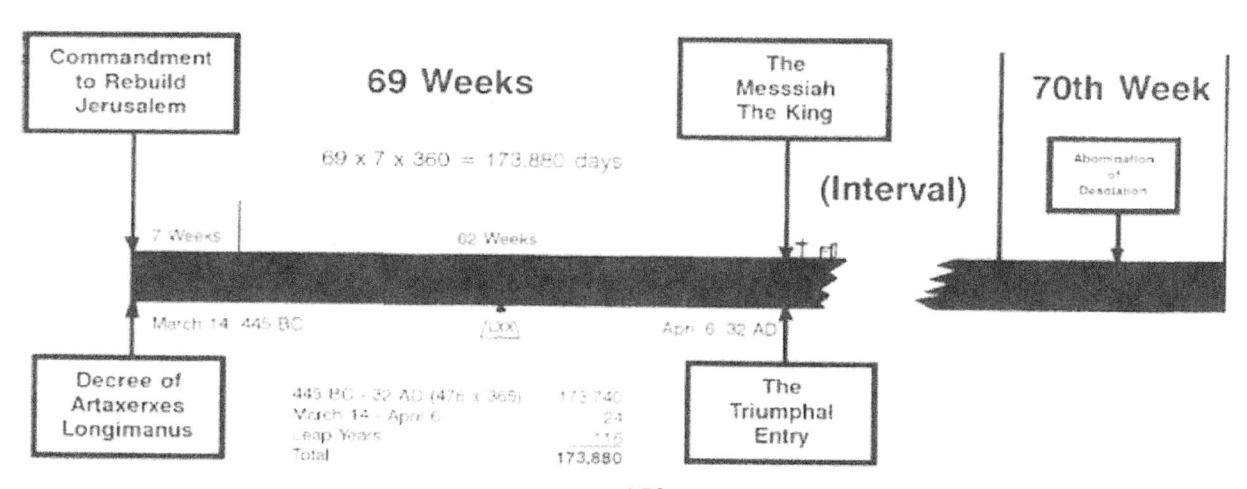

Abomination of Desolation – Middle of 70th Week
The Antichrist (prince who is to come) makes or confirms a covenant with the "Many" (worldly Hellenistic Jewish leaders)

The "Many" is a term used for the apostate Jewish leaders who have become Hellenistic (Humanistic) and have renounced the Torah (covenant) with God. We deduct this from the history of the Jews under Antiochus Epiphanes who was the prototype of Antichrist and the one referred to in Daniel chapter 11 (see verse 31), which seems to shift from the history of this man to a parallel history of Antichrist at the end of the age. Jesus makes reference to this event under Antiochus and repeated under Antichrist known as the Abomination of Desolation and the reader is supposed to understand what is being referred to (Mt 24:15).

One Week Left – *Referred to as Daniel's 70th Week*
- *It's broken into two halves – the last half is the Tribulation*
- *The Week begins with the confirming of a covenant (likely a Peace Treaty regarding the worship in the Holy Place (New Temple) and admits Israel to the EU*

It is sad that the church has been taught for so long that the Tribulation is 7 years long. This is simply not so and has caused great confusion. Daniel's 70th Week is 7 years long, but the Tribulation is the second half – 3½ years long. Both Jesus and Paul confirm this.

Jesus said that when you see the Abomination of Desolation (middle of 70th Week) the Tribulation would begin (Mt 24:15-21). And Paul in 2 Thessalonians 2:3-4, tells us that the Tribulation or the Day of the Lord, will not come until the Antichrist is revealed proclaiming himself to be God in the Temple – the Abomination.

Chapter 10 – Spiritual Warfare

Read verses 1-10

Daniel was on a partial fast and "mourning" for 3 weeks. He did not eat fancy food or meat or wine. This partial fast is often referred to today as a "Daniel fast." Then on the 24th day of the month, while he was on the bank of the Tigris, an angel appeared to him. It is assumed that this angel was also Gabriel who appeared to him in Chapter 9, however the text does not say. The powerful angel is described in detail and Daniel was weak and pale as a result. The men who were with him did not see the vision, but they were very afraid and hid themselves. Daniel fell on his face in a deep sleep and the angel lifted him trembling on his feet. Indeed, throughout the encounter he needed help from the angel to stand and speak.

Read verses 11-21

The angel refers to Daniel as a man of "high esteem." This is a remarkable commentary from heaven on this extraordinary man. He apparently was seeking God regarding the future of the people of Israel for this three-week period. Then the angel explains that he was released to bring the answer the moment Daniel began to pray but was held up by the resistance of the Prince of Persia. This "Prince" is a spiritual principality of darkness (Eph 6:12) that is over the kingdom of Persia but is about to give way to another dark principality called the Prince of Greece. The angel goes on to say that the only help he got was from Michael, one of the chief angelic Princes - the one that protects Israel.

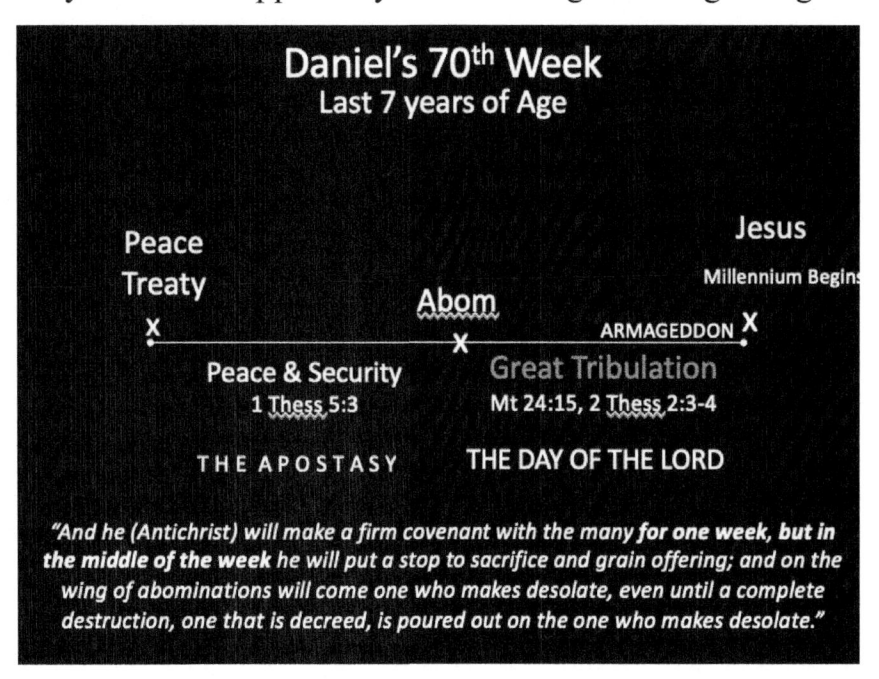

This is indeed a most fascinating passage in which we are given a glimpse inside the spiritual warfare in the heavenlies. Two other places give us a similar peek and they are Ephesians 6 and Revelation 12. Putting the passages together we can draw certain conclusions regarding the role angelic principalities play in the events that occur on earth.

There are principalities and powers in the heavenlies that work for satan. These appear to have been holy angels who were given authority by God over nations initially, but sometime afterwards rebelled and are now working for the devil.[60] Nevertheless, they can only operate as God allows. It also seems that each empire that develops under the influence of these dark forces, is also allowed, and thereby ordained by God to accomplish His purpose (Rom 13). When people worship gods and goddesses (which are really these principalities or demons under their rule) or when they engage in evil behavior, it gives strength to these dark angels. For instance, the angel is released to bring a message to Daniel, pursuant to his seeking God. Yet the Prince over the empire of Persia tries to prevent this word coming to Daniel because he obviously feels threatened by it. So these principalities that Paul says we wrestle with spiritually (though not directly), seem to be allowed to hinder the work of God at least until God's people pray, live godly lives, and do God's will. As Daniel continued to pray, Michael the chief Prince over Israel was sent to free the other angel on his mission. Thus, the stance of God's people on earth matters

---

[60] Deut 32:8 – Should be translated "sons of God" and not "sons of Israel." See the Septuagint version.

with regard to what happens in the heavens and what happens in the heavens directly impacts what happens on earth.

We see this again in Revelation 12 where it is said that the overcoming church defeats the devil and is taken up to God (vs 5,11). Then there is no longer a place found for satan and his army in the heavenlies and they are thrown to the earth. The enemy loses his legal ground and standing, if you would, and is cast down to earth for the final judgment to begin.

Chapter 11-12 - The Final Vision

"In the first year of Darius the Mede, I arose to be an encouragement and a protection for him." Dan 11:1

Because of the chapter break here, it is easy to assume that it is Daniel speaking in verse 1. However, this is not the case. The angel who was speaking with Daniel in Chapter 10 is merely continuing the same discourse. He, the angel of God, arose to help Darius in his first year. Thus we see that although principalities from the enemy prop up evil kingdoms, Gods angels also help out worldly rulers who seem to want to do right, regardless of their ignorance.

Now the angel brings to Daniel the rest of the history of the empire, and the one to come, which is the kingdom of Greece, and then he concludes with Antiochus Epiphanes who is a type of the Antichrist appearing prior to Christ's return.

- <u>(Verse 11:2)</u> **Three more kings to arise in Persia** – These were: ***Cambyses, Pseudo-Smerdis, Darius Hystapus***
- **A Fourth** – more riches – Arouses the kingdom toward Greece *(Xerxes)*
- <u>(Verse 3)</u> **Mighty King** – does as he pleases - *(Alexander the Great)*
- <u>(Verse 4)</u> *soon as he has risen,* he dies, and his kingdom is broken up between his four generals

The rest of the Book of Daniel deals with the warfare between two of these kingdoms – the Northern Kingdom (Seleucid Empire which included Syria) and the Southern Kingdom (Ptolemaic Kingdom which included Egypt) and the revelation of Antichrist of whom Antiochus Epiphanes is a type or pattern.

Chapter 11: read Verses 4-20 and then see the corresponding history below.

General Ptolemy became king of the southern kingdom and General Selucus became king of the northern kingdom. Their kingdoms battled back and forth for years until Antiochus II Theos, the grandson of Seleucus, married Ptolemy's granddaughter Bernice. Antiochus II was already married. He divorced his wife Laodice in order to marry Bernice. When

Bernice's father died, he divorced Bernice and remarried Laodice. Laodice was still angry about the way she had been treated. She poisoned her husband Antiochus II Theos and had Bernice, Bernice's servants, and Bernice's child murdered. She then appointed her son, Seleucus II, to be the new king of Syria. Bernice's brother, Ptolemy III, became king in Egypt. He invaded Syria to avenge his sister's death by executing Laodice. Selucus II went into hiding during the invasion. Ptolemy III looted Syria and carried great treasures back to Egypt. Seleucus II came out of hiding and attempted a counterattack, but he was unsuccessful. Years passed, and after these two kings died, they were replaced by their sons. Ptolemy IV Philopaton, king of the south, went into battle with Antiochus III, also known as "The Great, king of the north. Both kingdoms used elephants in the battle. Ptolemy IV's army won the battle. Years later, Antiochus the Great gave his daughter Cleopatra to Ptolemy V as a wife. He hoped that she would be able to keep Egypt from attacking his kingdom while he went into battle against Roman-controlled Greece. His plan failed because Cleopatra was a faithful wife. When Antiochus the Great died, his son Antiochus Epiphanes took over.

Antiochus Epiphanes was a type of Antichrist. He gave himself the title "Epiphanes" meaning "God Manifest." We have seen already, that at the end, Antichrist would come out of this kingdom.

Daniel 11 (continued)

Verses 21-35 cover his reign
We must keep in mind that Antiochus Epiphanes was a type of Antichrist, and these verses could, to some extent, be applied to him also.

Antiochus Epiphanes' army defeated the Egyptian king Ptolemy Philometor in battle. Antiochus was the Egyptian king's uncle because Cleopatra was his sister. The reason Ptolemy lost the battle was because he was betrayed by some friends. Antiochus took Ptolemy to Syria and pretended to be his friend but neither ever trusted the other. Antiochus attacked Egypt a few years later. However, the Romans came by ship from the west and stopped his attack. When that happened, he started back to Syria but on his way home, he took out his anger on Jerusalem. He defiled the temple and set up the **Abomination of Desolation** (abomination that makes desolate or causes horror). He set up an altar to Zeus in the Holy of Holies and offered pigs on the altar. Interestingly enough, Judea had been in a time of peace for about 30 years when Antiochus began his attack on Egypt and was turned around by the Romans. (Peace & Security then sudden destruction)

Seleucid coin depicting Antiochus IV Epiphanes, silver, circa 175-164 BC.

Many of the Hellenistic Jews (those who accepted Greek customs) became apostate (turned away from the faith) and began to live like Greeks. They set up a Greek Gym in Jerusalem. You can read all about this period of Jewish history under Antiochus Epiphanes in the Book of The Maccabees contained in the Apocrypha. During this period there was a great persecution of Jews. Many were brutally tortured and killed because they would not give up their faith in God (these are the ones referred to in Hebrews 11: 37-38). To survive many fled into the wilderness. Interestingly enough, three years later, Antiochus' reign of terror came to an end as Jerusalem and Judea was liberated by Judas Maccabees (The Hammer). The Temple was cleansed and reconsecrated on the anniversary of its defilement. The Jews continue to celebrate this event with the Feast of Hanukah.

The rest of Chapter 11 - verses 36 & onward describe the Antichrist

Verses 35 and 36 – The "End Time" – it is still to come at the "appointed time"

Then the king will do as he pleases

- Magnify himself above every so-called god or object of worship
- Speak monstrous things against the true God – great boasts - blasphemies (Rev 13:5)
- Will prosper until the indignation (the Tribulation - wrath) is finished (42 months – shattering the hand of the holy people - Chapter 12, verse 7)
- He will show no regard for the gods of his fathers, but he will honor a god of fortresses (war). In other words, he will be a military man and there will be continual war until the end of the Tribulation period.
- He will reward those who help him with land and make them rulers over those who have been conquered.
- Verse 40 - the King of the South (Egypt) and the King of the North (Syria)
  Notice: The King of the North is a term used up to this point to refer to the Seleucid kings, including Antiochus Epiphanes (up to verse 32) is now used of someone other than him (Antichrist). In this case the King of the North is either Syria or Russia.
- He will defeat them along with other countries, but he will not be able to take Jordan (Edom, Moab, Sons of Ammon). This might have something to do with Jordan's role in protecting the remnant of Israel (Mt 24:16, Is 63:1). He will also take great spoils from Egypt.
- Verse 44 – But rumors from the East and the North will disturb him and he will go forth with great wrath to destroy and annihilate many. This is most likely reports about the armies of Gog and Magog (Russia) and armies from the East (China, North Korea, etc.) coming against him in the land of Israel for the long-prophesied war of Armageddon.
- And he will pitch his tents (Headquarters- Capital) between the seas (Dead Sea and the Mediterranean) in the beautiful Holy Mountain (Jerusalem).

He will come to his end, and no one will help him – he will be destroyed by Jesus Christ the True Messiah on Yom Kippur.

Chapter 12: Verse 1

Now at that time (Period begun by the Abomination of Desolation)
- Antichrist moves his headquarters to Jerusalem, stops the regular sacrifice and sets up the Abomination of Desolation.

The period begun by the abomination of desolation is the <u>time of the end</u>. We see this clearly from these passages of Daniel and with this the rest of the Scriptures agree.

"And this gospel of the kingdom shall be preached in the whole world for a witness to all the nations, **and then the end shall come.** Therefore **when you see the abomination of desolation which was spoken of through Daniel the prophet, standing in the holy place** (let the reader understand), **then let those who are in Judea flee to the mountains**; let him who is on the housetop not go down to get the things out that are in his house; and let him who is in the field not turn back to get his cloak. But woe to those who are with child and to those who nurse babes in those days! But pray that your flight may not be in the winter, or on a Sabbath; **for then there will be a great tribulation, such as has not occurred since the beginning of the world until now, nor ever shall**. And unless those days had been cut short, no life would have been saved; but for the sake of the elect those days shall be cut short." Mt 24:14-22 NASV

Daniel 12:1

- Michael the Great Prince who stands guard over Israel will arise
- Since Michael already stands guard over Israel what would it mean to say he stands up? How then could his standing up usher in a time of distress such as has never occurred since there was a nation until that time? (See MT 24:21)

Could it be instead that Michael and his forces drive satan out of the heavenlies and into the earth? (Rev 12:7-12) On account of the great apostasy of Israel, and the spiritual warfare of the Bridal Remnant, satan is cast out and allowed to release wrath on Israel and the earth. Thus, Michael who is the restrainer[61] stops restraining the evil one and evicts him from the heavenlies with his principalities and powers. This begins the Day of the Lord's Wrath. A remnant of Israel, whose names are written in the book of life are rescued.

The sun will be turned into darkness, and the moon into blood, before the great and awesome day of the LORD comes. And it will come about that whoever calls on the name

---
[61] 2 Thess 2:7

of the LORD will be delivered; for on Mount Zion and in Jerusalem there will be those who escape, as the LORD has said, even among the survivors whom the LORD calls. Joel 2:31-32 NAS

And Isaiah cries out concerning Israel, "Though the number of the sons of Israel be as the sand of the sea, it is the remnant that will be saved; for the Lord will execute His word upon the earth, thoroughly and quickly. And just as Isaiah foretold, "Except the Lord of Sabaoth had left to us a posterity, we would have become as Sodom, and would have resembled Gomorrah." Romans 9:27-29 NAS

If this understanding of Daniel 12:1 is correct, and I believe it is, then it sheds much light on this very difficult and controversial passage in 2 Thess 2.

"Let no one in any way deceive you, for {it will not come} unless the apostasy (JEWISH) comes first, and <u>the man of lawlessness is revealed, the son of destruction, who opposes and exalts himself above every so-called god or object of worship, so that he takes his seat in the temple of God, displaying himself as being God</u> (Abom of Desolation). Do you not remember that while I was still with you, I was telling you these things? <u>And you know what (or who) restrains him now, so that in his time he may be revealed.</u> For the mystery of lawlessness is already at work; <u>only he who now restrains {will do so} until he is taken out of the way. And then that lawless one will be revealed</u> whom the Lord will slay with the breath of His mouth and bring to an end by the appearance of His coming; {that is,} the one whose coming is in accord with the activity of Satan, with all power and signs and false wonders, and with all the deception of wickedness for those who perish, because they did not receive the love of the truth so as to be saved. 2 Thes 2:3-10 NAS

Daniel 12:5-7
How long until the end of these wonders? A time (year), two times (2 years) and a half time (1/2 year) = 3 ½ years or 42 months

Dan 12:9-13

"He said, "Go your way, Daniel, for these words are concealed and sealed up until the end time. Many will be purged, purified and refined, but the wicked will act wickedly; and none of the wicked will understand, but those who have insight will understand. From the time that the regular sacrifice is abolished and the abomination of desolation is set up, there will be 1,290 days."

3½ years = 1260 days – Abomination of Desolation is set up in the middle of Daniel's 70th Week

There is an additional 30 days – possibly to Sukkot

Notice it's not – from sacrifice abolished to Abomination but from the time that both the sacrifices are abolished, and the Abomination is set up <u>until</u> the end there will be 1290 days

12 "How blessed is he who keeps waiting and attains to the 1,335 days!

Additional 75 days – probably until Hanukah and the cleansing of the Temple.

13 "But as for you, go your way to the end; then you will enter into rest and rise again for your allotted portion at the end of the age." NASU

The general resurrection of the righteous saints.

Notes

Ezekiel

Authorship: Ezekiel the son of Buzi, a priest who was brought to Babylon with the first group of exiles. He was a contemporary with Jeremiah who was bringing much the same word in Jerusalem.

Time: Approximately 597BC to 570BC

The book of Ezekiel could be broken into four parts.

1. Call and commission of Ezekiel.
2. The judgment of Judah
3. The judgment on the Gentile nations.
4. The restoration of Israel.

Read chapters 1-3

Chapters 1-3 - Called by God

Ezekiel began his ministry at age 30 as he received visions of God while at the river Chebar in Babylon, which today is in Iraq. Ezekiel is called by God to preach to the Jewish people, even though he is told that they are stubborn and stiff-necked and will not listen to him anyway. A very colorful prophet, Ezekiel is told to do many things that appear crazy to us but were powerful illustrations of what God wanted His people to know. When he receives his commission, Ezekiel is told to eat a scroll that had written on it lamentations, mourning, and woe. It was a scroll of judgment upon the kingdom of Judah for their idolatry and rebellion against God. It is very similar to a passage in the book of Revelation (as is much in Ezekiel) chapter ten where the apostle John is told to eat a scroll which is also judgment. As with Ezekiel's scroll, it tasted like honey in John's mouth, but it made his stomach bitter. This is undoubtedly the same bitterness which Ezekiel says filled his spirit in chapter 3, verse 14. His belly is filled with a word which the hearers will not hear nor respond to, even though it would save them, and thus the bitterness. At the same time Jeremiah is bringing the same word in the city of Jerusalem.

This illustration with the scroll also reveals that the messenger of God's word is not just a delivery boy who is uninvolved in the event. On the contrary, the prophets entered into the anguish of God's heart and were living testimonies of His suffering and also His compassion. Indeed, there was often great personal cost involved in understanding God's heart and making it known to the people in graphic word pictures. Examples of this are when the prophet is asked to lay on his side for 14 months, have his wife taken away who was "the desire of his eyes" without mourning for her. This was to illustrate how God felt about the destruction of Jerusalem and the Temple and not be able to mourn because of His great wrath over their sins.

By the river or canal Chebar, Ezekiel is caught up in a vision in which he sees the Throne of God and the Cherubim underneath (10:1). The Cherubim are glorious creatures that dwell in the presence of God and seem to guard the Throne. They are mentioned in Genesis 3:24 as guarding the entrance to the garden of Eden. There are two Cherubim above the Ark of the Covenant, and they also are seen before the Throne in Revelation chapter 4. It seems that satan himself was a cherub who covered and was in the Garden of Eden before his rebellion. It is likely that it was at this time that he fell after murdering Adam and Eve.[62]

The Cherubim mentioned here have four faces and four wings. Though the vision of the creatures is real and not symbolic, nevertheless they seem to represent all of creation – the four corners of the earth. Interestingly, there is much in mythology and ancient religions depicting Cherubim. It appears that the ancients knew about them, and the enemy has tried to distort these heavenly images to mislead.

Another group of angels that are mentioned in Isaiah are called Seraphim. These appear above the Throne and have six wings. From this some have concluded that Seraphim are higher in rank than Cherubim. Also, the four Cherubim of Ezekiel appear to be the same as the four living creatures of Revelation 4, except they have four wings instead of six. Therefore, there is still much mystery as to the order of the heavenly host that we long to see revealed.

Judgment of Judah
Read chapters 4 through 24.

Prophetic Parables
The section from chapters 4-24 is filled with prophetic images of the impending judgment on the city of Jerusalem for the rebelliousness of Judah. There were many false prophets in Judah at this time, as we know from Jeremiah's life, who opposed this message and were prophesying that everything was going to be ok.

The Siege (Chapter 4)
Ezekiel is told to illustrate a siege against Jerusalem by placing a brick on the ground and writing Jerusalem on it. He is then told to construct a siege mound and lay siege against it a proscribed number of days for the sins of Israel and Judah. This was a depiction of the coming siege and destruction of Jerusalem which took place in 586 BC. God first told Ezekiel to bake his bread over human dung to illustrate the uncleanness of the city, but later He had mercy on the prophet and changed it to cow dung.

---

[62] Ez 38:13-17, John 8:44

The Lord told Ezekiel that 430 years had ben decreed for the punishment of Israel and Judah at the end of which they would be restored. From that number we must subtract the 70 years of the Babylonian exile which was the beginning of this punishment. This leaves us with 360 years remaining. In 606BC, Nebuchadnezzar came up against Judah and captured it. He took Jehoiachin the king captive along with many of the Jewish nobility. Ezekiel himself was in this number, along with Daniel and his friends. Then Nebuchadnezzar appointed Zedekiah (Jehoiachin's uncle) as king and went back to Babylon. However, Zedekiah rebelled against the king of Babylon and the word of the Lord through Jeremiah, and Babylon came against him. In 586BC, Jerusalem and Solomon's Temple were destroyed, and Zedekiah and the rest of the nation was taken captive. Only a tiny remnant of very poor Jews was left. Then seventy years later in 536BC, in fulfillment of the words of Jeremiah, the first exiles returned under Ezra the priest. Thus the exile in Babylon was from 606BC to 586BC – 70 years.

Jewish Exile 606 BC - 536 BC = 70 years
Temple Destroyed 586 BC
Temple Rebuilding Finished 516 BC
586 BC - 516 BC = 70 years

Another interesting aspect of the exile in Babylon is the 20-year lag between the return of the people and the restoration of the Temple which was completed in 516BC. The exiles returned after 70 years, and the Temple was rebuilt after 70 years – 586-516BC. This same 20-year lag between the people and the Holy Place occurs again after the beginning of the State - 1947/48 to 1967.

Israel and Judah
Some will argue that the northern kingdom of Israel was separated from Judah since they were exiled by Assyria many years before the Babylonian exile. However, what they appear to be forgetting is that many from the northern tribes had already migrated south into Judah and Benjamin long before the Babylonian exile and thus were represented in Judah. For instance, Anna the prophetess, who appears in the gospels,[63] was from the tribe of Asher, and Paul was from the tribe of Benjamin.[64] Thus all Israel was represented in Babylon, and after the exile, all were called Jews.

2520 Years of Punishment
Now that we understand Israel was punished for seventy years in Babylon, let us go back to the prophecy of Ezekiel. According to the prophecy, four hundred and thirty years of

---
[63] Luke 2:36
[64] Rom 11:1

punishment are decreed. When we subtract seventy years from that, we conclude that after the exile three hundred and sixty years of punishment remain. Adding this number to the end of the exile in 536BC brings us to 176BC.

430-70 = 360 years remaining
(Subtract the 70 years of exile as part of the punishment)
Return was in 536 BC
-536 BC + 360 = 176BC
Thus, according to the prophecy, Israel's punishment should have been over in 176BC. However, at that time they were about to enter one of their most difficult periods of persecution under Antiochus Epiphanes. What then are we to do with the prophecy? The answer to this mystery seems to come from Moses himself.

"Yet if in spite of this, you do not obey Me, but act with hostility against Me, then I will act with wrathful hostility against you; and I, even I, will punish you seven times for your sins ......I will lay waste your cities as well, and will make your sanctuaries desolate; and I will not smell your soothing aromas. And I will make the land desolate so that your enemies who settle in it shall be appalled over it. You, however, I will scatter among the nations and will draw out a sword after you, as your land becomes desolate and your cities become waste." Lev 26:27-33

The people did not come back from Babylon in full repentance. In fact, only a small remnant returned, and they had to be admonished by the prophets Zechariah, Haggai, and Malachi to complete the work on the Temple. Thus, we can conclude that the remnant was lukewarm and had to be punished seven times more for their sins. When we multiply 360 years by 7, we get 2520 years. These 2520 years for the punishment of Israel must be converted from biblical prophetic years[65] to our calendar years. When we add this to 536BC, we arrive at 1948. The punishment of Israel ended with her re-gathering from all the nations to her ancient homeland
in 1948.

The Captivity of Israel
390 days for Israel - 40 days for Judah - 1 day = 1 year
390 years + 40 years = 430 years
430-70=360
360 x 7 = 2520 years
2,520 x 360 (days) = 907,200 days
907,200 days /365.25 = 2483.8
-536 B.C. + 2483.8 = **1948**

---

[65] Biblical prophetic years follow the ancient system of 360-day years versus the 365 ¼ days of our Gregorian calendar. See Gen 8:3-4

Captivity of Jerusalem (Holy Place)
-516 B.C. (Temple Restored) + 2483.8 = **1967**

Chapter 5 – Shaven Head

Ezekiel is told to shave his head (a sign of mourning) and use the hair to represent the house of Israel. He is to do this after the siege enactment. Then he is told to burn a third of the hair in the center of the city, another third he is to strike with the sword around the city, and the last third he is to scatter to the wind.

This prophetic symbolism expresses the broken heart of God for His rebellious people. He said that He placed Jerusalem at the center of the nations, but she has done more wickedly than the nations around her, rejected His statutes and ordinances, and flagrantly prostituted herself to idols, even bringing them into the Temple. Therefore, the Lord says He is against her and will bring great judgments against her. He will bring the Babylonians who will lay siege against Jerusalem and the famine will be so severe that fathers will eat their sons. It would seem that this horrible famine in the city and the cannibalism as a result, is what is being referred to as not happening again. Jerusalem was surrounded again by the Romans in 68AD and destroyed completely in 70AD and the same judgments enacted. The people were massacred, or taken as slaves, and the rest were scattered to the nations, where they were until the restoration began in the 20th Century.

As Ezekiel was told to symbolically enact the judgments on the thirds, it is explained to him what these judgments are. One third will die in the famine, one third will be slaughtered by the sword, and the other third will be scattered to the nations. Jeremiah speaks over and over of the same judgments but does not give numbers. Also, it seems clear that this was likely what happened in 70AD and what will happen in the Day of the Lord Tribulation. Zechariah 13:8-9 can be interpreted this way for the first century, but it also must be about the end of the age, since it concludes with Israel restored to God forever (9). This would of course explain why God said he had not done it before and never will again, since both exiles are one judgment that concludes at the end of the age. This is also consistent with the Biblical perspective on prophecy where there is more than one meaning and fulfillment. For instance, many messianic prophecies encompass both the first and second comings in what appears to be one event.

Another confirming fact is that in the first exile the people were sent to Babylon but in the second they were scattered to the nations (wind).

Ezekiel was also told to take a few hairs and hide them in his garment. Yet some of them he was to burn in the fire. This appears to speak of the tiny remnant that was left in the land and what they would suffer because of the treachery of Ishmael son of Nethaniah.

Chapters 6-7

Ezekiel is told to proclaim judgment against the mountains of Israel for all the wickedness performed in all their high places and valleys. The Lord declares that wrath is coming, and He will leave only a remnant. All their altars and idols will be destroyed, and the land will be desolate. The land itself has been polluted by the sin of Israel and must be cleansed. It is also clear that the land and the people are eternally joined together. They both will mourn, and both will be restored. The Lord will bring back a remnant from the nations that will turn to Him (6:8-10). Nevertheless, disaster has come because of continual idolatry, and nothing can be done to avert it.

Chapter 7:20-27 laments the idolatry that Judah has brought into the Temple and how it was defiled, most likely referring to the evil of Manasseh. As a result of all this, the Lord will bring the "worst of nations" to plunder it and take possession of its jewels.

Chapters 8-11

While Ezekiel is sitting in his house with the elders of Judah before him, he has a vision of someone resembling a man who was clearly an angel.

"Then I looked, and behold, something like the appearance of a man; from His waist and downward there was the appearance of fire, and from His waist and upward like the appearance of a glow, like gleaming metal. And He extended the form of a hand and took me by the hair of my head; and the Spirit lifted me up between earth and heaven and brought me in the visions of God to Jerusalem, to the entrance of the north gate of the inner courtyard, where the seat of the idol of jealousy, which provokes to jealousy, was located. And behold, the glory of the God of Israel was there, like the appearance which I saw in the plain."

The man stretched out his hand and snatched Ezekiel away and took him "in the visions of God" to the Temple in Jerusalem. What follows then are a series of visions which depict the idolatry of Judah and how they have hurt the Lord (6:9) and defiled the true worship of Yahweh depicted by their outrageous acts in the Temple. It is not that these things are literally happening in the Temple at the time, but God is pulling the veil back, so to speak, and showing what Judah is really doing in the land while they pretend to worship Yahweh and think He doesn't see. The Temple was the place where God had placed His glory among them, thus the abominations are pictured as happening right there before the Lord. The insincerity and idolatry in the hearts of the people is exposed as God prepares to bring destruction on them and the city and to destroy even the Temple itself.

The first thing Ezekiel saw inside the North Gate toward the Altar was the "idol of jealousy." We are not told what this idol is, but it could be Baal, or an Asherah. It was obviously, provoking the Lord to jealousy. But the Lord essentially says, "That's just the beginning. Wait 'till you see the rest of it." Then Ezekiel was taken to the entrance to the court where there was a hole in the wall. He is told to dig through the wall and when he did, he saw that all sorts of creeping things and beasts and detestable idols were carved into the walls. And standing in front of the idols were seventy elders of Israel with Jaazaniah son of Shaphan among them each of them with censers offering incense to idols. This is what is going on throughout the land. Then he was taken to the entrance to the North Gate and there, women were weeping for Tammuz.[66] Then finally he is taken to the inner court of the Lord's House, before the entrance to the Temple, between the porch and the altar. There he saw about twenty-five men with their backs toward the Temple prostrating themselves toward the east. They were facing east worshiping the pagan sun gods and defiling the Temple of God. This image depicts the offense caused by worshipping idols, which is snubbing the Almighty and turning their backs toward Him in the ultimate insult. Thus, the anger of the Lord is kindled against them and He is about to pour out His wrath on them.

Vision of God's Judgment
Then the prophet is shown six men coming from the North with weapons. Six is the number of man and this is a picture of the judgment that is coming at the hand of the Babylonians. It is God's judgment, but it is being carried out by human agency. And to underscore that it is God's judgment, there is a man dressed in linen (likely an angelic figure) among them who has an inkhorn. He is told to go through the city and put a mark on the forehead of everyone who sighs and groans over the abominations within it. The glory of the Lord, which was over the cherubim on the mercy seat, has moved to the threshold of the Temple and from there His word goes forth. The six men are told to go after the angelic scribe and slay all who do not have the mark, beginning at the Temple itself. They are to have pity on no one.

In the midst of judgment there is always a remnant saved. In the Day of the Lord when the wrath of God is poured out in the earth, the remnant of Israel is once again marked and sealed.[67]

"As they were striking the people and I alone was left, I fell on my face and cried out saying, 'Alas, Lord GOD! Are You destroying the whole remnant of Israel by pouring out Your wrath on Jerusalem?' Then He said to me, 'The iniquity of the house of Israel and

---

[66] Tammuz originated in the Babylonian idolatry begun by Semiramis the wife of Nimrod. He was worshiped as the son god – a satanic counterfeit of the Son of God. It seems that the enemy knew something of the gospel, yet not enough to keep him from killing the true Son of God. Tammuz shows up in many forms as does Nimrod and Semiramis (Ishtar, Ashtarte, Baal, Zeus, to name a few). Tammuz was supposed to die and come back to life with the seasons. Thus the demonic festival of mourning for him.

[67] Rev 7:3

Judah is very, very great, and the land is filled with blood and the city is full of perversion; for they say, "The LORD has forsaken the land, and the LORD does not see!" But as for Me, My eye will have no pity nor will I spare, but I will bring their conduct upon their heads.' Then behold, the man clothed in linen at whose loins was the writing case reported, saying, 'I have done just as You have commanded me.'" Ezek 9:8-11

The Glory Departs
We are given a description of the glory of the Lord which hovered over the Cherubim and the fire that was darting back and forth between them and the wheels. The voice of the Lord commanded the man dressed in linen (likely an angel) to take some of the coals of fire from between the Cherubim and sprinkle it over the city. And he did so. This is likely speaking of the divine judgment not only on the people, but the city itself and even the Temple. Then in the saddest picture of all, the Cherubim and the glory of the Lord depart from the Temple and hover over the East Gate.

Then Ezekiel is shown twenty-five men of the leaders of Israel, among whom are Jaazaniah son of Azzur and Pelatiah son of Benaiah. These are undoubtedly the same twenty-five shown earlier with their backs toward the Holy Place. Now they are at the entrance of the East Gate. These are the men who give evil counsel to King Zedekiah and say, "The time is not near to build houses. This city is the pot, and we are the flesh."

These evil leaders are advising against the word of the Lord spoken by the prophet Jeremiah. He told them to build houses in Babylon and serve the king because they would be there a long time (70 years).[68] But they said that we must fight against Babylon and be victorious. Jerusalem is like a pot, and they are the flesh in it. This maybe a taunt concerning Jeremiah's word about Babylon being the boiling pot from the north.[69] Jerusalem would be the pot with its fortifications to protect them. Then the Lord told Ezekiel to prophesy against them.

"Therefore, thus says the Lord GOD, 'Your slain whom you have laid in the midst of the city are the flesh and this city is the pot; but I will bring you out of it. You have feared a sword; so I will bring a sword upon you," the Lord GOD declares. "And I will bring you out of the midst of the city and deliver you into the hands of strangers and execute judgments against you. You will fall by the sword. I will judge you to the border of Israel;

---
[68] Jer 29:1-9
[69] Jer 1:13-16

so you shall know that I am the LORD. This city will not be a pot for you, nor will you be flesh in the midst of it, but I will judge you to the border of Israel." Ezek 11:7-11

Though there will be many slain in the city which will be like a pot for them, the Lord says that He will not allow the Babylonians to destroy them, but He will instead bring them out of the city and take them into exile. Yet, there will be judgments within the borders of Israel. All this will come about because of their wickedness which they have done even worse than the nations around them.

Then it came about as Ezekiel prophesied that Pelatiah died. Thus, the prophet cried out to the Lord once again for the nation and begged Him not to destroy the whole remnant. Then comes the beautiful promise of restoration at the end of the age, which we are so privileged to have witnessed and continue to witness in our day.

"Therefore say, 'Thus says the Lord GOD, I will gather you from the peoples and assemble you out of the countries among which you have been scattered, and I will give you the land of Israel. When they come there, they will remove all its detestable things and all its abominations from it. And I will give them one heart, and put a new spirit within them. And I will take the heart of stone out of their flesh and give them a heart of flesh, that they may walk in My statutes and keep My ordinances and do them. Then they will be My people, and I shall be their God. But as for those whose hearts go after their detestable things and abominations, I will bring their conduct down on their heads," declares the Lord GOD." Ezek 11:17-21

Just as the Lord had spoken through Isaiah, Jeremiah and all the others, He now declares it again trough Ezekiel the prophet in exile. Though Israel is scattered to the nations, God will bring back a remnant at the end of the age to their own land. He will change their hearts and give them a heart of flesh. He will bring them into this New Covenant in Messiah, and they will no longer follow idols. This promise of the New Covenant is spoken of again in chapter 36[70] and also by Jeremiah.[71] These passages make it clear that there is a two-stage restoration of Israel. First, they are brought back to the land and then they are spiritually restored to their God. The natural restoration was completed in 1967 and the spiritual restoration, which has been going on since then, is close to completion in our day.

The Cherubim
The descriptions of the Cherubim are striking in chapter one and chapter ten. Great detail is given on the movement of the wheels and how the spirit of the living beings was in the wheels. So, they were not just wheels. Also in chapter one, the vision by the river Chebar describes the four living creatures as each having the face of a man, an ox, a bull, and an

---
[70] Ezek 36:24-29
[71] Jer 31:31-34

eagle. Then in chapter ten,[72] the face of a cherub is mentioned instead of a bull, but we are told that the vision was the same as chapter one. Thus, it would imply that the face of a bull is the same as the face of a cherub.

The vision of the four living creatures described in Revelation chapter 4 is very similar to that of Ezekiel. However, there is no mention of wheels, and they have six wings instead of four. Perhaps they are a different kind of Cherubim. Also, what Isaiah saw were Seraphim. This is clearly stated in the text.[73] They each had six wings and we are told that with two of those wings the Seraph covered his face. Thus, we can deduct that Seraphim have one face, but we are not told what it is like!

This section ends with the glory of the Lord above the Cherubim leaving the Temple and hovering over the Mount of Olives. Then Ezekiel is taken back by the Sprit to Babylon where he explains to the exiles all that he has seen. Interestingly when Messiah returns, the glory of God will come from the east and rest in the Temple once again. Many Scriptures indicate this.[74] Being aware of the prophecies, the Ottoman Sultan Suleiman in 1541 sealed the Eastern Gate and created a cemetery outside of it to keep the Jewish Messiah from entering. Nice try, but the Lord will return to His Temple.[75]

Chapter 12
Ezekiel is told to prepare his bags and go somewhere through a hole in the city wall (in Babylon) and pretend that he is going into exile as a sign to the people of the coming exile of the Jews from Jerusalem. He is to bring his baggage out during the day and dig the hole in the wall and go through it in the evening, with his eyes covered, and in the sight of the exiles. When they ask him what he was doing, he is to tell them that this is a sign concerning Zedekiah as well as the people of Jerusalem. Zedekiah would load his bags, and they would bring him through a hole in the wall in the dark of night. He would cover his eyes so as not to see the land. Then the Lord would set a trap for him, and he would be caught. He would be taken to Babylon where he would spend the rest of his life. However, he would never see it because he would be blind. This same prophecy was brought by Jeremiah to Zedekiah.[76] Yet he did not listen but hardened his heart.

---
[72] Ezek 10:14
[73] Is 6:2
[74] Is 63:1-6, Rev 19:11-16, Zech 14:4-6
[75] Mal 3:1-4
[76] Jer 32:1-5, 52:6-11

The chapter continues to speak of the calamity that will come upon Jerusalem and the land of Israel. The inhabited cities will be laid waste and the land will be a desolation. The proverb that has become popular saying, "The days are long, and every vision fails" is about to cease. The Lord says that there will be no longer any false vision or flattering divination within the house of Israel. He will speak the word and perform it in their days. They say that the words of the prophet are for a long time off, but the Lord says that none of His words will be delayed any longer. Whatever word He speaks will be performed!

Chapter 13 – False Prophets Condemned

The word of the Lord came to Ezekiel concerning the false prophets in Jerusalem. They are prophesying a false vision or lying divination. They are listening to their own spirit and prophesying what they want to happen and then saying that the Lord has spoken to them. Many in the church today are doing the same thing. They are prophesying what they want God to do. In fact, the prophetic movement of today has been teaching people to decree things that they believe rather than speak what God is actually saying. This is the same grievous sin of the false prophets of Israel who misrepresented the Lord and misled God's people telling them there will be peace when there is no peace. They speak out of their own imagination and lying dreams and visions. They presume that because God had spoken that before it must also be right now. Yet, they deny that God is angry with the people and refuse to call for repentance. Thus, the Lord says they will not be part of Israel's council or history ever. One must also assume that those who make a habit of prophesying falsely and misrepresenting the Lord today will suffer the same fate.

The false prophets are depicted as whitewashing a wall and trying to put a pretty face on something evil. It is reminiscent of what Jesus said to the Jewish leaders when He called them "whitewashed tombs." The Lord says he will send a mighty wind and flooding rain and hail that will consume the wall. And those who plastered it will be destroyed with it. This is a picture of God's wrath which will be poured out on Jerusalem by Nebuchadnezzar king of Babylon.

Ezekiel is also told to confront the women in the city who were leading people astray using witchcraft and magic bracelets and veils and claiming to speak for God. They are seen as hunting down lives and bringing people into bondage. The Lord will bring judgment on them because they are bringing the righteous into sin and thus the judgment of God. For handfuls of barley and fragments of bread they are leading people astray with lies and assuring their destruction. The Lord says He will tear off their bands and veils and they will no longer see visions and practice divination. The Lord will deliver the people out of their hands!

Chapter 14

Some of the elders of Israel[77] came to Ezekiel seeking a word from the Lord. Scholars have suggested that this is a delegation from Jerusalem. However, there is no indication of this in the text - it is purely speculative. The Lord says that they have idols in their hearts, and it is the same as putting them before their faces in His presence. They must repent of the idolatry that caused their captivity if they are to come before the Lord to inquire of a prophet. Therefore, the Lord says that He will not be consulted by them and will answer them personally. He will set His face against them to cut them off from Israel. He will also do the same to the prophet who attempts to speak to them on His behalf rather than confronting their idolatry.

Again, the Lord speaks to Ezekiel regarding the punishment and destruction He is bringing on Jerusalem. He lists four different judgments that could be brought against a country and even if Noah, Daniel, and Job were in its midst, they could only save themselves because of their righteousness. While this is a stunning commentary on these three friends of God who were highly esteemed, it is also a damning indictment of the wickedness of Judah and Jerusalem, that not even they could intercede for it. In a similar way the Lord told Jeremiah not to pray for the people because He was not going to listen.[78] Four different judgments are coming, famine, sword, plague, and wild beasts. The city will be destroyed but God will bring out a righteous remnant and this will be a comfort to them.

Chapter 15 - The Useless Vine

Here we have an illustration of how useless the wood of the vine is compared to the wood of all the other trees. Nothing can really be made from it. But if it is burned and charred it is even more useless. It is only good for the fire. In the same way the Lord says he will give up the inhabitants of Jerusalem and the city will be consumed. The land will be desolate because of their iniquity.

Chapter 16 – God's Heart for Jerusalem

This lengthy chapter, with highly metaphorical and allegorical language, tells the story of Jerusalem as the wife of God and her adultery and betrayal. She was a Canaanite city in her youth that was loved by Yahweh, who took pity on her and adopted her as His own.

---

[77] Please notice how over and over again the Jews in Babylon are referred to as Israel.
[78] Jer 7:16, 11:14, 14:11

He made a covenant of marriage with her, and she grew and became beautiful among the kingdoms. However, she was unfaithful and played the harlot with all the idols of the nations. Her abominations and harlotries were so great that they even excelled those of her northern sister Samaria and even Sodom who is also referred to as her sister in the South. It is not clear why Sodom would be referred to as her younger sister and Samaria her older sister since by our reckoning this seems reverse. The age of the cities is being measured apparently by the time period built rather than the years of existence. Sodom being first is the younger, and Samaria which came after the Solomonic period is the older. Thus, Jerusalem is the middle sister in age and geographics. In any event, Jerusalem has committed more abominations that the other two. The point is even made that harlots usually commit their adultery for gain, but Jerusalem paid others to take advantage of her. Consequently, Jerusalem makes even Sodom and Samaria look better by comparison. Thus, she will be judged as women who commit harlotry and shed blood are judged. The Lord will give her over to the Babylonians who will burn her with fire.

Restoring their Captivity
The passage speaks of the restoration of Jerusalem and also of Sodom and Samaria. Though the allegorical language is obviously speaking of the sins committed by the people in these cities, it is still speaking of the cities themselves. Also, the reference to their daughters concerns the cities that were under them or related to them. Jerusalem was over the cities of Judah and Samaria was over the cities of the Northern Kingdom of Israel. Sodom also had cities that were connected with her. Thus, the daughters are these cities. Therefore, when it says their captivity will be restored it can only mean that the cities themselves will be restored. Yes, Israel was promised over and over that she would be brought back from all the nations to which she was exiled. However, the people of Sodom were all wicked and there were no survivors. Therefore, the promise is about the restoration of Jerusalem to righteousness under the Messiah in the Millennium, and apparently Samaria and even Sodom may be restored as well in that day. There is no promise here that wicked people will be saved as the Universalists suggest.

Another point that is made is that Sodom was always spoken of in derision by those in Jerusalem and rightfully so. Now however, the prophet says that the Edomite and Philistine cities will be able to say the same of Jerusalem.

Chapter 17 - The Eagles and the Cedar
This illustrates the foolishness of King Zedekiah in rebelling against Nebuchadnezzar and looking to Egypt for help. God would punish him for his disobedience and hand him over to the king of Babylon.

The passage ends with a promise of restoration. The Lord Himself will take a sprig from the top of the Cedar, or the royalty of Judah, and plant it on the high mountain of Israel (undoubtedly the Mountain of the Lord in Jerusalem). This is a reference to the Messiah who will reign there over the remnant that is restored from all the lands. All the nations will come to Zion and all the nations (trees of the field) will know that Yahweh is the Lord.

Chapter 18 – The Soul who Sins will Die

The Lord confronts a Proverb which says, "The Fathers eat sour grapes and the children's teeth are set on edge." In other words, the children will answer for the sins of their fathers. The Lord says instead that the soul that practices sin will die. This does not mean that sins of the father's do not come down the family line, but that the Lord holds each soul responsible for its own sins. He gives several examples of this principle. The man who walks in righteousness and does not worship idols but obeys the commandments and statutes of the Lord is righteous and will live. But if he has a son who disobeys the statutes of the Lord and is wicked, that son will die for his own sins. The soul who sins (practices sin) will die. But if, on the other hand, a son has a father who is disobedient to Torah, but he himself refuses that example and instead obeys the Lord and walks in righteousness, that son will live but his father will die for his iniquity. The son will not bear the punishment for the father's iniquity nor the father for the son's iniquity. Each will bear the punishment for his own iniquity. In the same manner if a wicked man turns from his ways and practices righteousness, all the transgressions he has committed will be forgiven him and he will live because of his righteousness. But if a righteous man turns away from righteousness and instead practices iniquity, his righteous deeds will not be remembered. He will die because of his iniquity. Thus, the Lord says His ways are righteous and just and that the way of Israel is evil. Consequently, He will judge each one based on their deeds.

The point of this word is to call, not only the nation, but each individual to repentance so that they will not die in the wrath that is coming. God takes no pleasure in the death of anyone including the wicked. Those who repent and receive His word, will presumably be spared from the destruction coming from Babylon. Those who do not will die in the wrath and in their sin.

Chapter 19

This chapter laments the destruction of Jerusalem and its Princes. She was like a lion with her cubs. In verse 4, one of her cubs is captured and taken to Egypt (Jehoahaz)[79] Another one is taken to Babylon in hooks (Zedekiah)[80] Now there is none to rule.

---

[79] 2 Kings 23:34
[80] 2 Kings 25:4-7

Chapter 20: 1-32

The elders of Israel in Babylon come to Ezekiel to inquire of the Lord, and he is given the word to speak to them. It is a lengthy word which recapitulates all of God's workings with Israel in the desert and their continual rejection of His love and His statutes. And when they came into the land, they were even worse, rebelling against Him continually to offer sacrifice on every high hill. Thus, the Lord says His judgment has been decreed and He will not be sought by them.

Throughout this passage God says that He gave Israel His laws and statutes that when followed bring life. However, in verse 25 he says:

"So I gave them other statutes that were not good and laws through which they could not live..."

To take this verse out of context and suggest that God gave them laws that were not good and did not lead to life, would be a grave mistake. Let's put it back in context and get the intended meaning.

"Also I swore to them in the wilderness that I would scatter them among the nations and disperse them among the lands, because they had not observed My ordinances, but had rejected My statutes and had profaned My sabbaths, and their eyes were on the idols of their fathers. I also gave them statutes that were not good and ordinances by which they could not live; and I pronounced them unclean because of their gifts, in that they caused all their firstborn to pass through the fire so that I might make them desolate, in order that they might know that I am the LORD."'

God told the people through Moses in the desert that He would scatter them among the nations for their sins. They rejected His laws and decrees and desecrated His Sabbaths by their worship of their father's idols and by the abominable practice of offering their children in the fire to Baal and Molech. Thus the Lord says He gave them over (a better translation) to the laws and statutes of the idolatry to which they engaged and allowed them to experience the horrors of it and the punishment so that they may know that He is the Lord and the only one who gives life.

Verses 33-44 – The Restoration

Once again, the prophet speaks of their restoration, a theme that consumes the last fourteen chapters of the book. This promise of restoration comes after they have been scattered to the nations and severely disciplined and judged. When we consider all that Israel has been through over the centuries, it is clear that God is faithful to His word. Moses said that the Lord would draw out a sword after them and He certainly did. It seems clear here, and in all the restoration prophecies, that the return from Babylon is not the fulfillment spoken off. Though it was indeed the return of a remnant nation, the vast majority never came back. Thus, the diaspora began and was completed in 70AD when the whole nation was scattered to the ends of the earth.

In the 20th Century God fulfilled His promise to bring back the remnant nation to the land. Yet there is more to come. They must come back to the God of Israel and the Messiah Yeshua and fulfill their calling to walk in holiness and righteousness and be a light to the nations. God will purge from them all the disobedient and rebellious. When Messiah comes, He will gather all the remaining Jews that continue to live abroad and judge them. The rebellious and wicked among them will not be allowed to enter the land or the Millennium. This promise is for a purged holy remnant that will be faithful to Him forever.

Verses 45-49 – Prophesy Toward South
Teman was a city in Edom which is today part of Jordan. Ezekiel was told to set his face toward this city and the Negev, which is the south of Israel. The prophecy speaks of the forests of the Negev being set aflame. The Negev is a desert today, so it is not clear if the fire is a figurative reference to the coming judgment of Babylon on Judah, which occupied the south, or perhaps a reference to the judgment of Edom and the coming of Messiah who will bring with him a righteous remnant from that area.[81]

Chapter 21:1-27 – A Sword Against Jerusalem
Ezekiel is told to prophecy against Jerusalem and the sanctuaries and the land of Israel. Since "sanctuaries" is plural perhaps the second Temple destruction was also in mind. A sword is coming – the Lord has pulled His sword out of its sheath, and He will not return it. The king of Babylon is coming, and he will set his face against Jerusalem. The Lord will clap his hands and satisfy His wrath for all their sin and rebellion.

Ezekiel is told to mark two ways for the king of Babylon to go who is pictured at the head of the ways using divination to set his course. He is to destroy Rabbah of the sons of Ammon and the fortified city of Jerusalem. The coming siege of Jerusalem is described, and the end of the wicked prince Zedekiah is celebrated, and indeed the end of the kingdom of David in Jerusalem until the Messiah comes to whom it belongs (vs 27). Notice that it will be a ruin until that time. This is clearly about the coming kingdom since the word is about the prince, but it is also about the Temple which is still a ruin and must be rebuilt and cleansed by Messiah. Here again we see the dual scattering and dual regathering with the latter days always coming to the fore – the Day of the Lord. Also remember the prophecy of Moses that since they did not come back from Babylon in genuine repentance and obedience, God would punish them seven times more.[82]

---
[81] See Isaiah 63
[82] Lev 26:18

"And you, slain, wicked one, the prince of Israel, whose day has come, <u>in the time of the punishment of the end</u>,' this is what the Lord GOD says: 'Remove the turban and take off the crown; this will no longer be the same. Exalt that which is low, and humble that which is high. Ruins, ruins, ruins, I will make it! <u>This also will be no longer until He comes whose right it is</u>, and I will give it to Him.'" Ezek 21:25-27

Verses 28-32 – Judgment on Ammon

Because of their evil enmity toward Israel and their insults they will be as fuel for the fire. The Lord will pour out His wrath on them and they will be remembered no more.

Rabbah, Capital of Ammon

The Ammonites are also mentioned in chapter 25, but they were not heard from again after this time. All that remains of this Ammonite kingdom is archaeological ruins.

Chapter 22:1-17 – The Sins of Israel
Once again, the sins of Israel and their rulers are documented in detail.

- The shedding of Innocent blood.
- Defilement of Idolatry.
- Oppressing the stranger, the orphan, and the widow.
- Despising the Holy things.
- Profaning the Sabbaths.
- Dishonoring parents.
- Immorality, adultery, incest, uncleanness.
- Taking of bribes.
- Charging interest (usury).

Ezekiel is asked if he would pronounce judgment. The Lord says He will act and scatter them to the nations. There they will defile themselves in the sight of all the nations and He will eliminate their uncleanness from them.

Verses 17-22 - The Fiery Furnace
This illustration explains how God is going to purge the people through the siege of Jerusalem as metals are purified in a furnace. The Lord's wrath will be poured out on them.

Verses 23-31 – Compromised Leaders
The conspiracy of the prophets who speak from their own imagination rather than the Spirit of God. They have conspired together to deceive God's people, and what they have agreed upon is their own agenda - what they want God to do. The priests have done violence to God's Law, defiling the holy things, and making no distinction between the holy and the profane. They don't teach people the difference between what is clean and unclean, and they defile the Sabbaths. The leaders are all like wolves tearing the flock and causing all these judgments to come on the people. The prophets are painting with whitewash seeing false visions and divining lies – putting a positive spin on everything.

The same things can be said concerning the leaders of the church today and all the false prophets and teachers who whitewash everything and never teach holiness or sanctification.

The Lord says that He sought someone to build up a wall where it is broken down or stand in the gap where there is a hole. Although we can use this to speak of intercession, it is certainly intended to be more than praying. It must also include challenging the false prophets and leaders and teaching the truth of God's Word.

Chapter 23 - Two Harlots
The two harlots of chapter 23 symbolize the harlotries of Israel (the Northern kingdom) and Judah (the Southern kingdom). The language is graphic and is intended not only to expose their sin but to express the heart of God for Israel who was betrothed to Him. Both sisters were loved by Him and belonged to Him, but they continually lusted after their neighbors, looking to them for help and worshipping their gods. Oholah which means "tent" is Samaria and "Oholibah" which means "my tent is in her" is Jerusalem. The northern kingdom with its capital in Samaria, is referred to as the elder or greater,[83] whereas; Judah with its capital Jerusalem, where the Temple of God was, is the smaller. God says that both sisters were His, but they have been harlots since their youth in Egypt. This is an obvious allusion to idolatry and spiritual unfaithfulness, a theme that runs throughout the prophets and the New Testament as well.

The bigger sister Samaria had played the harlot so much with the Assyrians that God finally gave her over to them and they destroyed her and took her sons and daughters away into exile. However, upon seeing this Judah did not repent but committed even more harlotries than her sister. They worshipped idols in Jerusalem and even passed their sons through the fire. They profaned the Sabbaths and defiled the Temple. Thus, the Lord will bring her lovers against her – the Egyptians, the Assyrians, the Chaldeans. These will slay their sons and daughters and burn their houses with fire and take them off into exile.

---
[83] The same as chapter 16 where Samaria is said to be the older and Sodom the younger.

Chapter 24 - The Boiling Pot

This is yet another illustration of how God is going to purge Jerusalem and turn up the heat through the siege of the Babylonians. On the very day that the siege began[84] Ezekiel receives this word. Jerusalem is a rusty pot whose rust will not go away. The rust is its stain of bloodguiltiness which continues in it. It is to be brought to a ferocious boil with its inhabitants inside. The Lord says that He would have cleansed them had they repented, yet now they will not be cleansed from their filthiness until His wrath is spent on them.

Then the Lord speaks to Ezekiel in what is perhaps the saddest of language concerning the destruction of Jerusalem and the Temple. His wife is to be taken from him and he is not to mourn for her but to groan inwardly. He spoke to the people in the morning and in the evening his wife died. Thus, he understands and feels the pain of the Lord over His people and His house in Jerusalem which is to be destroyed. Thus, Ezekiel will be a sign for the people who are told to do what he has done concerning his wife's death, when they hear the news of Jerusalem. Also, he is to speak to the exiles who will come and be a sign to them as well.

Judgment of the Gentile Nations
Please read chapters 25-32

As Jerusalem was destroyed by the Babylonians the nations roundabout were undoubtedly pleased for their hearts were against Israel as they are today. But Ezekiel is told to turn toward those nations and prophesy the destruction that is coming upon them. Here we see a demonstration of the power of God's spoken word, not only to declare His plans ahead of time but to speak things into existence.

Chapter 25:1-7 – Against Ammon
Because of her continual enmity against Israel and her gloating over the destruction of the Temple, God is going to remove them as a people and their territory will be given to the people of the East. Some believe this may be a referral to its being possessed by Babylon and later Persia and Greece. However, it is likely that it became occupied by nomadic tribes from Arabia such as the Nabateans. Ammon ceased to exist after the Babylonian conquest.

Verses 8-11 – Against Moab
The same judgments that were pronounced on Ammon were also pronounced on Moab. She would disappear as a people and her territory given to the Nabateans and Arabians.

---
[84] 2 Kings 25:1

Verses 12-14 – Against Edom
Edom, whose people were the descendants of Esau, Israel's brother, had been cruel to Israel from the beginning and refused them passage through their land. Because of their vengeance against Israel, God says He will exact vengeance against them and cut off man and beast from Teman in the north to Dedan (or Ababia) in the south. It is believed that Edom was eradicated by Babylon and later taken over by the Nabateans. However, after the destruction of Judah, it would appear that they held onto their territory in the Negev. Thus at the time of Jesus their ancient mountainous territory is referred to as Nabatea and the Negev territory as Idumea (Edom) including Hebron. King Herod was an Edomite. After the second destruction of Judah by the Romans, they migrated further north likely settling in Gaza as well. Thus, the people known as the Palestinians today are most likely descendants of the Edomites and the other dispossessed nations.

Though the judgment on Edom seems to have been fulfilled by the Babylonians, it would appear from other Scriptures that it is singled out for an end-time judgment as well.[85]

Verses 15-17 – Against Philistia
Philistia, of course, was always trying to destroy Israel. They possessed the territory which is today known as Gaza. The term Palestine was coined by the emperor Hadrian, after the Philistines, to eradicate the memory of the Jews from the land. Philistia was taken over by the Assyrians and also by Nebuchadnezzar and soon thereafter became extinct as a nation.

Chapter 26 & 27 - Judgment of Tyre
One of the most notable prophecies contained in these chapters, is the prophecy over the city of Tyre, a very wealthy seaport city on the Mediterranean, which was to be attacked by Nebuchadnezzar and subsequently destroyed (see page 35 - Isaiah 23). This city had two parts, the mainland city, and an island city.

Nebuchadnezzar laid siege to Tyre for thirteen years beginning in 586BC. When he finally entered it, he discovered that most of the people had moved out to the island city in the sea. So he destroyed the mainland city and left. Alexander the Great came against the island city of Tyre in 333BC, and being unable to penetrate it, he gathered navies from nations that he had conquered to aid in the fight. However, to get to the city with his battering rams, Alexander used the stones from the rubble of the mainland city to build a bridge to the island city.

Chapter 27 is a lengthy lament over Tyre, which was perhaps the most famous trading and shipping port in the area at the time.

---
[85] See Obadiah 15-21, Isaiah 34, 63:1

Chapter 28 – The King of Tyre

While addressing the king of Tyre in chapter 28, as is typical with the prophets, Ezekiel parallels the king of Tyre with satan himself and we get a glimpse into the time when he was cast out of God's presence. The passage is similar to Isaiah 14, which flips from the king of Babylon to satan.

The first time the word of the Lord came to him in verse 1, he is told to speak to the "leader" of Tyre. Apparently, this leader was very arrogant even thinking he was a god. The Lord asks him if he is wiser than Daniel. This is the second mention of Daniel and his high esteem, who was at that time number two in Babylon, and undoubtedly the wisest person there. But this ruler of Tyre was very haughty even thinking he could prevail against the mighty king of Babylon. The Lord said he would be brought down to the pit and die the death of those slain in the heart of the seas. We do not know for sure where he died, but when the Island City finally made a deal with Nebuchadnezzar, he was either killed or taken to Babylon and killed.

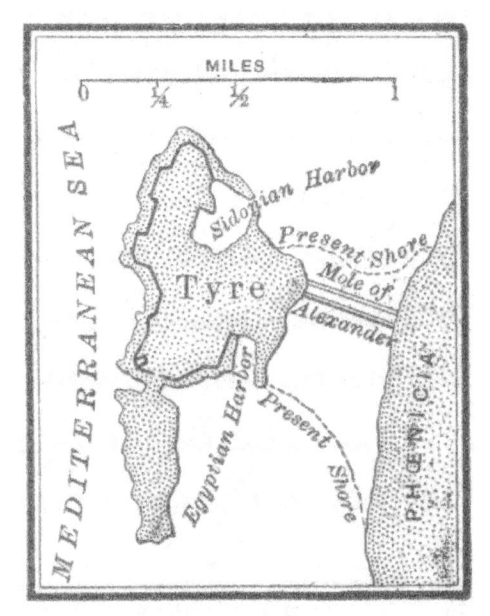

Then in verse 11, Ezekiel says that the word of the Lord came to him again and he is told to take up a lament concerning the downfall of the king of Tyre, however, it is not the ruler of Tyre mentioned earlier, but satan himself who was obviously the real power behind the Baal worshiping leader of Tyre.

"You had the seal of perfection, full of wisdom and perfect in beauty. You were in Eden, the garden of God;......You were the anointed cherub who covers, and I placed you there. You were on the holy mountain of God; you walked in the midst of the stones of fire. You were blameless in your ways from the day you were created, until unrighteousness was found in you. By the abundance of your trade you were internally filled with violence, and you sinned; therefore I have cast you as profane from the mountain of God. And I have destroyed you, O covering cherub, from the midst of the stones of fire." Ezekiel 28:12-16

When we combine Isaiah 14 with this passage, we get significant insight into the fall of satan. He was an anointed cherub and was in the garden of Eden which is also referred to as the mountain of God.[86] He had a special role in the presence of God and walked among the stones of fire. He was perfect in wisdom and beauty, but he became arrogant and wanted to be like the Most High. For this he was cast from the presence of God.

---

[86] Many believe that Mt Zion in Jerusalem (the mountain of God) was in fact the site where the Garden of Eden also was.

In has been thought for centuries that satan had fallen and taken a third of the angels with him some time before the creation. However, there is no text that gives any information prior to creation, thus it is mere speculation based on what we see happening at the end of the age.[87] Recently, we have been challenged by the understanding that since satan was in the garden as an anointed cherub, perhaps his behavior in deceiving and murdering humanity was in fact the time when he fell and was cast out.[88]

Verses 20-24 – Judgment of Sidon

The judgment against Sidon, named after Canaan's oldest son, is that she will be attacked, and blood will run in her streets. This was likely fulfilled by the Persian King Artaxerxes who beat it into submission. It is not clear to what extent Nebuchadnezzar afflicted Sidon, but he did conquer it. What is clear is that she ceased to be a thorn in Israel's side.

Verses 25-26 – Restoration of Israel

These verses contain the promise of Israel's regathering from all the nations and God's judgment on those nations round about that scorn them. God will manifest His holiness through Israel in the last days and she will live securely on the land that was given to Jacob. This will soon be fulfilled in the Millennium reign.

Chapter 29 - 32 - Judgment on Egypt

Israel's ancient enemy is now mentioned. She too is going to receive the judgment of God through Nebuchadnezzar. In the tenth year, Ezekiel is told to prophesy against Egypt. She is to be laid waste and her inhabitants scattered for 40 years, after which time they will return. The king of Babylon invaded Egypt and plundered it in 571BC. The land was devastated, and a large quantity of its skilled people exiled with only a remnant remaining.[89] After 40 years, when Babylon fell to the Persians many returned and the country was revitalized, although it was never to be a major power again.

The judgment of Egypt is clearly a result of its treatment of Israel. It proved to be a reed that gave way whenever Israel leaned on it, and Israel was always injured. Nevertheless, Judah continued to seek it's help until the end in its rebellion against God.

In chapter 29, verse 17, we are told that in the 27th year the word of the Lord came to Ezekiel regarding Nebuchadnezzar's defeat of Tyre and his coming plunder of Egypt. The prophet says that the King of Babylon and his army worked hard in Tyre but got no payment, presumably because they were unable to capture the island city. Nevertheless, they will be abundantly rewarded because God will give Egypt into their hands, and they

---

[87] Revelation 12:4-9
[88] Gen 3:14-15, John 8:44
[89] The invasion of Egypt by Nebuchadnezzar is denied today by many historians. One has to source older accounts such as the works of Josephus. Ezekiel and Jeremiah and Isaiah prophesied this invasion and its destruction, and it most definitely happened.

will plunder it and take much spoil. It will be payment for what they have done since they have carried out God's will. This happened in 567BC.

Verse 21 says that God will make a horn sprout for the people of Israel and Ezekiel will prophesy in their midst. A horn is a picture of strength. God will once again strengthen Israel.

Lament for Egypt
Though the opening verses of chapter 30 are reminiscent of the Day of the Lord at the end of the age, it is specifically speaking of the destruction of Egypt, and all the nations of the middle east, by the hand of Nebuchadnezzar. It is a repeat of the destruction of chapter 29, only with more detail. Many of the cities and districts of Egypt are mentioned and specific judgments exposed. The gods of Egypt will be judged, and the people will be scattered, and the Pharoah will be killed.

The Same Fate as Assyria
A year later the word of the Lord came to Ezekiel regarding Pharoah king of Egypt and his hordes (armies). What follows in chapter 31 is a lengthy description of Assyria and its power and pride. It was like one of the tallest trees in Lebanon, which is said figurately to have surpassed the cedars in God's Garden of Eden. It was a great and mighty kingdom that ruled over many nations, until it was crushed by the Babylonians. This same fate was to befall Egypt. Just as Assyria had fallen to Sheol so would Egypt meet the same fate. Though Egypt did not disappear as the Assyrian Empire did, it was never a powerful nation again.

Chapter 32 is a lengthy lament for Pharaoh king of Egypt. The first prophesy in the chapter is dated after the fall of Jerusalem which took place in 586BC. Pharaoh is said to think of himself as a lion among the nations, but instead he is a monster in the seas. God said He would catch him in His net and throw him on the land where the birds and wild beasts would feed on him. This was all to be fulfilled by the sword of the king of Babylon (vs 11). Egypt and all its hordes will go down to Sheol. The pride of Egypt will be devastated.

Three months later the word of the Lord came to the prophet again. "Wail for the hordes of Egypt and bring it down, her and the daughters of the powerful nations, to the nether world, with those who go down to the pit." Then he lists the other nations that are there in Sheol, Assyria, Elam, Edom, Meshech, Tubal, and the Sidonians. All the nations will lament the destruction of Egypt. It was always a powerful force in the region but alas no more. The time of judgment has come.

The Restoration of Israel
Please read chapters 33-48

Chapter 33:1-20 – The Watchman
These verses are a response to the complaints of the people regarding the judgment they have received. "The way of the Lord is not right," they say, when it is their way that is not right. First the message is to Ezekiel that he is a watchman on the wall. His responsibility is to see what is coming and warn the people. If they listen, they will save their lives, but if they do not listen, they will die in their sin and the prophet will have no responsibility. However, if the watchman does not warn them, they will die in their sin, and he will be responsible for their blood. This is a very somber warning to all who are called to minister to God's people, both then and now. We must be faithful to speak the truth and those who reject it will suffer the consequences, yet we will have been obedient to God. Ezekiel is the messenger. He has been faithful as was his contemporary Jeremiah. Thus, they bear no responsibility for the sins of the nation.

Though this passage defines God's justice, it also expresses His heart of compassion and mercy. He takes no pleasure in the death of the wicked. Inflicting punishment is not something He wants to do but it is something He must do. If the wicked repent from their wickedness and do righteousness God will save them and their sin will not be remembered. On the other hand, if those who walk in righteousness become so confident in their own righteousness that they turn to iniquity, they will die in their sin and their righteousness will not be remembered. Thus the soul who sins will die and those who turn from their sins and do right will live.[90] Even now in Babylon, if they will repent and turn from their sin they will live and be restored to their land at the appointed time.

Verses 23-29
In the twelfth year of the exile on the fifth day of the tenth month the refugees from Jerusalem came to Ezekiel and told him that Jerusalem had been taken. The hand of the Lord was heavy on the prophet the night before, and when the refugees came the next morning, he was able to release the prophecy. The word concerned the tiny remnant that were left in the land of Israel. It appears they were thinking that since they were left behind, the judgment had passed them by, and they would now possess the land as Abraham had. After all he was only one person, and they are "many" who are his descendants. In other words, they would start over and be the inheritors of the promise. But the comparison was flawed. They were still living in disobedience to God and His Torah and could not be given the land. The Lord would give them over to the sword, pestilence, and wild beasts. As for the land it was to be desolate because of their abominations until the seventy years of the exile were completed as was spoken through Jeremiah.

---
[90] Ezek 18:4, Rom 2:9

Verses 30-33
The Lord affirms the ministry of Ezekiel. The people in the exile with the prophet have been coming to him to hear the latest word from the Lord, but they have not taken them seriously. They are still following the lusts of their hearts. They looked to Ezekiel as one looks to a musician for entertainment rather than how they may obey the Lord. They were like the multitudes of Christians today who follow celebrities and comb the internet for the latest word to tickle their ears, rather than obeying the truth of God's word. However, the Lord says that when the word comes to pass and the land is desolate and the exile is complete, they will know that a true prophet has been among them.

Chapter 34 – Woe to the Shepherds
This word is spoken against the leaders of Israel, the kings, princes, priests, false prophets, and elders of the people, who have not cared for God's flock but instead looked out for their own interests. Shepherds are responsible to feed the flock, but they have fed themselves. They have taken the fat of the flock to eat and left the others to fend for themselves. They did not help the weak, heal the sick, bind the broken, gather the scattered ones or look for the lost. They are worthless shepherds who have dominated and abused th
e people of God. Thus, the Lord says He is against the shepherds and will take His flock away from them and they will not be allowed to have sheep anymore. This certainly was fulfilled in the exile when the kingdom was taken away. However, Israel continued to have corrupt leadership after that and even now. Therefore, there is a final fulfillment that takes place during the Day of the Lord.

The Lord says that He Himself will gather back His scattered flock from all the nations to which they were banished on a cloudy and gloomy day. This of course covers both the exile to Babylon and the final scattering in the 1st Century. Yet, remarkably in the middle of the 20th Century these words have been fulfilled. Almighty God has gathered back the Jewish people from the four corners of the earth to their own land and to the holy city of Jerusalem. And even though the Aliyah continues, the physical restoration is complete. The Lord has done it and not man. And even though modern Israel has had some good leaders, it is very clear that the Lord is watching over them. Indeed, their adoption of a Western style democracy may be part of this. Nevertheless, currently what we see is a very fractured leadership in Israel and an inability to form or maintain a government. That is likely the fulfillment of these verses. God will judge between the sheep and will not allow their leaders to dominate and abuse them again. He promises to give them one shepherd – his servant David will feed them, and Yahweh will be their God. This of course is the Kingdom of Messiah Yeshua (Jesus), which is about to be restored to them. Jesus the Son of David will reign from Jerusalem during the Millennium. However, it is also possible that David himself will be on the throne as well.

Verses 25-31 will be fulfilled in the Millennium. Israel will be the head of the nations and live securely on her land with no one to make her afraid. They will no longer endure the insults of the nations as they do now but will be renowned throughout the earth. The Lord will be their God and they will be His people.

As we examine this passage about the worthless shepherds of Israel abusing and exploiting the flock, it is hard not to notice the leadership of the church today that is guilty of the same sins. Woe to the shepherds of Israel who feed themselves and not the flock and woe to the those who claim to be shepherds of the church who do the same thing. God will judge the ones who exploit God's people and get rich off them and do not feed them the truth of God's word. Indeed, the judgment upon the false shepherds in the church has already begun. God is separating them out. Anyone who is called to be a leader in the church of God would do well to read and reread the following passage from the epistle of Peter and make sure it is the way you live.

"Therefore, I urge elders among you, as your fellow elder and a witness of the sufferings of Christ, and one who is also a fellow partaker of the glory that is to be revealed: shepherd the flock of God among you, exercising oversight, not under compulsion but voluntarily, according to the will of God; and not with greed but with eagerness; nor yet as domineering over those assigned to your care, but by proving to be examples to the flock. And when the Chief Shepherd appears, you will receive the unfading crown of glory. You younger men, likewise, be subject to your elders; and all of you, clothe yourselves with humility toward one another, because GOD IS OPPOSED TO THE PROUD, BUT HE GIVES GRACE TO THE HUMBLE." 1 Pet 5:1-5

Chapter 35 – Edom Again
Again, the destruction of Mt Seir and Edom is predicted. Esau's jealousy of his brother Jacob has become his legacy. Edom continued in jealousy and hatred of Israel and rejoiced in their destruction by the Babylonians. It also seems that they even participated in it. Nevertheless, they were destroyed and laid waste. Their land was taken over by the Nabateans and is a waste place today. Their remnant appears to have settled in southern Judah and the Palestinians today may be some of their descendants. Notice how they lay claim to all of Israel. For more on the identity and judgment of Edom see this commentary on Ezekiel 25, Isaiah 34, 63, Jeremiah 49, Amos 1, and Obadiah.

Chapter 36:1-13 – Mountains of Israel
As judgment has been pronounced on Edom is chapter 35 and her motives laid bare, to possess the mountains of Israel, now the prophet speaks to the mountains. The enemies of Israel which are mentioned here by the Lord are the nations round about, and more

specifically Edom, who appropriated His land (My land) for themselves with wholehearted joy and scorn of soul. This land today is referred to by the nations as the West Bank and they deny that it belongs to Israel and want to make it a Palestinian State. Yet the word of the Lord is that it is His land, and the mountains are still the mountains of Israel. They have been made a prey and a derision by the nations round about and by the descendants of Edom. Though this began millennia ago, it has come to a head in our day as the Lord has brought back His people. The settlers of Israel have built many cities on the mountains, and they are home to stay. Now the fulfillment of these verses is near. The Lord says that the insults they have spoken against His people and the mountains of Israel will now fall back on their own heads. The Lord in His jealousy pronounces judgment on these nations. The mountains will be inhabited by Israel, and they will never again be bereaved of their children.

Verses 16-23 – For His Name Sake

The word of the Lord to Ezekiel is that He is about to act for His Namesake. While they were in the land, Israel defiled it by their idolatry and shedding of innocent blood and the Lord cast them out. Now He says that everywhere they went they profaned His holy name, since the nations said, "These are the people of the Lord, yet they have come out of His land." Therefore, the Lord says that He will no longer allow His name to be profaned among the nations. He is going to act for the sake of His holy name. He will bring Israel back and vindicate the holiness of His great name among them. Then the nations will know that He is the Lord.

Verses 24-38 – Restoration Promise and Pattern

"For I will take you from the nations, gather you from all the lands and bring you into your own land. Then I will sprinkle clean water on you, and you will be clean; I will cleanse you from all your filthiness and from all your idols. Moreover, I will give you a new heart and put a new spirit within you; and I will remove the heart of stone from your flesh and give you a heart of flesh. I will put My Spirit within you and cause you to walk in My statutes, and you will be careful to observe My ordinances. You will live in the land that I gave to your forefathers; so you will be My people, and I will be your God." Ezekiel 36:24-28

The Lord promised to restore Israel in two phases.

Phase One is the Promise of Physical Return.

"For I will take you from the nations, gather you from all the lands and bring you into your own land."

Remember the Lord said He would do it for the sake of His holy name. Therefore, it was His sovereign act and was not dependent upon the actions of the Jewish people. This physical regathering began in 1897 with the convening of the World Zionist Congress in Basel Switzerland by Theodor Herzl, who had also written the book, "The Jewish State." Fifty years later the dream was realized with the UN partition plan (Nov. 1947) and the founding of the state in May 1948. And seventy years later in 1967, the dream was complete as Israel was reunited with her ancient city of Jerusalem. Since then, we have been in Phase Two.

Phase Two is the Spiritual Return.

"Then I will sprinkle clean water on you, and you will be clean; I will cleanse you from all your filthiness and from all your idols. Moreover, I will give you a new heart and put a new spirit within you; and I will remove the heart of stone from your flesh and give you a heart of flesh. I will put My Spirit within you and cause you to walk in My statutes, and you will be careful to observe My ordinances. You will live in the land that I gave to your forefathers; so you will be My people, and I will be your God."

The spiritual restoration of Israel to God began in 1967. And in the same manner as the physical regathering, no one took it seriously. Then it happened. The same is about to happen once again. In 1967, Israel captured the Old City of Jerusalem (Biblical City) including the Temple Mount from the Jordanians. However, the secular leaders made an agreement to let the Temple Mount be managed by the Muslim Waqf even though they maintain sovereignty. That situation persists today. But what is often missed is that when Israel recaptured the site of the Temple, fulfilling the words of Jesus,[91] the nation was ill equipped to carry out the Biblical mandate to restore the Temple. They had no knowledge of what was needed. However, once the Temple Mount came back in their hands, a number of religious Jews formed organizations, such as the Temple Mount Faithful and later the Temple Institute, to begin the painstaking and expensive work of preparation to build. Since then, they have prepared the vessels, the priestly garments, the blueprints of the Temple, trained the Levitical priesthood, and bred the Red Heifer in Israel. All of these were necessary to rebuild the Temple which is an essential step in their return to God.

It is hard for Christians to see the building of the Temple as a spiritual return of the Jews. However, much of Biblical Judaism is centered around the Temple. Besides the Scriptures are clear that it must be rebuilt. This is the event that will turn the hearts of the Jewish people back to the God of Israel. We also know that this same Temple will be defiled by the Antichrist and this event will begin the Tribulation and the reconciliation of the remnant

---
[91] Luke 21:24

of Israel with the true Messiah, Yeshua. Since this process began in 1967 and, presuming it lasts the same amount of time as the physical regathering, we are within a decade of the Temple's appearing.

The rest of the chapter will all be fulfilled when the Millennium begins.

Chapter 37:1-14 – The Dry Bones

This passage is really a continuation of chapter 36 and the regathering of Israel. It is the same message which is foretold by a vision given to Ezekiel. He is taken into a valley that is filled with very dry bones. The Lord asks, "Can these bones live?" Most would say no, but Ezekiel told the Lord he was the only one who knew. Then he is commanded to prophesy life and flesh to the bones. Then there was a rattling, and the bones came together, and flesh and sinews came on them. Then he was told to call on the breath to enter them. This of course is a reference to the Holy Spirit infilling them. The prophet obeyed and the spirit came into them, and they stood on their feet an exceedingly great army. Then for those who care to actually read the text, the Lord explains the vision. The dry bones are the whole house of Israel scattered in the nations who say their bones are dry and their hope is completely gone. The Lord says He will bring them up out of their graves (dead hopeless condition) and bring them back to the land of Israel. This is Phase One – the physical regathering. Then the Holy Spirit will be poured out on them, and they will possess the land completely and they will know the Lord has spoken it and done it. The is the completion of Phase Two – the spiritual regathering.

Many in the church today use this passage in a spiritual sense and apply it to the church and revival, without ever acknowledging what it actually says. This is due to Replacement Theology which still permeates their thinking. Thus the nations want to steal the land from Israel and the church wants to steal her promises.

Verses 15-28 – The Two Sticks

Ezekiel is told to take two sticks, one that represents the kingdom of Judah and another that represents the northern kingdom of Israel known by the name of Ephraim who was Joseph's son, since the capital Samaria was in Ephraim. The two sticks represent all the tribes of Israel. Then he is told to join them together as one stick in his hand before the exiles and tell them that they are one in God's hand, and He will gather them from all the nations and bring them back as one people to the land and there will be one king over them. Thus there are no lost tribes today or two houses existing. There is one people Israel, identified as Jews and they are from all the tribes of Israel. Before the exile to Babylon the northern tribes had many that had migrated to Judah and Benjamin on account of the idolatry of the northern kingdom. We see this in the New Testament when Anna is mentioned as being from the tribe of Asher.

The Lord promised to bring back Israel as one people, as He has done, and they will be reconciled to God and David their king in the last days. The Lord will bring them into the New Covenant and will put His sanctuary (the Temple) among them forever. Then the remaining remnant of the nations will know that He is the Lord.

Chapter 38 & 39 – Gog and Magog

Gog is the Prince of Magog, which most Bible scholars believe is Russia. It is the far north territory of what were the Scythians in New Testament times. All the nations mentioned are aligned with Russia today. Up until the 20th Century, most of these nations were aligned with the West, including Russia, but now they are all against them. The formation of this Gog and Magog alliance, after the restoration of Israel, is in itself, one of the proofs we are in the end of the age.

The Magog alliance of Meshech (Moscow) and Tubal (Tobolsk) includes Persia (Iran), Cush (Ethiopia, Somalia, Sudan), Put (Libya and Algeria), Gomer and Beth Torgamah (Turkey). Older translations include Rosh, but since Rosh means "head" it is now generally translated as the "Head" or "Chief" prince of Meshech and Tubal.

Map of Possible Confederates in the Invasion Against Israel in Ezekiel 38-39

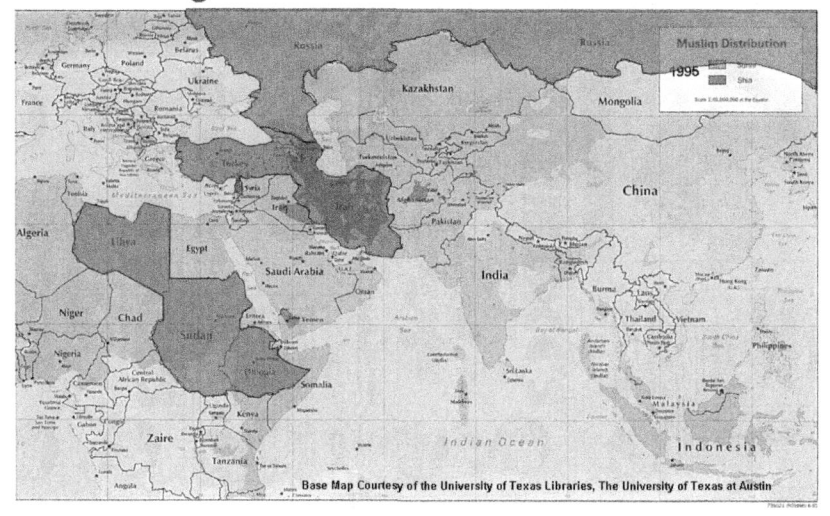

The Gog and Magog war is the final war at the end of the age where God Himself has promised to bring all the nations of the earth against Jerusalem.[92] These nations are in alliance today against Israel. Some bible teachers believe that this Gog and Magog battle is one that takes place before the covenant of peace beginning Daniel's 70th week (Daniel 9:24-27), but for many reasons we believe it is the same battle that occurs at the end of the Tribulation and is part of the Armageddon campaign. We conclude this from the description of the battle in these chapters, and what God says He will do through it. The following are some examples:

---
[92] Joel 3:1-2

- Many nations with you (Ezek 38:15)
- After this battle God will no longer allow His name to be profaned (inconceivable to have the Great Apostasy and the rise of Antichrist after this)
- Nations will know God's blessing on Israel (Ezek 39: 23-29)
- People of Israel living securely ("Peace and Security" Ezek 38:14, 1 Thess 5:3) which is not the case now
- Great earthquake in the land of Israel (everything shakes in God's presence - mountains thrown down)
- Pestilence and blood - "I shall rain on him, a torrential rain, with hailstones, fire, and brimstone"
- Making firewood out of weapons (Ezek 39:10)
- Every man's sword will be against his brother (Ezek 38:21, Hag 2:21-22, Zech 14:13)

Chapter 40 – 48 – The Millennial Temple

Ezekiel is transported once again in a vision to Jerusalem where he is greeted by an angel with a measuring rod. The rod is to give him the actual dimensions of the Temple to come, but also measuring is a means of testing something to see if it is pleasing to God or not.[93] The angel tells him to remember and record everything he is shown because he is to share it with the whole house of Israel.

Right away we see that this is not the Jerusalem that the prophet knew, but a future restored Jerusalem. It was a high mountain with a city on the south of it. Mount Moriah or Zion could hardly be called a high mountain since it is surrounded by higher mountains. Evidently there has been a topographical change which does not take place until the Day of the Lord and the Millennial Reign.[94] Also the very detailed measurements of the Temple and all its courts and gates that is given in chapters 40-42, make it clear that it is much larger than the second Temple which was destroyed in 70 AD. This Temple cannot be built without changes in Jerusalem, which is likely why it was not attempted when the Second Temple was rebuilt.

A Literal Temple

Many Christians today interpret these passages non-literally and apply them to the church which they claim is now the Temple of God. However, this Replacement Theology view is unbiblical and false. The church has not replaced Israel and neither is it the Temple of God. The apostles of the Lord never taught that the church was a replacement for the physical Temple in Jerusalem. What they taught consistently and carefully was that the church is called to be a temple in the Spirit and not the Temple. The church is a spiritual

---

[93] Dan 5:27, 2 Kings 21:13
[94] Isaiah 1:2, Zech 14:10-11

house, but Ezekiel's Temple is a physical house. Furthermore, the Bible is clear that the Temple is to be restored by the Messiah when He comes.

"Then say to him, 'Thus says the LORD of hosts, "Behold, a man whose name is Branch, for He will branch out from where He is; and He will build the temple of the LORD. Yes, it is He who will build the temple of the LORD, and He who will bear the honor and sit and rule on His throne. Thus, He will be a priest on His throne, and the counsel of peace will be between the two offices."' Zech 6:12-13

The Branch is clearly Messiah whom it is said will bring the two offices together (king & priest) and sit on His Throne and be a priest on His Throne. He is the one who will build the Temple. This Temple will be the one which is outlined in these chapters of Ezekiel. It was also promised by many other prophesies such as Isaiah chapter 2 and Micah 4. Indeed, almost all the prophets spoke of the restoration of Jerusalem and the Mountain of God and all the nations coming up to Jerusalem during Messiah's Millennial reign to worship the God of Israel. At that time Jerusalem will be the capital of the earth and Ezekiel's Temple will stand on Mount Moriah. This Temple was also mentioned in Ezekiel chapter 37, after God promises to restore Israel to the land and bring them into the New Covenant in Messiah, He promises to "set His sanctuary in their midst forever" (37:26).

Why the Temple?
Christians today find the idea that Jesus is going to rebuild the Temple very hard to comprehend. To them it is back peddling. "Why would God do that," they say. Jesus has made the way and taken away sin by His sacrifice. Why would the Messiah bring back the physical Temple and even animal sacrifices? This is too much for them to accept since it appears to be going against Christian Teaching. Replacement Theology has so turned Christians against Biblical Judaism and the Temple in Jerusalem, that most view it as something that God was happy to do away with. In fact, they find it hard to understand why it was ever instituted. Jesus wept over its destruction, but they cheer. Some have even gone so far as to suggest that the God of the Old Testament was different than the Father of Jesus on account of the Levitical priesthood and the apparent "harshness" of some of the commands of Torah. However, the Bible is clear. This is not some small detail of the Kingdom of Christ. It is the high point, the crescendo, the fulfillment of the Scriptures. The Millennial Temple in Jerusalem is the focal point of His reign, the very seat of His Throne. Thus, false teaching and thinking about the Temple is the last stronghold of Replacement Theology which all of us must renounce to receive correct understanding on the age to come.

The difficulty we Christians have with the rebuilding of the Temple, has a lot to do with our understanding of Christ's Millennial reign, and our view of the purpose of animal sacrifices. Firstly, the Millennial reign is glossed over by most Bible teachers, if they believe in it at all. They generally would prefer to skip it and just go to the final state, where there is no longer an Israel or Temple but only Peter and pearly gates. However, this Augustinian thinking is at the root of the problem. The Millennial reign on earth is the Kingdom of Christ which we pray will soon come and for which we have given up everything to seek. There will be a remnant of nations to repopulate the earth after the Tribulation. Israel will be the head nation and Christ will rule from Jerusalem and a restored Temple with His Bride by His side. Yet there will still be sin, crying, pain, rebellion, and even death.[95] And there will still be unclean things that cannot be in the presence of God. The Levitical priesthood will be restored, but it will fulfill God's original intent and minister to the nations who will now have to go up to Jerusalem as Israel did in ancient times. So apparently there is still a need for the Temple, which underscores how little we understand of its significance and centrality to Biblical Judaism. Jesus loved the Temple calling it His Father's House. He also brought sacrifice there, unless you think that He went on Passover, Shavuot (Pentecost), and Sukkot (Tabernacles) emptyhanded in disobedience to Torah. The early church worshipped in the Temple every day and continually brought sacrifices there even though they knew Jesus was the Lamb of God who took away their sins. So, what did they know that we don't? And if Jesus had not wanted them to do that, then why did He not tell them to stay away.

Symbolic or Functional?
It is generally argued by Christians that animal sacrifices under Torah were symbolic and merely a teaching tool that pointed forward to the sacrifice of Messiah. If this is true, then it can also be argued that in the Millennium they will be like a memorial - a teaching tool pointing backwards to what Christ has done. But were the sacrifices merely symbolic or did they have a function in ancient Israel? Those who claim they were symbolic only, have a very skewed view of Temple worship. First of all, the Temple was at the center of Biblical Judaism which is why the Jews have mourned its loss the last 2000 years. Also, sacrifices were not begun by Moses when he constructed the Tabernacle. The patriarchs offered sacrifices regularly and considered them quite functional and necessary in their response to God. To suggest that all the sacrifices offered from the Tabernacle in the wilderness to the destruction of the Temple in 70AD were merely symbolic, is a testimony of the deep roots of Replacement Theology in the church. How could we ever think such as thing? On Yom Kippur if the High Priest failed in His ministry of sprinkling blood on the mercy seat the people would not be forgiven, and he would die. The scapegoat that went into the wilderness carried the sins of the people after hands were laid on him. We can say it was symbolic, but it was functional also. People could not come into the presence of God if they did not bring the prescribed sacrifice and if they brought a sick animal, it was offensive

---
[95] Zech 14:16-19, Is 65:20

to God. The spilling of the blood was not merely symbolic, it was necessary for forgiveness. This is the testimony of the book of Hebrews which does not say the sacrifices were merely symbolic. On the contrary, it says that without the shedding of blood there was no forgiveness in Torah.

"And according to the Law, one may almost say, all things are cleansed with blood, and without shedding of blood there is no forgiveness." Heb 8:22

If there had been no sacrifices, there would have been no forgiveness for the people. There were, of course, some sins that had no forgiveness in Torah, such as premeditated murder, but if there had been no sacrifices there would have been no forgiveness for anything. This would have rendered the covenant useless and God's promises to them null and void. I realize that many Christians already have such an attitude toward the old covenant, but herein lies the problem. This understanding is terribly wrong. The book of Hebrews does not teach that the Levitical sacrifices were symbolic. Consider the following:

"But when Christ appeared as a high priest of the good things to come, He entered through the greater and more perfect tabernacle, not made with hands, that is to say, not of this creation; and not through the blood of goats and calves, but through His own blood, He entered the holy place once for all, having obtained eternal redemption. For if the blood of goats and bulls and the ashes of a heifer <u>sprinkling those who have been defiled sanctify for the cleansing of the flesh</u>, how much more will the blood of Christ, who through the eternal Spirit offered Himself without blemish to God, cleanse your conscience from dead works to serve the living God?" Heb 9:11-14

What is being presented here is a contrast between what Christ has done and what the Levitical system did. Christ's sacrifice was only needed once. He went into the heavenly sanctuary and not the earthy one. His blood cleanses the conscience of the repentant believer and takes away the consciousness of sins. This is something the blood of bulls and goats could not do. They had to be offered repeatedly yet we are told that they did sanctify for the cleansing of the flesh of those who were defiled. In order for the people of Israel to fellowship with God in the Temple, there was a need for cleansing, forgiveness, and sanctification of the flesh. God's glory among them in the Holy of Holies required this.

The Glory Returns
Ezekiel is taken to the Eastern gate where he saw in a vision the glory of the God of Israel returning to the Millennial Temple. He is then lifted by the Spirit and taken to the inner court to see that the glory of the Lord had filled the House. Then he said, "One spoke to him from the House" which is clearly the Lord, yet the way it is worded may suggest that it is the Messiah speaking. This is the Millennial Temple which does not exist when Messiah comes in His glory but will be built by Him. Therefore, the glory that appears is not the Messiah's return, which is also in glory, but the Shekinah of the God of Israel. The

Lord declares that this is the place of His Throne and the soles of His feet where He will dwell among the sons of Jacob forever. Never again will it be defiled by the harlotries and defilements of Israel or the nations.

Ezekiel is again charged to describe the Temple and make it known to Israel that they may be ashamed of their iniquities. If they are ashamed, then he is to make known to them the design of the house with all its statutes and laws that they may do them.

Altar and Sacrifices
Immediately after the mention of the glory coming to the Millennial Temple, we are given the dimensions of the altar and how the Levitical priests (sons of Zadok) are to cleanse and sanctify it with blood and sacrifices. This is very difficult for Christians to understand since Christ is the Lamb of God who takes away the sin of the world. How can the Levitical system return in a Millennial Temple? They shake their heads in disbelief and say it cannot be. But there it is clearly in the Biblical text. Furthermore, there are many other passages that teach the same thing. The Messiah will build the Temple, anoint the Most Holy Place, from which He will reign over the earth with the Bride of Christ at His side. So, it must be settled in your mind that this is going to happen. The only question that matters is why? Why is the sacrifice of Jesus on the Cross not applied to the people on the earth in the Millennium? Let us consider what the answer might be.

The Temple & The Garden
First of all, we have concluded that the sacrifices of the Levitical priesthood were not symbolic but functional. They provided forgiveness for the people who trusted God and were a means of fellowshipping with Him. Secondly the Tabernacle and later the Temple were ordained by God to be His dwelling place among the Israelites. Of the Temple in Jerusalem the Lord proclaimed it would be

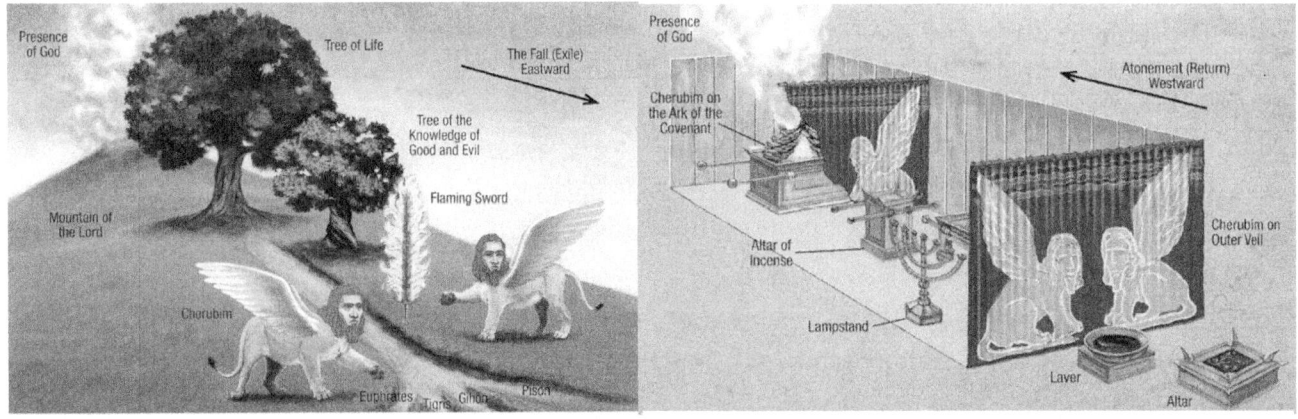

His resting place forever. Christians are predisposed to view the Temple as being about blood and sacrifices, but this is not the case. The glory of God filled the Holy of Holies and to come to the Altar was the closest a non-priest could get to the Shekinah. In a very real way, the Temple was like the garden of Eden. When mankind was driven from the Garden, the Cherubim were stationed at the gate on the East to guard the way to the Tree of Life and the Presence of God. Yet, Adam and His descendants were able to come to the entrance to worship and fellowship with God.[96] In the same way, the presence of God was in the Temple and the Cherubim were guarding the entrance. The priests were able to go into the holy place to minister before the Lord and they came out to minister to the people. All the Israelites were able to bring their offering and worship the Lord at the altar at the entrance to the Temple. In the Millennium, the nations will come to a more perfect Temple, which is the Throne of Messiah, to worship the Lord and be taught from Torah.

"Now it will come about that in the last days the mountain of the house of the LORD will be established as the chief of the mountains, and will be raised above the hills; and all the nations will stream to it. And many peoples will come and say, "Come, let us go up to the mountain of the LORD, to the house of the God of Jacob; that He may teach us concerning His ways and that we may walk in His paths." For the law will go forth from Zion and the word of the LORD from Jerusalem." Isaiah 2:1-3 Emphasis Mine

Mortal Bodies

"Now I say this, brethren, that flesh and blood cannot inherit the kingdom of God; nor does the perishable inherit the imperishable." 1 Cor 15:50

When the remnant of Israel comes to the Messiah during the Tribulation, they will enter the New Covenant, but they will enter the Millennium in mortal bodies. Also, the sheep and goat judgment of Matthew 25 concerns the survivors from the nations who have come through the Tribulation but are not Christians. They have escaped the mark of the beast and have shown great compassion in caring for persecuted Jews and probably also Christians – the brothers of Jesus. It is on this basis alone that they are told they have a place in the kingdom. They will populate the earth during the Millennium, but they will be in mortal bodies that have sin and corruption in them and cannot be in the presence of God's glory. Remember flesh and blood cannot inherit the heavenly kingdom and glory. They will be required to come to Jerusalem to the Millennial Temple to worship where they will be taught Torah by the Levitical priests and will be ruled over by a righteous Israel that walks in the New Covenant and the Davidic kingdom of Messiah. Nevertheless, they will not have eternal life. They missed the opportunity to be in Christ's body, since they lived through the period of the preaching of the gospel and did not seek Him. Therefore, the cleansing of His Blood is not offered to them. At the end of the Millennium,

---

[96] Gen 4:3-4, 16 (Notice they "brought" their offerings "to the Lord." Also, Cain "went out from the presence of the Lord."

all who are dead, including those who died during the Millennium, will be resurrected, and judged. It is also presumed that those who are alive of the nations at the end of the Millennium will enter a new earth in the same perfect state that Adam was in when He was created.

It is important to note that the Millennium Reign is not heaven, It is the kingdom of heaven on earth, but it is not actually heaven where God Almighty dwells. For those who are not immortal there will still be death, crying, pain and rebellion to deal with. When the final state comes all these things will be done away with and the new heavens and earth will be one.

Israel in the Millennium

"It shall be the prince's part to provide the burnt offerings, the grain offerings and the drink offerings, at the feasts, on the new moons and on the sabbaths, at all the appointed feasts of the house of Israel; he shall provide the sin offering, the grain offering, the burnt offering and the peace offerings, to make atonement for the house of Israel." Ezek 45:17

It is very clear that Israel in the Millennium, although reconciled with the Messiah, and having the heart change of the New Covenant, are still required to bring the appropriate sacrifices for atonement. This is difficult for us Christians to grasp, especially because so many have been indoctrinated to think of the sacrifices as the Old Covenant that is done away with. But if we read the passages on the New Covenant carefully, we understand that for Israel, the Law and ordinances of God are not done away with but are written on the heart. Consider what Ezekiel said earlier:

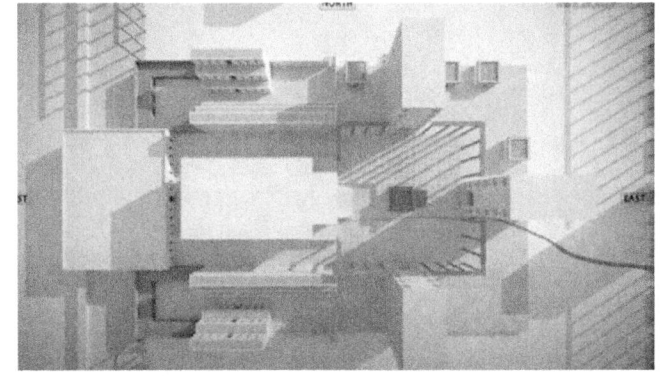

"Moreover, I will give you a new heart and put a new spirit within you; and I will remove the heart of stone from your flesh and give you a heart of flesh. I will put My Spirit within you and cause you to walk in My statutes, and you will be careful to observe My ordinances. You will live in the land that I gave to your forefathers; so you will be My people, and I will be your God." Ezek 36:26-28

This is Israel in the Millennium. The land is renewed, the people are renewed, the covenant is renewed, the Temple is renewed, the priesthood is renewed, and the earth is renewed. However, they are in mortal bodies that do not have eternal life and are incapable of being near the glory of God without atonement and the cleansing of the flesh. For this God has made provision through the Temple sacrifices and offerings. It seems clear then, that although they have the Spirit, they do not have the eternal redemption that is offered to us in Christ. We who have received this redemption in His blood, when we get our new heavenly bodies, we will be with Him where He is, forever. Thus, we inherit the heavenly kingdom and not just the earthly.

The Prince

Since we already know that Jesus reigns over the earth from Jerusalem and the Millennial Temple, which is said to be the Throne of God, it is difficult to imagine that the Prince of the Jewish people mentioned here is the Messiah. First of all, he is not presented as the King of Kings and Lord of Lords, but as a representative of the people. He must bring sacrifices for himself as well as the nation and he is worshiping with them. Also, he is given a portion of land outside of the holy allotment for the priests, which would make no sense at all, and there is mention of him possibly having children. Some have suggested that David Himself will be Israel's king in the Millennium. It seems clear that David will be resurrected to play his millennial role, yet it is hard to see him operating in this position in a glorified body. Who then is this Prince that is mentioned here? Incidentally, Ezekiel does not use the word Melech for king but the word Nasi, which today is translated president, and in ancient times was used for the leader of the Sanhedrin. Perhaps this is an indication that this is a leader of Israel that is chosen by Messiah or the apostles who are told they will judge the twelve tribes during this time.[97]

Water From the Temple

For centuries the church, having lost its Jewish roots, and believing in Replacement Theology (the church has replaced Israel), interpreted this prophesy of Ezekiel in a "spiritual" sense and applied it to God's presence in the church. Many times, throughout the years I have heard about the river of God flowing and reaching the angles, then the knees, and then the waist. While it is acceptable, I suppose, to use it in this way, we must not steal it from its context. A river flowed out of Eden and broke into four rivers. Once again, a river will flow from the Millennial Temple and flow down into the Dead Sea which will come to life and be teeming with fish. It will likely continue until it reaches the Red Sea. On its banks will be all kinds of trees for food that will bear fruit every month and their leaves will be healing for the nations. Notice that in the final state, in the New Jerusalem, there will also be a river flowing from the Throne of God, and it will also have the Tree of Life on its banks bearing twelve kinds of fruit every month and its leaves are also said to be for the healing or health of the nations.

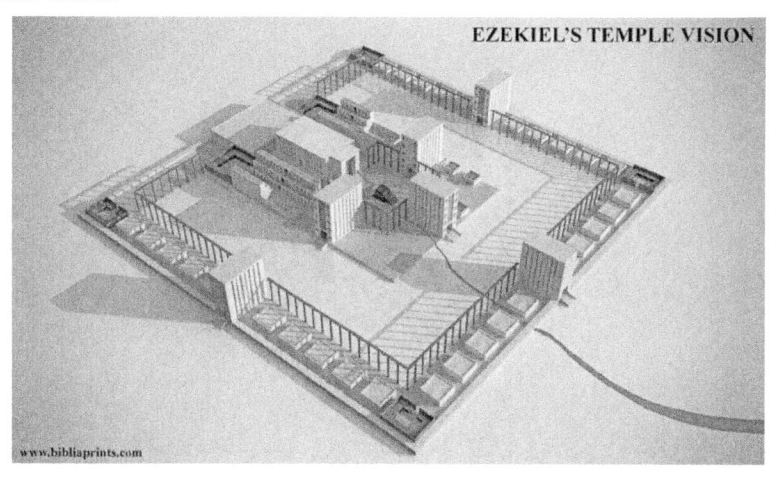

---

[97] Mt 19:28

Division of the Land

The book of Ezekiel ends with the division of the land between the twelve tribes with a holy portion for the Lord and the Priests which is about 9 miles long from East to West and about 3 ½ miles wide. Jerusalem and the Temple are in the center of the Holy Portion and the city has 3 gates on all 4 sides. And the name of the city is called, Yahweh Shammah – Yahweh is there.

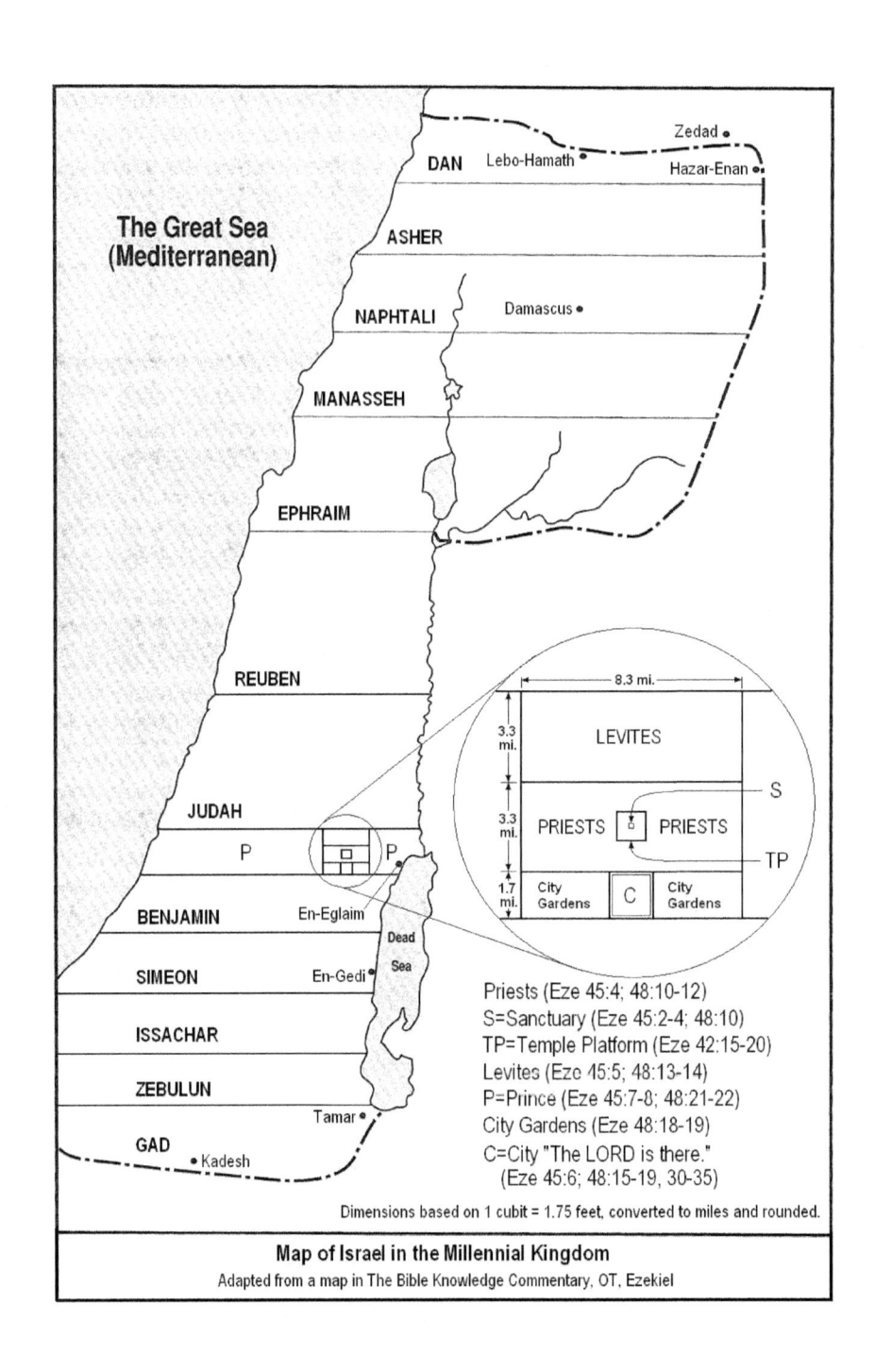

Map of Israel in the Millennial Kingdom
Adapted from a map in The Bible Knowledge Commentary, OT, Ezekiel

Priests (Eze 45:4; 48:10-12)
S=Sanctuary (Eze 45:2-4; 48:10)
TP=Temple Platform (Eze 42:15-20)
Levites (Eze 45:5; 48:13-14)
P=Prince (Eze 45:7-8; 48:21-22)
City Gardens (Eze 48:18-19)
C=City "The LORD is there."
(Eze 45:6; 48:15-19, 30-35)

Dimensions based on 1 cubit = 1.75 feet, converted to miles and rounded.

Notes

Haggai

Haggai and Zechariah were both prophesying around 520 BC. The people had come back to the land but not with a full heart for God. The foundation of the Temple had been laid in 536 BC, but the work had been abandoned due to opposition from the surrounding peoples. Haggai and Zechariah were raised up by God to call the people to repentance and to finish the work which had begun on the Temple. The response was immediate, and the Temple was finished under Zerubbabel (516 B.C.).

Chapter 1- Paneled Houses

The people had concluded because of the opposition against them that the time had not come to rebuild the Temple. Haggai admonished them saying, "Is it time for you yourselves to live in paneled houses while this house lies desolate." The real issue was not the opposition to the building of the Temple but the complacency in their own hearts. Interestingly, the people of Israel, though they are back in the land today, have the same attitude toward the Temple Mount. Also, from Haggai chapter 1, we see that the people were not blessed, indeed their work was cursed, because they were disobedient to the Lord by not building the Temple. Therefore, the issue was not one of timing but of obedience. This is often true in our lives as well. We have lots of excuses for not doing the right thing. Opposition, or the fact that it is hard, is no excuse. We need to rely on God and obey his will.

Verses 12-15

Zerubbabel the governor and Joshua the high priest and all the people were stirred up by the words of Haggai the prophet and they showed reverence to the Lord and to His word. Therefore, they began to work on the house of God is Jerusalem and we are told that this work began on the 24th day of the 6th month in the 2nd year of Darius the king.

Chapter 2:1-9 – The Latter Glory

When the Temple was being built under Zerubbabel, many of the older men who had seen the previous Solomonic Temple began to weep because they realized it would pale in comparison. But Haggai the prophet comforts them with the word of the Lord and the promise that during the Day of the Lord, when He would shake the heavens and the earth, that the Temple built then would be far more glorious. He promised that, instead of all the opposition they were getting from the nations, that in That Day, the nations would bring all their wealth up to Jerusalem to rebuild the Temple. "The silver is mine, and the gold is mine, declares the Lord of hosts."

The author of Hebrews quotes verse 6 to reaffirm that at the end of the age the Lord will shake not only the earth but also the heavens. Though this shaking has begun in many ways, it will be severe during the Tribulation period – the Day of the Lord. This shaking of the heavens is the cosmic signs mentioned by all the prophets and by Jesus Himself.[98] However it does not merely speak of the shaking of the physical heavens but also the judgment of the spiritual beings.[99]

Verses 10-19

On the 24th day of the 9th month it appears the foundation of the Temple was laid. Haggai spoke to the people reminding them how the Lord had cursed their work and their produce because of their disobedience. But from this day forward the Lord would pour out blessings on them.

Verses 20-23

The word of the Lord came a second time to Haggai on this date to encourage the governor Zerubbabel, who undoubtedly felt intimidated by the threats of his enemies around Judah who wanted to have the work cease. He is to know that Yahweh Sabaoth (Yahweh of Armies) will overthrow the kingdoms and rulers of the nations by the sword of each other. He is not to fear them because the Lord has chosen him, and he will make him like a signet ring. When a king used his signet ring it was a seal of the highest authority in the land. Thus, the Lord is telling Zerubbabel that he will be like His signet ring in the midst of these nations. He has divine authority and recognition.

---

[98] Joel 2:30-31, Mt 24:29
[99] Isaiah 24:21

Notes

Zechariah

Chapter 1:1-6

About a month after Haggai's first message, Zechariah begins with a call to the people to repent and return to the Lord and not be like their fathers who disobeyed the prophets and wouldn't listen. Then he receives a series of eight visions which speak of the restoration of Zion and the Temple, judgment on Gentile nations that have continued to mistreat Judah, and God's promised purification of the people of Judah.

Verses 7-17 - Horses Among the Myrtle Trees
They are patrolling the earth and seeing the nations at ease while Jerusalem is in ruins. God is angry with the nations who have furthered the disaster and promises to restore Zion and the House of the Lord.

"Therefore thus says the LORD, 'I will return to Jerusalem with compassion; My house will be built in it,' declares the LORD of hosts, 'and a measuring line will be stretched over Jerusalem.' Again, proclaim, saying, 'Thus says the LORD of hosts, "My cities will again overflow with prosperity, and the LORD will again comfort Zion and again choose Jerusalem."'" Zech 1:16-17

Verses 18-21 - The Four Horns and Four Craftsmen
A vision of four horns and four craftsmen that will remove them. The horns represent the strength or power of the kingdoms that scattered Israel, Judah, and Jerusalem. These nations will be terrified and thrown down by the Lord.

Chapter 2 - Man with a Measuring Line
Zechariah saw a man with a measuring line measuring Jerusalem. Then an angel gave him the word concerning Jerusalem whose walls were broken down.

"'Jerusalem will be inhabited without walls because of the multitude of men and cattle within it. For I,' declares the LORD, 'will be a wall of fire around her, and I will be the glory in her midst.'" Zech 2:4-5

The word is that Jerusalem will once again be inhabited without walls because there will be so many people in it. This is fulfilled in our day. The city is much larger and is controlled by the remnant of Israel that has come back from all the nations.

Verses 6-13 are clearly referring to the end of the age and the Millennial Reign of Messiah when He has restored Jerusalem and Judah after bringing judgment on the nations that plundered them, since they are the apple of His eye. He promises to come and dwell among them and once again chose Jerusalem. All flesh is told to be silent since the Lord is coming out of His holy habitation to pour out His wrath on the nations.[100]

Joshua as imagined by Guillaume Rouille, from his 1553 work

Chapter 3:1-7 - Cleansing of Joshua the High Priest

Zechariah saw Joshua standing next to the angel of Yahweh and satan next to him accusing the High Priest of uncleanness, as he accuses all of us. But the angel rebukes him saying, "Yahweh rebuke you satan. Indeed, Yahweh who has chosen Jerusalem rebuke you. Is this not a brand plucked from the fire?" Now Joshua had filthy garments on, and the angel ordered that clean clothes be put on him and for him to be robed in his priestly robes. This represents his sins and iniquity being removed. Thus, the accusations of satan are invalidated. Then the angel admonishes Joshua to walk in the ways of God and perform His service, and he will govern His house and his courts and have free access before the Lord.

Verses 8-10 - The Branch

"Now listen, Joshua the high priest, you and your friends who are sitting in front of you—indeed they are men who are a symbol, for behold, I am going to bring in My servant the Branch."

This prophecy looks to the future and the work of the Messiah. Joshua and the men with him are symbols of what the Branch, the Messiah, is going to do. Joshua is a type of Messiah who will both be the King and the High Priest. This typology appears again in Chapter 6, when a symbolic crown is placed on Joshua who has the same name as the Messiah (Yeshua).[101] Then there is a stone set before Joshua with seven eyes which represent the Spirit of God who looks throughout the earth.[102] The Lord will write a description on the stone and the iniquity of the nation will be removed in one day. This will be fulfilled in the Millennial reign of Christ when the nation receives their Messiah who was pierced for them. Thus, they will enter the kingdom, and each will sit under his vine and fig tree with no one to make them afraid anymore.

Chapter 4 - The Golden Lampstand and the Olive Trees

This is a picture of the Golden Menorah which belonged in the Temple being supplied with oil. The message is "not by might nor by power, but by My Spirit says the Lord of Hosts."

---

[100] Is 2:21
[101] Joshua is the English translation of Yehoshua or Yeshua which means Yahweh saves.
[102] Zechariah 4:10

This means that it will not be human strength and power that rebuilds the Temple but the Spirit of God who accomplishes the task through Zerubbabel (chapter 4:10), with the aid of the two prophets represented by the two olive trees. Those two prophets are undoubtedly Zechariah and Haggai who were instrumental in encouraging the work to be done.[103] The revealing of the vision to Zechariah was obviously to encourage him to continue bringing the word to Zerubbabel and the builders. His hands have started the foundation and they will finish it. What is this great mountain of opposition? It will become a plain before Zerubbabel. He will bring forth the capstone with shouts of, "favor, favor to it."

Chapter 5 – The Flying Scroll
This is a vision of the word of the Lord going forth to purge the land. It is a word of judgment going forth, which brings a curse that will enter the house of the thief and the one who swears falsely.

The Woman in the Basket (Ephah)
The woman who represents wickedness is placed in a basket (Ephah)[104] and brought by two women with stork wings to Babylon where a house is prepared for her and where she will be set on her own pedestal. The flying scroll purges the land, and the wickedness is put in a basket and taken away. The women are not angels. They are the servants of wickedness, and their wings are from an unclean bird. The Lord puts the wickedness of the land in a basket with a lead covering and sends it to Babylon where at the end of the age it will come to fruition. Babylon represents the wickedness of the nations and the four empires that conquer and enslave Israel. It is also the place where all idolatry originated with the tower of Babel. It is the home of wickedness. Its end-time manifestation is the kingdom of antichrist with the false prophet religious system centered in Rome (Mystery Babylon) riding on top of it.

Chapter 6 - The Four Chariots
This vision likely has to do with God's judgment on Babylon and bringing peace through the Persians so that the work could be accomplished.

Four chariots were going out from between the two mountains which were of brass. These chariots are said to be the four spirits of heaven that are before the Lord of the earth. These are likely the princes of

"Four Chariots Zechariah 6" by Texas artist Donna Johnson

---

[103] The apostle John was shown that the two witnesses were prophets and the same symbolism of the two trees was used. In this case, it is Moses and Elijah being referred to. They also finish their ministries to Israel when the Holy Place is desecrated a final time.
[104] Basket for measuring grain.

the four empires that dominate Israel as revealed in Daniel.[105] The mountains may be the two mountains that encompass the Temple and its rituals – Mt Moriah and the Mount of Olives. The empires are represented by the chariots pulled by different colored horses. The red horses are likely Babylon, the black horses Media-Persia, the white horses Greece, and the strong spotted horses Rome. The red horses are not mentioned again since Babylon has been defeated by the black horses representing Persia. Then the white horses of Greece go to the North and defeat the black horses. Thus, the horses that went north appeased the wrath of the Lord.

The Crowning of Joshua
Then the prophet is told to take a collection from certain exiles and make a crown and set it on Joshua the High Priest. Though this is a word to Joshua to encourage him, it is more importantly a prophecy concerning the Messiah to come, the Branch, who will have the same name (Yeshua). This Branch will be King and Priest on His Throne and in Him the two offices will be combined. This Messiah will build the Millennial Temple and all the Gentile nations will come and help in the project. This is the same message of Haggai.

Chapter 7 – The Fast That Pleases God
On the 4th year of Darius, on the 4th day of Chislev, the word of the Lord came to Zechariah regarding two officials from Bethel who had been sent to the priests and prophets to inquire if they should continue the fast of the 5th month – the 9th of AV. The prophet was told to speak to all the people the following response:

'When you fasted and mourned in the fifth and seventh months these seventy years, was it actually for Me that you fasted? When you eat and drink, do you not eat for yourselves and do you not drink for yourselves? Are not these the words which the LORD proclaimed by the former prophets, when Jerusalem was inhabited and prosperous along with its cities around it, and the Negev and the foothills were inhabited?'" Zech 7:5-7

The people are reminded of all their rebellion against the Lord and the prophets who warned them over and over, that religious rituals without true justice, were the reason He punished them so severely. Dispense true justice and practice kindness toward one another, they are told. And do not oppress the widow, the orphan, or the stranger. Then their fasts will be meaningful to the Lord.

Chapter 8 – Restoration and Peace Promised
The Lord of Hosts, or armies, says that He is exceedingly zealous for Zion. Indeed, with great wrath He is zealous for her. He will return to Zion and dwell in the midst of Jerusalem. Then it will be called the City of Truth and the Mountain of the Lord the Holy Mountain. Old men and old women will sit in the streets and the sound of boys and girls playing will

---
[105] Daniel Chapter 2 & 7

be heard. Then comes the astonishing statement that nothing will be too difficult to the restored remnant.

These beautiful words were only partially fulfilled with the return of the remnant from Babylon. They will reach their fullness in our era as the Lord has restored the remnant of Israel from all the nations and established them in their homeland. The Lord is turning their hearts back to Him. The time is soon coming when the zeal of the Lord of Hosts will once again choose Jerusalem and make His presence known in the earth as the Messiah begins His reign. But first His wrath will be poured out on the nations who oppose His people and His holy city.

The Lord will gather all His remnant from the east and the west. This is clearly a reference to what has happened in our day. They will live in the midst of Jerusalem and the Lord will be their God and they will be His people. No longer will He treat them as He did when He was angry with them. He will do good to Jerusalem and to the house of Judah. And just as the house of Israel and Judah were once a curse to the nations, the Lord will save them and make them a blessing instead. The fasting of the 4th, 5th, 7th, and the 10th months, which all have to do with the destruction of Jerusalem and the Temple, will no longer be sad times but joyful and cheerful feasts for the house of Judah. All the nations will come to worship and seek the favor of the Lord in Jerusalem during the Millennium. Ten men from the nations will grab the garment of a Jew saying, "Let us go with you for we have heard that God is with you."

Nevertheless, amidst these great promises of joy and gladness, the people are reminded once again to speak the truth to one another and judge with truth for peace in their gates. They must not devise evil in their hearts, nor love perjury, for these are the things the Lord hates.

Chapter 9:1-7 - Word of the Lord Against Neighboring Places

"The burden of the word of the LORD is against the land of Hadrach, with Damascus as its resting place (for the eyes of men, especially of all the tribes of Israel, are toward the LORD)..."

Hadrach seems to be a place around Damascus in Syria. Hamath is also mentioned. It is a city north of Damascus called Hama today. Also, Tyre and Sidon in Lebanon are mentioned. Nebuchadnezzar destroyed Tyre but he was unable to destroy the Island city which remained even though he was there for 13 years. Alexander the Great however, finished it off in 322BC.

Alexander fighting Persian king Darius III. From Alexander Mosaic of Pompeii, Naples, Naples National Archaeological Museum

Sidon was beaten into submission by the Persian King Artaxerxes,[106] and subsequently taken over by Babylon and Greece.

Also spoken against are the Philistine cities of Ashkelon, Ashdod, Ekron, and Gaza. Though they were conquered by Nebuchadnezzar, and some of them destroyed and rebuilt by a remnant of survivors and migrants, they were finished off by Alexander the great. Alexander had the king of Gaza dragged through the streets.[107] Ashkelon was abandoned and the whole area was brought under Jewish control, as was the remnant of Edom, during the Hasmonean era. Thus, the prophecies were fulfilled and many of these people converted to Judaism and blended into Israel.

Verse 8 seems to be speaking about the army of Alexander that will come and fulfill the previous verses, but he will pass through Israel and do no harm because the Lord will make His camp around His House – the Temple in Jerusalem. But then it seems to suggest that the Greeks will return later. This occurred during the Ptolemaic and Seleucid wars when Israel was caught between them. And of course, the Antichrist prototype, Antiochus Epiphanes, desecrated the Temple and was defeated by the Maccabees. The nation had peace for about 100 years until Herod, who was empowered by Rome. Then of course the Messiah came, and the next verse describes His entry into Jerusalem on what the church has called Palm Sunday.

"Rejoice greatly, O daughter of Zion! Shout in triumph, O daughter of Jerusalem! Behold, your king is coming to you; He is just and endowed with salvation, humble, and mounted on a donkey, even on a colt, the foal of a donkey." Zech 9:9

Verse 10 speaks of the Millennial kingdom when Messiah begins to reign as the King of Kings and Lord of Lords. As with all the Messianic prophecies, the ministry of the suffering servant (His first coming) and the Reigning King (second coming) appear together and must be discerned.

Public domain. From the book: Paintings in sacred and Church history: the Greatest holidays of Orthodoxy. St. Petersburg 1876

"I will cut off the chariot from Ephraim and the horse from Jerusalem; and the bow of war will be cut off. And He will speak peace to the nations; and His dominion will be from sea to sea, and from the River to the ends of the earth." Zech 9:10

---

[106] See Ezekiel 28, Pg. 154
[107] Interestingly, Palestinians do this as vile punishment in Gaza today.

Verses 11-17 – Victory over the Greeks

After briefly mentioning the Messiah - the ultimate Shepherd of Israel who will save them from the final manifestation of Antiochus Epiphanes (Antichrist), these verses return to the Maccabean revolt of 168BC. Antiochus forbid the people to practice any form of Judaism, including circumcision, and he murdered all who did. Judas Maccabee and his father and brothers and a brave remnant, fled the city and hid out in the Judean hills. God says that on account of His blood covenant with them, he would deliver their prisoners from the waterless pit – likely empty cisterns. The faithful remnant who had hope could return to the fortress Zion and be aroused against the sons of Greece. The Lord Himself would fight on their behalf and restore twice as much to them. The Lord God will save them on that day like a faithful shepherd saves his flock. How else could this small group of untrained soldiers defeat the army of Antiochus unless the Lord of Armies was fighting for them? However, God said that they would not only prevail against the Greeks, but He would restore twice as much to them, by giving them their own kingdom for many years.

"They will sparkle in his land like jewels in a crown. How attractive and beautiful they will be!" Zech 9:16-17

Chapter 9:1-5 – False Shepherds

The Lord says He is the provider of rain to everyone and plants of the field. It is Him they need to seek and ask for these things. Idols give false signs and diviners false visions and false hope. Therefore, the people wander oppressed like sheep.
The Lord says his anger burns against their leaders and He will punish them and He Himself will shepherd His flock – the people of Judah. From Judah will come the cornerstone which is, of course, the Messiah. The tent peg is the foundation and support of the tent which is the same idea as the cornerstone. From Judah will come all the rulers and the Lord will give them victory. The passage looks to the future fulfillment at the end of the age.

Verses 6-12 – The Future Restoration

These verses, although they refer somewhat to what Israel would face with the Greeks, are more specifically directed toward the end of the age. This is very typical of the writings of the prophets since it was all future to them. Therefore, they often made no distinction.

We know these verses are future because God said that, even though he would scatter them to the nations, they would remember Him in the distant lands and return. The exile is Babylon, although it was the beginning of the diaspora of Israel, was not the scattering that is mentioned here. That happened under the Romans in 70 AD and onward. But the Lord says He will bring them back from all the places He scattered them, and they will be very numerous. However, they will first pass through the sea of trouble which will be no more. The Lord will bring back the remnant of Israel in the last days, and He will also bring them back to Himself, and in His Name they will live securely.

Chapter 11- The Flock is Doomed

The chapter begins with a message of doom to the land. The Cedars of Lebanon and the Oaks of Bashan are symbolic of the glory of the nation that is yet to be destroyed. It could also be referring to false leaders. Another likely meaning is that the invaders will come from the north as the Romans did and devastate the land. This destruction will come in the future, and it is connected with Israel's rebellion and rejection of the True Shepherd the Messiah Yeshua (Jesus), who figures prominently in the rest of the book.

Many believe that Zechariah is told to shepherd a flock doomed to slaughter as some sort of prophetic picture of what is coming. But it is not at all clear in the text that the prophet is the one being spoken to. It could be the Lord speaking to the Messiah to pasture his flock (feed His sheep) doomed to slaughter.

After speaking of the false shepherds who always used the flock to enrich themselves, the Lord says He will no longer have compassion on the people of the land.

"For I will no longer have compassion for the inhabitants of the land," declares the LORD; "but behold, I will let the people fall, each into another's power and into the power of his king; and they will crush the land, and I will not rescue them from their power." Zech 11:6

God says that He let them fall into the hands of another and into the power of his king. This is not speaking of some internal struggle among the Jews, because it says they will crush the land and the Lord will not rescue them from his power. Consider how the NIV translates it:

"For I will no longer have pity on the people of the land," declares the Lord. "I will give everyone into the hands of their neighbors and their king. They will devastate the land, and I will not rescue anyone from their hands." Zech 11:6 NIV

This is clearly when God gave the nation over to the devastation of the Roman empire.

"So I shepherded the flock marked for slaughter, particularly the oppressed of the flock. Then I took two staffs and called one Favor and the other Union, and I shepherded the flock. In one month I got rid of the three shepherds." Zech 11:7-8 NIV

The Good Shepherd[108] began to shepherd the flock of Israel, particularly the oppressed of the flock. How fitting this is for the ministry of Jesus. Then He took two staffs in His hand – one called Favor and the other Union. These staffs represented the favor of God's covenant with the people and the other the union of the nation.

---

[108] John 10

The three shepherds the Good Shepherd got rid of were likely the Scribes, the Pharisees, and the Sadducees. These were the corrupt leaders of Israel that were removed when the Romans destroyed Jerusalem.

"The flock detested me, and I grew weary of them and said, 'I will not be your shepherd. Let the dying die, and the perishing perish. Let those who are left eat one another's flesh.'" Zech 11:9 NIV

The Jewish leaders hated and rejected Jesus and He had no choice but to abandon them to the destruction as was prophesied.

"Jerusalem, Jerusalem, who kills the prophets and stones those who have been sent to her! How often I wanted to gather your children together, the way a hen gathers her chicks under her wings, and you were unwilling. Behold, your house is being left to you desolate! For I say to you, from now on you will not see Me until you say, 'BLESSED IS THE ONE WHO COMES IN THE NAME OF THE LORD!'" Mt 33:37-39

"And I took my staff Favor and cut it in pieces, to break my covenant which I had made with all the peoples. So it was broken on that day, and so the afflicted of the flock who were watching me realized that it was the word of the LORD." Zech 11:10-11

And so it was that God took His favor and the blessing of His covenant away from Israel and they were driven from their land and scattered throughout the nations, until the time of the promised restoration when they would be restored and unified in their ancient homeland.

"And I said to them, 'If it is good in your sight, give me my wages; but if not, never mind!' So they weighed out thirty shekels of silver as my wages. Then the LORD said to me, 'Throw it to the potter, that magnificent price at which I was valued by them.' So I took the thirty shekels of silver and threw them to the potter in the house of the LORD. Then I cut in pieces my second staff Union, to break the brotherhood between Judah and Israel." Zech 11:12-14

This passage details the betrayal of Jesus by Judas Iscariot for a measly 30 pieces of silver. The leaders of Israel paid this money for Jesus and thus they valued Him. The money was not put in the treasury but was used to buy the Field of Blood – the Potter's Field.

"Then when Judas, who had betrayed Him, saw that He had been condemned, he felt remorse and returned the thirty pieces of silver to the chief priests and elders, saying, "I

have sinned by betraying innocent blood." But they said, "What is that to us? You shall see to it yourself!" And he threw the pieces of silver into the temple sanctuary and left; and he went away and hanged himself. The chief priests took the pieces of silver and said, "It is not lawful to put them in the temple treasury, since it is money paid for blood." And they conferred together and with the money bought the Potter's Field as a burial place for strangers. For this reason that field has been called the Field of Blood to this day. Then that which was spoken through Jeremiah the prophet was fulfilled: "AND THEY TOOK THE THIRTY PIECES OF SILVER, THE PRICE OF THE ONE WHOSE PRICE HAD BEEN SET by the sons of Israel; AND THEY GAVE THEM FOR THE POTTER'S FIELD, JUST AS THE LORD HAD DIRECTED ME." Mt 27:3-10

Matthew seems to create confusion when he says that Jeremiah spoke this prophecy. However, it is likely that he had both Zechariah 11, and Jeremiah 19 in mind, since both passages are about the same period when the Lord will make the Valley of Hinnom the Valley of Slaughter, when the city of Jerusalem is destroyed. This happened in 70AD. It could also be speaking of the slaughter of the Day of the Lord as additional fulfillment.[109]

Hakeldama - Field of blood in the Hinnom Valley

The ancients divided the Tanakh into three parts, The Law, the Prophets, and the Writings, and in the rabbinical order of the books, Jeremiah was normally first. Thus, it was acceptable to refer to the entire body of the prophets as Jeremiah. In fact, Christ Himself designated the third body of the Tanakh, the Writings, as the Psalms, since that is the first book. Also, in many places where Zechariah is quoted from in the New Testament his name is not mentioned.[110] It merely says, "What was spoken by the prophet," or "The Scripture says," or "It is written." Another example of this literary practice of the era is Mark 1:2-3.

"… just as it is written in Isaiah the prophet: 'BEHOLD I AM SENDING MY MESSENGER BEFORE YOU, WHO WILL PREPARE YOUR WAY; THE VOICE OF ONE CALLING OUT IN THE WILDERNESS, 'PREPARE THE WAY OF THE LORD.'" MK 1;2-3

Mark quotes Isaiah and Malachi but only mentions the better-known prophet.

Another issue that must be resolved regarding the Field of Blood is who bought it. Matthew says the Jewish leaders, but the apostle Peter says Judas did.[111] What appears to have happened, is that Judas made the deal for the property and could not finalize it because of

---
[109] Joel 3:2
[110] Mt 21:4-5, 26-31, John 12:12-15, 19-37
[111] Acts 1:18

the Sabbath. However, he then had a change of heart when he saw what happened to Jesus and threw it back at the Jewish leaders. They then went and finished the deal. The field became a burial place for strangers.

Verses 15-17 – The Worthless Shepherd
Since the Good Shepherd has been rejected, God says He will raise up a worthless shepherd worse than the others. He will not care at all for the people but will use and abuse them. Though this could be referring to the corruption of the Hasmoneans and later Herod and the Romans, it is undoubtedly aimed at the false Messiah or Antichrist that will deceive the Jews at the end of the age. Consider what Jesus said to the Jewish leaders.

"I have come in My Father's name, and you do not receive Me; if another comes in his own name, you will receive him." John 5:43

Chapter 12 – All the Nations Against Jerusalem
The theme of the Day of the Lord comes to the fore in the closing chapters. So far, the Greek period up until the coming of Messiah has been outlined for us. Now there is a jump to the end of the age and the final salvation of Israel.

As the end of age approaches, Jerusalem will be like a heavy stone for all the peoples. We are living in the time when these events have begun to happen. For half a century, nations have been trying to advance the so called "Peace Process" by dividing Jerusalem and they have all failed. Indeed, we can say that they have been injured as a result. After many years leading the charge the United States is now divided itself. Yet, during the Tribulation period (last 3 ½ years of the age) all the nations will lay siege to Jerusalem and the Lord Himself will enter into Judgment with them.[112] It will not be like the 1st Century when God allowed them to be defeated and scattered. This time He will fight for them and even the weakest will be as David – a mighty warrior. Yet they will suffer greatly, and the majority will perish. But the Lord will rescue a remnant and pour out His Spirit on them. The Messiah Himself will deliver the remnant and destroy all the nations that have come against Jerusalem.[113]

"I will pour out on the house of David and on the inhabitants of Jerusalem, the Spirit of grace and of supplication, so that they will look on Me whom they have pierced; and they will mourn for Him, as one mourns for an only son, and they will weep bitterly over Him like the bitter weeping over a firstborn. In that day there will be great mourning in Jerusalem, like the mourning of Hadadrimmon in the plain of Megiddo." Zech 12:10-11

These beautiful verses give us great detail of the reconciliation of Israel during the Day of the Lord Tribulation. When the Antichrist is revealed, the remnant of Israel will come to

---
[112] Joel 3:2
[113] Rev 19:11-19, Is 63:1-6

their senses, and repent of their great apostasy. Then they will turn to the Messiah and see the one they have pierced. They text says they will look on Me, which means they not only acknowledge Him as the Messiah but as God Himself. There will be a time of national mourning like that which took place over Josiah when he was slain by Pharoah Neco in the valley of Megiddo. The Messiah Himself will deliver them and be reconciled to them. Jesus referred to this mourning also. He seems to say that it is not only in Israel but around the world.

"And then the sign of the Son of Man will appear in the sky, and then all the tribes of the earth will mourn, and they will see the SON OF MAN COMING ON THE CLOUDS OF THE SKY with power and great glory." Mt 24:30

Chapter 13 – Strike the Shepherd
Verse 1 is a continuation of the spirit of grace and supplication that is poured out on the remnant of Israel. The fountain for sin and impurity is Christ Himself and the New Covenant in His blood.

Verses 2-6
The Lord will cut off the idol from the land and their names will never again be mentioned. He will also remove the prophets and the unclean spirit. Idols and false prophets will not be tolerated in the Millennium. If a prophet dares to speak in the name of the Lord, even his parents will be horrified and "pierce him through" (kill him). And contrary to the behavior of false prophets at that time who put on hairy robes drawing attention to themselves, they will be so ashamed in that day that they will try to disguise themselves claiming to be a farmer or a slave. Then comes verse 6 which appears to have a double meaning.

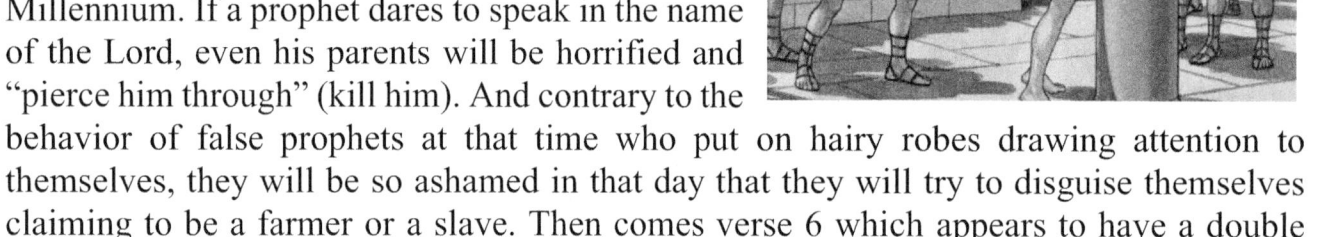

"And one will say to him, 'What are these wounds between your arms?' Then he will say, 'Those with which I was wounded in the house of my friends.' Zech 13:6

It is generally thought that this verse is referring to the habit of false prophets of cutting themselves.[114] In other words, even though the prophet may deny his identity someone may say to him, "What about the scars or wounds on your body?" Then the man would say that he had received the wounds through a fight or an accident at a friend's house. Anything but admit that he was prophesying.

---
[114] 1 Kings 18:28

Though this meaning is likely, there is a double meaning here and a clear play on words. Jesus, who was the True Prophet, foretold by Moses and all the prophets, was rejected by the nation as a false prophet and beaten and pierced. He continues to display the scars. Indeed, just a few verses back in chapter 12, it is said that they will look on Me whom <u>they have pierced or pierced through</u>. Furthermore, the next verse (verse 7) is clearly about the rejection of Messiah a fact to which Jesus Himself testified.

"And Jesus said to them, 'You will all fall away, because it is written: 'I WILL STRIKE THE SHEPHERD, AND THE SHEEP WILL BE SCATTERED. But after I am raised, I will go ahead of you to Galilee.' But Peter said to Him, 'Even if they all fall away, yet I will not!' And Jesus said to him, 'Truly I say to you, that this very night, before a rooster crows twice, you yourself will deny Me three times.' But Peter repeatedly said insistently, 'Even if I have to die with You, I will not deny You!' And they all were saying the same thing as well.'" Mark 14:27-31

Verses 7-9

"Awake, sword, against My Shepherd, and against the Man, My Associate," Declares the LORD of armies."

The Messiah is here referred by Yahweh as My shepherd and associate. When He is struck the disciples are scattered and the nation is subsequently scattered for their rejection of Him. Two thirds of them perish, but the other third is brought through the refining fire. This remnant is that which comes through the fire of the Tribulation. They are reconciled with the Messiah, and they will be His people and Yahweh will be their God.

Chapter 14 – The Day of the Lord

The Day is coming when the spoils taken from Israel will be divided among them. The Lord of armies will gather all the nations to Jerusalem for battle. However, though the Lord will fight for them, another purging is allowed. The city will be conquered, houses plundered, women raped, and half of the people exiled (refugees).[115] Then the Lord will go forth and fight against those nations as when He fights in a day of battle. Woe to them when the Lord almighty wages war on them. Judah (Israel) will fight also against them as the weapon of God. Then the angel of the Lord will place his feet on the mount of Olives,[116] and it will split apart leaving a very large valley. The people in Jerusalem will flee through

---
[115] Perhaps these refugees go to the mountains of Jordan as Jesus warned (Mt 24:15-21).
[116] Many have taught that this is the Messiah who puts his feet on the Mount of Olives here in verse 4, but He is said to come in verse 5 after the earthquake and the destruction of the armies of Antichrist in Jerusalem.

the valley to escape the armies of Antichrist who will subsequently be swallowed up by the earth, just as Pharaohs army was drowned in the sea.[117] Then the Lord, the Messiah, will come and all the holy ones with Him.[118] Verse 6 is covered in my book, "The 7 Lost Keys of End-Time Prophecy."

"But immediately after the tribulation of those days the sun will be darkened, and the moon will not give its light, and the stars will fall from the sky, and the powers of the heavens will be shaken, and then the sign of the Son of Man will appear in the sky, and then all the tribes of the earth will mourn..." Mt 24:29-31

On Rosh Hashanah at the end of the Tribulation, when the New Moon is supposed to take place, a new light appears. It is not the new, renewed light of the moon, neither is it the light of the Sun, but, rather, the "sign of the Son of Man." When this sign appears, there will be great mourning in the earth, particularly in Israel. This mourning is in keeping with Rosh Hashanah, the Day of the Awakening Blast, but this time it is mourning over Him who was pierced. Zech 12:9-14

Another passage in Zechariah Chapter 14 seems to agree with this and perhaps identifies the feast of Rosh Hashanah (Zech 14:1-7).

The prophet indicates that all the nations will be gathered to Jerusalem to battle. And just when they are planning to finish off the remnant of Israel there will be a great earthquake and a valley created through the Mount of Olives on the East through which the remnant will flee. When it says that "His feet will stand on the Mount of Olives," we have tended to think that it is a reference to Jesus Himself. However, it may not be Jesus but instead the angel of the Lord since two verses later it says, "Then the Lord, my God will come." Also, if the feet are the feet of Jesus the remnant would be seen as fleeing from Him. In any event, we see that the day is a Unique Day and there is not light because the luminaries have dwindled. This is a reference to the cosmic signs spoken about by many of the prophets and the Lord Himself. Then it says that in the midst of the darkness there will be light. Perhaps this light is the sign of the Son of Man that appears throughout the Days of Awe.

The time between Rosh Hashanah and Yom Kippur (Atonement), on the tenth of Tishri, was called "the days of awe." It appears that during these ten days the powers of the heavens will be literally shaken, and the sign of the Son of Man will be visible to the earth. Perhaps these cosmic disturbances are caused by the great conflagration known as Armageddon which takes place prior to and during this time. In any event, ten days later, on Yom Kippur the Son of Man is seen coming on the clouds with power and great glory."

---

[117] Rev 12:13-16
[118] All the Old Covenant saints including the previously raptured Bride of Christ and the angels.

Verse 8 says that living waters will flow out of Jerusalem, half toward the Eastern Sea (Dead Sea) and half toward the Western Sea (Mediterranean). We know from many other passages that this living water will flow from under the Temple.[119] The water will flow in summer and winter.

Verses 9-10

The topography of the land will change. Jerusalem will rise on its current site[120] and all around it from Geba in the north of Jerusalem to Rimmon in the south, will become a plain. Currently Jerusalem is rugged and mountainous all around, but that's going to change. The city will stand out and be seen far and wide and it will have peace and security.

Verses 12-15

These verses describe the plague that the Lord brings on those who come to war against Jerusalem. It sounds very much like what happens because of a nuclear blast. Considering this, it is interesting that the burial of Gog and his horde over seven months, and the process involved, also hints at that possibility. Nevertheless, since God is changing the topography, He will also protect His remnant and His city from any harmful effects. The land will be cleansed and renewed.

The nations that come against Jerusalem will end up fighting with Israel and with each other. Perhaps Israel's government moves its headquarters and can launch attacks from the Negev where most of its facilities are. In any event, a panic from the Lord falls on these armies and they lose control of their strategy and fight each other. And Israel will take great spoils from them.

Verses 16-21

Then the survivors from all the nations[121] will be required to come up to Jerusalem once a year to worship the King of Kings and celebrate the Feast of Booths or Sukkot. And any nation that does not come up will not receive any rain. Interestingly, at the end of the feast there was always prayer for the rains to come. So too there will be prayer and great rejoicing in the Millennium kingdom.

---

[119] Ezek 47:1-12
[120] Isaiah 2:2
[121] Mt 25:31-46

When it says that the bells on the horses and all the cooking pots in Judah and Jerusalem will be holy, it seems to be saying that holiness and righteousness will be the norm, and there will be no Canaanite, who has become symbolic of evil,[122] allowed in the house of the Lord.

---
[122] The dishonest merchant in Hosea 12:7 is literally the "Canaanite."

Notes

The Book of Malachi

Malachi is the last of the prophets. Little about him is known and since his name means "My Messenger," some have thought it was a pen name. Nevertheless, he was raised up by God to exhort the people and to complete the message of the prophets. His ministry likely took place during the time of the governor Nehemiah (444BC) and the rebuilding of the walls of Jerusalem. The Temple had been completed many years earlier, yet the fervor of the people had waned significantly. They were being unfaithful with the tithe and were also intermarrying again with foreigners and doubtful of the promises and the Messianic era. The priests were very careless and there was a drought in the land and the crops were failing. At that time Judah was being restored and Edom had been destroyed.

Chapter 1:1-5

The word of the Lord to Israel is that He loves them. Yet, they question that love.

"'How have You loved us?' 'Was Esau not Jacob's brother?' declares the LORD. 'Yet I have loved Jacob; but I have hated Esau, and I have made his mountains a desolation and given his inheritance to the jackals of the wilderness.'" Mal 1:2-3

Esau, who despised his birthright was rejected by God, who knew what he would be like before he was born.[123] His descendants were enemies of Israel. As the prophets had foretold, his mountains, the habitation of Edom, would be destroyed. This has happened while Judah and Jerusalem are being restored. The Lord points to this as proof of His love for Israel and that He fulfills His promises. Esau, He has hated, but Jacob He has loved. Though Edom says they will return and rebuilt, God says He will tear it down again. They will be a perpetual waste and will be known as the ones with whom God is indignant forever. The prophet says that Judah will see this and understand that God is glorified beyond the borders of Israel.

Verses 6-14 – The Priests Confronted

A son honors his father and a slave his master, yet the priests dishonor and disrespect the Lord by offering sick, blind, and lame, animals to Him. God says that what they are doing is pure evil. He asks them if they would offer such an animal to the governor, and if they did, would he be pleased with them? Obviously not. Yet they treat the Lord this way and expect Him to be pleased. The Lord says He is not and would rather that someone shut the

---

[123] Rom 9:10-12 quotes this passage but does not say that God hated Esau in the womb as many conclude. Only that he was to serve Jacob and not receive the birthright. However, Esau hardened his heart and passed on his grudge to his descendants.

gate and not let them offer any fire at all on His altar. He reminds them that He is a great King and that the time is coming when all the nations will worship Him and bring offerings in purity and His name will be great among them. Yet they who are His priestly nation are profaning His name. They acknowledge that the table of the Lord is defiled yet they don't care and treat it as a trivial thing to bring what is sick and what has been stolen. But the Lord will not accept it and they bring a curse on themselves by their disobedience. Also, the swindler who has a male in his flock and vows it to the Lord and then brings a blemished animal instead will be cursed. Yahweh says He is a great King who is feared among the nations. Therefore, how dare they bring such offerings to Him.

There is much here to convict us today concerning the way we worship God. We must always be enthusiastic and never treat worship as trivial and always give our very best, not only in the way we sing to him, but in the way we live our lives!

Chapter 2:1-9 – Curses on the Priests
The Lord says that if they do not listen and take their service to heart and honor Him, their blessings will be cursed and indeed it is already happening. The Lord will discipline them severely and make their feasts like refuse on their faces. The Lord will do this so that He may continue his covenant with Levi. Then the Lord speaks kindly of His covenant with the tribe of Levi and how they had revered Him and walked in righteousness and turned many back from iniquity. For the lips of a priest should preserve knowledge and men should seek instruction from him for he is a messenger of the Lord. But they have corrupted the covenant and shown partially in the instruction and caused many to stumble. Because they have not followed His ways God is making them despised and abased before the people.

Verses 10-12 – Foreign Wives
The people are confronted who have married foreign wives. They have married women who were non-Jews and who would lead them into idolatry. This was clearly against Torah and was a serious sin. Malachi refers to it as marrying the daughter of a foreign god. Nehemiah confronted this also and made them put away their foreign wives.[124]

Verses 13-17- Divorce
The people weep and wail at the altar because God no longer regards their offerings, yet they deal treacherously with their wives. In other words, they are being unfaithful to their wives and divorcing them without any cause. It is treachery and adultery. The Lord says that he is a witness between a man and the wife of his youth. God hates divorce and he who divorces his wife without a Biblical cause, is covering his garment with violence, since he is one with her and covenanted to protect her. The term "wife of your youth," implies that

---
[124] Neh 13:23-29

men can be led to divorce their wives merely because she has gotten older. The Lords considers it treachery and He hates it.

Chapter 3 – The Messenger

"Behold, I am sending My messenger, and he will clear a way before Me. And the Lord, whom you are seeking, will suddenly come to His temple; and the messenger of the covenant, in whom you delight, behold, He is coming," says the LORD of armies." Mal 3:1

When we study these passages as with all the Scriptures, we are blessed with hindsight in that it is all not future. We can determine the verses that speak of Messiah coming first as the suffering servant, and then secondly as the victorious King. In each case Messiah, who is identified as Adonai, will come suddenly to His Temple in Jerusalem after He has sent a messenger before His arrival. The messenger prepares the people as John the Baptist did and as Elijah himself will do before He appears again in Jerusalem. However, the messenger John the Baptist is the next prophet to appear after this last prophet has spoken. Those who did not receive the messenger did not receive the Lord.

"But who can endure the day of His coming? And who can stand when He appears? For He is like a refiner's fire, and like launderer's soap. And He will sit as a smelter and purifier of silver, and He will purify the sons of Levi and refine them like gold and silver, so that they may present to the LORD offerings in righteousness. Then the offering of Judah and Jerusalem will be pleasing to the LORD as in the days of old, and as in former years." Mal 3:2-4

This warning was true of Jesus' first coming and even more so when He comes again. His presence and teaching confronted the false leaders and sinners among the Jews. His words cut them to the heart and burned them like a smelters fire. That whole generation was exposed as perverse, and they were judged and scattered throughout the nations. The prophecy also contains the second coming of Christ who will purify His remnant, and the sons of Levi will once again offer sacrifices to the Lord in righteousness and be pleasing to Him. This, of course, will be fulfilled in the Millennial Reign.

The Lord will remove from them the sorcerers, the liars, and those who oppress the workers, the orphan, and the widow, and those who turn away the stranger from justice. The Lord says that He does not change, and He is not done with Jacob even though they have always disobeyed His statutes. He pleads with them to return to Him, and He will return to them. However, they think they have returned to Him. They are self-righteous and have not sought to be pleasing to Him since they are withholding the tithe from the storehouse. They are robbing God in tithes and offerings. They are stealing from the Almighty and are selfish and living for themselves and not Him.

Christians who withhold the tithe from the local church today are guilty of the same sin even though many pastors reject the tithe and say it does not apply to the church. But this is clearly false. The principle of giving the First Fruits and the Tithe (10%) goes all the way back to Adam and was practiced by the Patriarchs.[125]

"Bring the whole tithe into the storehouse, so that there may be food in My house, and test Me now in this," says the LORD of hosts, "if I will not open for you the windows of heaven and pour out for you a blessing until it overflows. Then I will rebuke the devourer for you, so that it will not destroy the fruits of the ground; nor will your vine in the field cast its grapes," says the LORD of hosts. "All the nations will call you blessed, for you shall be a delightful land," says the LORD of hosts." Mal 3:10-12

In some cases, they were robbing God by not bringing the tithe, but generally it was that they were only bringing a portion of it and lying about the rest. As a result of this sin, their crops and vines were being devoured and the Lord could not bless them. Yet if they will repent and bring in the full tithe, the Lord promises to open the windows of heaven and pour out a blessing that they could not contain. So much so that all the nations would see it and call them blessed.

Verses 13-15 – Arrogant Words
The Lord chastises them again for their words of complaint and arrogance against Him. He sees the heart and knows the thoughts of the mind. They say that it is vain to serve God and that even when they do, they still end up losing and mourning. It's like we say today, "What's the use?" As a result of this attitude, they are excusing sin by calling the arrogant blessed and building up the doers of wickedness.

Verses 16-18 – Book of Remembrance
This passage is not necessarily saying that God has a special book called the Book of Remembrance. It is merely stating that the Lord knows the righteous[126] and they know Him and each other and He will save them, and they will be His. Just as He did then, the Lord will rescue a righteous remnant in the Day of the Lord and righteousness will prevail.

---
[125] Gen 14:20, 28:22
[126] 2 Tim 2:19

Chapter 4 – The Day of the Lord

"For behold, the day is coming, burning like a furnace; and all the arrogant and every evildoer will be chaff; and the day that is coming will set them ablaze," says the LORD of hosts, "so that it will leave them neither root nor branch. But for you who fear My name, the sun of righteousness will rise with healing in its wings; and you will go forth and skip about like calves from the stall. You will tread down the wicked, for they will be ashes under the soles of your feet on the day which I am preparing," says the LORD of hosts. Mal 4:1-3

As the prophet sums up His words and the words of all the prophets, He reminds them of the Day of the Lord and the coming of the Messiah. As always, his first coming is interspersed with the second and the Millennial Reign.

The day is coming burning like a furnace. This is the Day of the Lord when all the arrogant and evildoers will be as chaff – meaning they will be burned up.[127] Then we are told that the sun of righteousness will rise. This verse is a reference to the Messiah coming on day four or the fourth millennium. Since the sun was created on the fourth day "the sun of righteousness" is a reference to Yeshua who came at the end of the fourth millennium bringing deliverance to Israel. The wings referred to were the "Tzi-Tzit" or tassels of his garments.[128]

"Remember the law of Moses My servant, even the statutes and ordinances which I commanded him in Horeb for all Israel." Mal 4:4

Then the people are warned to remember the law of Moses and the statutes and ordinances that he commanded them. This will keep them and prepare them for the Messianic era for which they wait.

"Behold, I am going to send you Elijah the prophet before the coming of the great and terrible day of the LORD. He will restore the hearts of the fathers to their children and the hearts of the children to their fathers, so that I will not come and smite the land with a curse." Mal 4:5-6

Then as a fitting ending, they are told that the next prophet to come will be Elijah. But as we have already seen, the first one is John the Baptist who comes in the spirit and power of Elijah.[129] When he was asked if he was Elijah, he said no.[130] He instead identified as the

---

[127] Isaiah 2:12-22, 1 Cor 3:12, 2 Pet 3:10
[128] Mt 9:20
[129] Luke 1:17
[130] John 1:21

fulfillment of Isaiah's words regarding the one crying in the wilderness.[131] Jesus clarified this when he says that John the Baptist was a fulfillment of this prophecy, but also that Elijah Himself would come at the end of the age.[132] For him the Jews put out a chair and a cup at every Passover Seder. And his coming is very close now.

With this the words of the Hebrew Prophets end. How greatly privileged we are to live in the generation in which all their words come to pass!

---

[131] Isaiah 40:3
[132] Mt 17:11-12

Notes

Printed in Great Britain
by Amazon